FIGHT
THE
POWER

FIGHT THE POWER

Rap, Race, and Reality

**Chuck D
with
Yusuf Jah**

Delacorte Press

Published by
Delacorte Press
Bantam Doubleday Dell Publishing Group, Inc.
1540 Broadway
New York, New York 10036

The trademark Delacorte Press® is registered in the U.S. Patent and
Trademark Office.

Book design by Susan Maksuta

Library of Congress Cataloging in Publication Data
D., Chuck.
Fight the power : rap, race, and reality /
Chuck D. with Yusuf Jah.
p.   cm.
ISBN 0-385-31868-5
1. Rap (Music)—History and criticism.   2. Hip-hop—United
States.   3. Popular culture—United States—History—20th century.
4. Race relations.   I. Jah, Yusuf.   II. Title.
ML3531.D2   1997
782.421649—dc21   97-22780
                                                            CIP
                                                            MN

Manufactured in the United States of America
Published simultaneously in Canada

October 1997

10 9 8 7 6 5 4 3 2 1

BVG

THIS BOOK IS DEDICATED TO MY CHILDREN:
DOMINIQUE, DJIRA, AND JEREMY

CONTENTS

Foreword by Spike Lee   ix

Prologue   xi

Chapter 1 Welcome to the Terrordome   1

Chapter 2 Black Community: Where Ya At?   25

Chapter 3 Prelude to Public Enemy   57

Chapter 4 Athletes and Entertainers   95

Chapter 5 RockRap   127

Chapter 6 Africa   153

Chapter 7 Apocalypse '91: The Enemy Strikes Black   183

Chapter 8 Black and Jewish Relationships   205

Chapter 9 Gangs   241

Epilogue   263

Recommended Reading   267

Discography   271

Tours   272

Acknowledgments   273

FOREWORD
BY
SPIKE LEE

For the millions of fans who are familiar with Chuck D from his huge success as lead vocalist of the Rap powerhouse, Public Enemy, you will not be disappointed. *Fight the Power: Rap, Race, and Reality* will take you where you'd expected to go and further. To those who are not familiar with Chuck D this book is a *must read.* Do yourself a favor and get acquainted with one of the most politically and socially conscious artists of any generation. This is a book that every person should read.

When I needed a song for my movie *Do the Right Thing*, I knew the person I needed to go to was Chuck D; he came back with "Fight the Power." The song was crucial to the impact of the film.

As lead vocalist of Public Enemy, Chuck has been able to inspire other rappers to redetermine the content and direction of their music. And right about now, with the tragic deaths of Tupac Shakur and Notorious B.I.G., the Rap world and society at large could use some more Chuck Ds. People who are able to inspire other young people to redirect their energies and thoughts for more positive and constructive objectives.

Chuck D is unique among rappers because he is a by-product of the volatile and turbulent environment of the 1960s, and has traveled and performed in over forty countries. He has witnessed firsthand the *global* issues of racism, ethnic prejudice, classism, and fanatical nationalism, and like a sponge he has incorporated his world experiences into a clear and concise commentary on a variety of issues and their possible solutions from his worldview.

Chuck has been criticized as being "angry," "militant," or "radical," as have many strong, uncompromising voices who have stood up to present a point of view that subverts the mainstream. *Fight the Power* allows readers the opportunity to get beneath the

surface, and get to *really* know the scope of Chuck's informed philosophies. His basic credo—there's good and evil, right and wrong, God and the Devil—what side are you on? The views expressed in *Fight the Power: Rap, Race, and Reality* are a long way from being a diatribe that would create increased tension between Black and whites, or Blacks and Jews. Instead, Chuck focuses his expression on things that the Black community can do to help itself, and ways that concerned individuals from other communities can help bridge gaps.

Consistent with the hard-hitting sounds of a Public Enemy jam, Chuck D addresses contemporary topics in an equally bold, brave, and straightforward way—addressing controversial and popular issues including the role and responsibility of athletes, entertainers, and celebrities; Gangsta Rap and the current state of Rap music; education, community and economic development; Black–Jewish relationships, international touring, the music business, Black media, mainstream media, and one of my personal favorites, Hollywood.

Fight the Power is a message from the Commissioner. Do the right thing by reading this book. . . . *Spike Lee*

PROLOGUE

THE CORPORATE PIMPS OF SOUL

Monday, February 24, 1997—12:00 noon
Soul Cafe, New York City

Ten years since the release of "Public Enemy Number One," my first single for Def Jam, and here I was sitting among reporters, TV and radio people, between Flavor Flav and Professor Griff. This was just the beginning of a hectic day and a crazy week, the prelude to the History of Hip-Hop concert being sponsored by Radio WQHT aka Hot 97 in New York. Being a part of this event had me wondering how the control of Hip-Hop and Rap music had changed hands and got swallowed up by the corporate pimps of soul. Aside from celebrating the history of this great music, one purpose of the performance was to balance out the growing stigma that Hip-Hop concerts are unsafe.

Flavor, Griff, and I took turns talking, setting the stage for what's in store for the coming months. Flavor, who's been back and forth in the media for a host of personal reasons, was abrasively upbeat about turning the page on our tenth year. Griff, on the other hand, was cordial and cool and let the room guess about the future plan and his ideas. Obviously, there was an appetite for what Public Enemy could bring to the public.

Personally, I felt rejuvenated after a four-year challenge-filled hiatus. My challenges were trying to sustain my art within a crumbling art form and trying to resuscitate that art form. It's damn near like scaling a slick mountain with roller skates, especially after the murder of Notorious B.I.G. three weeks later. I felt the career toll of controversial scars on my mind, body, and soul had healed a bit for future wars in store. The Rap game had changed

to a point where my competitive nature could no longer operate. Rap tours had all but vanished, an area that allowed Public Enemy to prove all our doubters wrong. Radio stations had to be paid heavy money to play Rap records. Record companies flooded the gap with payola, expensive video marketing, and oversaturated replicated marketing campaigns. And Gangsta sound became the lead topic on R&B formatted music, something that wouldn't offend a white corporation and still rotate easily on white-owned Black radio stations without losing a female audience.

Here I was performing for a corporation claiming to be the "Hip-Hop Voice of New York," only agreeing to do it providing I retained the rights to the World Wide Webcast of the event. That broadcast never happened, so I was committed to the task of performing merely for romantic reasons that night. KRS One and Run-DMC opened and closed the show respectively, lighting up the stage in the process, and there we were, in between, for the first time in a year and a half. We thundered through the set: Flavor, Terminator, The S1Ws, Brother James Norman, Roger, Mike and the Crew and, once again, Griff. We showed all, that if we had to do it, we could.

I must admit, I was surprised at the amount of media people who clustered inside the Black-owned Soul Cafe that Monday. All media were banned from the event, so I'll bet most of them were pissed off about not being able to see the show. I opened the floor talking about my multimedia ventures leading up to the twenty-first century; a new Public Enemy record, a PE Archive label, Slam Jamz, the Internet, and a host of ideas including this book, *Fight the Power: Rap, Race, and Reality.*

The purpose of this book is to expose to the reader the beauty and depth of Rap and Hip-Hop. For too long I've felt that this art form is tossed aside as a ghetto game for Black youth and that limited opinion is ignorant. Through the many controversies that my peers and I have weathered, the facts have been passed over for distortions and hysterical stigmas, not only by the mainstream, but by my own community as well.

This book damn sure ain't a passive introduction to this world, nor is it an autobiography. I've never stressed the importance of me. I am a man first and a Black one to the core. If those facts offend some, fuck it. *Fight the Power* will ruffle.

I'm offended that few know that my peers are worldly, engaging, entrepreneurial, have traveled, have families, have college degrees, and pay taxes like everybody else. I'm here to set the record straight.

But this book is not solely my own opinion. It has been shaped by the hundreds of conversations I've had across the planet over the past twelve years with everyone, including presidents, political leaders, athletes, leftists, conservatives, religious leaders, pimps, racists, international people, drug dealers, average men and women, homeless people, military prisoners, as well as my fellow Rap and Hip-Hop peers.

Personally, these past four years I've been a rebel, never going for the easy take, always taking the difficult road to the goal for the satisfaction of the battle and here I was in this interview room back where I started. Making statements and guessing the outcome, trying to be more than what I was considered as a rapper, an artist. Taking on the odds as a Black man.

The years 1994 through 1997 have been formulative ones, and I'm planning now to reach some of the goals I set then, one of them being this book. Wherever I go, increasingly people ask, "Yo, when are you coming out? We need you." Well, in order for me to cut through, I have to be multimedia man—books, CD ROMs, Internet, television, radio, and, of course, records—to get my point across. Once upon a time, records and video snuck information across battle lines. Now I have to have full media programming to rescue minds from the corporate pimps of soul. So here it is BAM and you say G . . . Damn. . . .

WELCOME TO THE TERRORDOME

The 1990s have been filled with Black men being systematically ripped down and overexposed in the media like we're the worst criminals on the planet. An increasingly hostile climate has developed in America toward Black people and our struggle: the Republican-proposed "Contract with America," the Supreme Court decision striking affirmative action programs, the Welfare Reform Bill, which will leave many people in a vaccum because there is no companion jobs-creation bill, and the "Crime Bill," which will lead to increased numbers of Black men filling the jails to spend the rest of their lives. Black culture became more marketable during the eighties, and white corporations found that they could make big bucks off of it. An example is the rise of Public Enemy, Rap music, and Black male celebrities like Mike Tyson, Michael Jordan, Michael Jackson, and Arsenio Hall. Once Black images started to infiltrate mainstream white society via Black celebrities and white kids began to imitate Black people, not only from a physical standpoint like in athletics, but also mentally and culturally, that's when a big problem began.

In the early nineties a new era began for the creation of the Black celebrity. Black music became a force invading the pop music scene in record numbers, including Black artists from Janet Jackson and Whitney Houston down to Kriss Kross and Arrested Development. Signings of Black artists went from about twenty to sixty percent. What occurred during that period was a visual explosion of Black celebrities. Music videos became more pervasive and entertaining, Black movies made a strong return, and simultaneously the NBA and NFL combined with major corporations to magnify and emphasize the individual. To the point whereby in 1995 and 1996 there was a subliminal message that stated, "If you're not a ballplayer, or entertainer, and you're not living a lavish lifestyle then you ain't shit."

The same thing happened during the seventies when there was an explosion of Black celebrities in film and music. Actors were all over the TV acting in sitcoms, and there was an explosion in music from both independent and major record labels, but by the early 1980s there weren't any Black celebrities to be found anywhere, unless they were ballplayers. Michael Jackson's *Thriller* became such a big deal in 1983 because he came after a Black celebrity drought.

I remember in 1989 when Samuel Jackson appeared in our video for "911 Is a Joke." That was before he was famous. A lot of Black actors had to take what they could get at the time. The dramatic rise in popularity of Black culture created the onslaught of the Black celebrity. Almost every male actor who became popular in the early nineties came through Spike Lee: Wesley Snipes, Laurence Fishburne, Samuel Jackson. There's more Black celebrities now than ever before, and less Black power.

The question for the 1990s is will the creation of the Black celebrity be used to fuel people with inspiration, or distract people from realistic goals? The Black celebrity has become like a cartoon image, someone who exists in the form of song, video, or moving picture, but who is never really seen or heard by people in real life.

I'm a firm believer, especially nowadays, in the African proverb, "It takes a whole community to raise a child." I spend as much time as I possibly can with my two daughters in order to provide a balanced view, and to help them think as independently as possible.

It's very important for athletes and entertainers, especially Black men, to say something uplifting and inspirational whenever they get an opportunity, because many children do not see strong Black men in their communities, and the Black men they do see are projected in the most derogatory manner: the "player," the pimp, or the temporary hustler. So the projection of the Black man's voice is important.

Many in the world of Hip-Hop have begun to believe that the only way to blow up and become megastars is by presenting themselves in a negative light. The two recently slain Hip-Hop artists, Tupac and Notorious B.I.G., as well as other Rap artists who have come under criticism like Dr. Dre, Snoop Dogg, Ice Cube, or whoever you want to name, talk positivity in some of their records, but those records have to be picked by the industry executives and program directors to be magnified. MC Eiht talks about "I don't want to get caught in this, I'm trying to go right, but society won't let me go right, but it's hard." The media just doesn't focus on those positive songs, they'd rather dwell on the negative.

That's what I feel happened with Tupac. Tupac had a loyalty to Black people without a doubt. His early albums sound like a combination of Public Enemy and N.W.A. He was raw. Tupac found that when he said things that were proBlack and militant, people were not paying any attention to what he was saying so he decided to go more and more into the side of darkness, like Bishop, the character he played in the movie *Juice*. "Fuck that. Thug life like a motherfucker." The more he played the "bad boy" or "rude

FIGHT THE POWER

boy" image, the bigger and bigger he got. The unfortunate thing is I think Tupac had a plan to bring everybody to the table with the "Thug for Life" image, and then he was going to flip the tables at the last minute and have people thinking. He was rooted in that. He was a brother who was strongly influenced by the Black Panther ideology, and by Black revolutionary political prisoners like Geronimo Pratt, Mumia Abu-Jamal, and others. On Pac's latest release, *Makaveli*, he has a song on the album called "White Man'z World" in which he states, *"Use your brain! It's not them that's killing us, it's us that's killing us."* In the aftermath of Tupac's murder the conscious, revolutionary, uplifting aspects of Tupac Shakur's existence were played to the side as being unimportant and irrelevant. Another victim of this white man'z world.

In 1994 my partner, Walter Leaphart, and I began shopping for a development deal at the major television networks and syndication companies for a show we proposed, which would serve as a *Larry King Live* targeted to the "Generation X" crowd, and come across with an interesting and new viewpoint, which would make people think. Larry King is a journalist I respect, and someone who can be seen all over the world. I began pushing for my own television show because I was, and still am, totally pissed by the derogatory characters depicted on TV. My aim was to confront Hollywood, and demand that a proper perspective on how Black people and people of color in general are presented. We shopped a couple of show ideas, one called *Chuck D on the Real,* which got turned down by every network and syndication company.

After one pitch, a senior programmer said to our agent at the time, "We like the star quality, but he has an agenda that we

> TUPAC HAD A PLAN TO BRING EVERYBODY TO THE TABLE WITH THE "THUG FOR LIFE" IMAGE, AND THEN HE WAS GOING TO FLIP THE TABLES AT THE LAST MINUTE.

don't want to put on TV." They're damn right I have an agenda, everybody on TV has an agenda. If I had Shaquille O'Neal on my show I would be asking him a different set of questions. Every powerful person in politics, religion, business, entertainment, athletics, or whatever industry would be asked, "What's your take on race relations?" I'm out to confront issues that we all face daily, but are very rarely presented from a Black frame of reference. For example, you can see the agenda of Paramount Television/UPN as clear as day, because it often has four shows in a row all designed to make people laugh. There's nothing wrong with laughter, but that's not all Black people are good for. There has to be some balance.

Once I realized that I'm a voice that people listen to, I realized I had to fill my voice with something of substance. Through Rap music I've seen people all over the world magnetized to thoughts and ideas. My goal is to be used as a viaduct, as a dispatcher of information. Television is the last plateau. We need programs representing our voice and interpretation, which come out and say the things that need to be said, and can be challenging and entertaining at the same time. A person like Chris Rock is someone who is attempting to bridge the gap with intelligence and entertainment. He is a key person in a key area.

The image of Black people on the tube has not drastically changed over the decades. We're either singing, dancing, telling jokes, telling one-liners in a sitcom, talking about a triple-double, touchdown, or stolen base, or getting locked up in a squad car on *Cops*. They'll go into a house in Cleveland and catch our people at their absolute worst.

There's only a few serious Black roles on TV. We have to put pressure on the networks and station groups where pressure hurts. Some say, "You have to hit them in their pocket." Fuck that. I'll repeat this statement, I'm a firm believer: hit them in their head, and challenge them on a mental level with logic, and they'll start finding ingenious ways to balance out the derogatory programming. It's such a serious issue because the derogatory programming leads to a point where life imitates art, and a blur develops be-

FIGHT THE POWER

tween fantasy and reality. I believe that television is one of the main reasons for the criminal mindedness of Black youth. In the book *Split Image: African-Americans in the Mass Media*, Jannette Dates and William Barlow refer to historian Joseph Boskin's statement: "To make the black male into an object of laughter, and conversely, to force him to devise laughter, was to strip him of masculinity, dignity, and self-respect. Sambo was, then, an illustration of humor as a device of oppression, and one of the most potent in American popular culture. The ultimate objective for whites was to effect mastery, to render the Black male powerless as a potential warrior, as a sexual competitor, as an economic adversary." The authors trace the Sambo character as far back as 1781, in a play called the *Divorce*, where he was cast in the all-too-familiar role of "singing nonsense songs and dancing around the stage."

> THERE'S ONLY A FEW SERIOUS BLACK ROLES ON TV. WE HAVE TO PUT PRESSURE ON THE NETWORKS AND STATION GROUPS WHERE PRESSURE HURTS.

Black intellect is rarely projected from a Black viewpoint. Black comedy is. Black family life from a funny point of view is. Black athleticism is. Black style and dress are. It's countercultural. Intelligent Black people on television like Oprah Winfrey and Bill Cosby do us well. Unfortunately, for every Oprah or Bill Cosby, there are twenty-five people trying to tell a joke, a hundred and fifty people trying to sing, and thousands of people trying to dribble a basketball or score touchdowns and dance in the end zone. As Bill Cosby said, "Get people from anywhere in the world and they'll have a negative view of the Black man, because of what they've seen in the media, not what they know."

The networks, UPN, which I say stands for the "United Plantation of Niggers," and WB, which in my mind stands for "We Buffoons," are presenting a far too one-sided slice of Black life. The most-seen Black man on TV today has got to be Urkel. That's nothing against Jaleel White, who plays Urkel, but the projection is saying that the most influential Black male is a guy who's in shorts shooting a basketball, or if he's acting he wears glasses, has high waters, and speaks with a high-pitched, squeaky voice. I wonder what goes on in the boardrooms filled with decision makers at these TV stations. "Here's an idea, how about *Homeboys from Outer Space?*" "That sounds like a great idea. Let's do it." What the fuck? In spite of the many intelligent Black filmmakers and scriptwriters who have submitted viable projects, at the end of the day they decide on *Homeboys from Outer Space* and *Sparks?* What kind of crazy shit is that? Again, that's not an attack on my man Michael Collier, who is a very talented political comedian and an actor on *Homeboys from Outer Space,* or any of the other actors who are cast on that or any other show. I understand the realities of life in the entertainment business. The knock is on the networks and station groups and the imbalanced picture that gets presented. And people wonder why a person like me is mad?

The executives at the stations defend their choices by saying things like, "Well, that's what the people want." The people will only want bullshit if their intelligence is continually insulted with bullshit. After a long-enough period of time, the insult of their intelligence turns into an intelligent insult. In other words, it begins to work. After a five- to ten-year period of being constantly barraged with similar programming, the audience loses grip on what is good and what is bad. The Fox network was built off of Black viewership: *In Living Color, The Simpsons, Martin, Living Single. Rock.* Now they're able to compete for the rights to broadcast the World Series and Super Bowl because of the foundation that was partially built off of Black viewers.

There are white shows to make people laugh too, but they also have white everything else. White people control the news networks, which according to *Split Image: African-Americans in the Mass Media,* edited by Jannette Dates and William Barlow, "explain, instruct and justify practices and institutions . . . linking symbols, formulas, plot and characters in a pattern that is *conventional, appealing* and *gratifying.*" Don't be confused when

FIGHT THE POWER

7

you see Black people reporting the news the way mainstream America wants to hear it. To see a Black person come across with no point of view is crazy.

My plan is to penetrate news. News is the last frontier, and still is one of the hardest industries left for Blacks to crack in this country. They want to continue to control the information that gets out. The FCC controls the television and radio, and they're trying to control the Internet. The FCC is the government. The government controls the information.

News is an area where a Black perspective is not allowed to come across anywhere close to prime time. A show featuring a Black perspective on serious issues will come on at 6:05 on Sunday morning. Why? Because they don't want that point of view expressed. That point of view is probably racist. I'll tell you what is racist, the belief that every time a Black person opens his or her mouth canned laughter has to come out three seconds after. That's racist in a subliminal way.

Bryant Gumbel, Ed Bradley, and the Black anchorpeople that report the five and eleven o'clock news, or cover the weather, they're Black faces covering American issues. That's no knock on them, they're doing their jobs, and they're some of the best at what they do, but somebody needs to be there for Black people telling them how the "American issues" will affect their Black lives. I'm going to always be in the mix telling people what's going on, and to challenge information and get involved in the process. My involvement with the Rock the Vote campaign during the 1996 Presidential campaign and elections gave me a platform to be able to challenge people and to instruct others to challenge themselves. It's very important for me to be involved with MTV, BET, the major networks, and Internet on that level.

My involvement in Rock the Vote had nothing to do with telling people to be a Democrat or a Republican. It was about telling people to be aware of the process that's going on. You can vote or not vote, just be aware of the process. I have to get to first base before I tell them about stealing third. My agenda is to be a voice in the community and take advantage of media time to get across the message to *just think*. Don't be a robot. Make a decision and put pressure on the person you vote for, because if that person ends up winning the election that person has to come up with some answers. Having control of our local environment means a lot more than understanding the national picture. Having control of your local environment means that you're able to control the decisions that go down every day that affect your community via council members, the Board of Education, and local judges. Right now people get into those positions unchallenged by the Black community, and are unwilling to represent the best interests of the community.

America has become a headline-reaching country. People only want to know the headline, fuck the rest of the story. People rarely hear about Michael Jordan when he was in the ninth grade and got cut from the basketball team, and started practicing by himself and trying to learn his schoolwork. We don't hear about that story as much as you hear about "Jordan scores forty." People say they'd like to be Michael Jordan. Jordan says, "Being Michael Jordan for a whole lifetime is a different story."

Favorite Rap Publications:

Rap Sheet: Content thorough, star wars, tight, fair representation.
Source: A lotta ads, regardless a must pickup.
Rap Pages: Cover deeper issues than most.
Vibe: Dedication to Rap not full but madd exposure.
Beatdown: Readers review albums, innovative.
Word Up: An archive of photos through the years make it worth.
One Nut Network: Attempts to make it spicier, have worked gossip rap-mag.
Yo: Made for kids under eighteen but sometimes interesting for survey.
Hip-Hop Connection: This London-based mag actually second only to *Rap Sheet.*
XXL: This list was made before the first issue but knowing these guys, it should crack the top four.

For the most part the American news machine has become that of filth and garbage. There's some press that come across with integrity, but then there's what I call the "piss press." The piss press are those that figure they'll do anything to make a dollar. They make a parody of life, and fuck the result. We have to look at the "fuck the result" doctrine and see what that causes.

The commercial success and popularity of tabloid programs like *A Current Affair,* which started the whole trend, and *Hard Copy* have caused the local, national, and world news programs, which used to have more substance in their reporting, to become more tabloidistic in order to keep up their ratings. Everything should not be about ratings, there has to be an accountability factor as well.

MAKE NO MISTAKE RICKI LAKES
EATIN MAD STEAKS
OFF YOUR BAD BREAKS
FUNERALS AND WAKES
SOME OF THAT SHIT IS FAKE YEAH!
—"Talk Show Created the Fool"

When I embarked on my solo album *Autobiography of MistaChuck* in 1995, one of my titles was "Talk Show Created the Fool." Previously, on the *It Takes a Nation of Millions to Hold Us Back* album I wrote the jam "She Watch Channel Zero," which focused on soap operas and how we as a people, especially some sisters, believe what we see on TV and soap operas, when there's really nothing there for *us*. "Talk Show Created the Fool" talks about how the mass production of talk shows takes Black individuals and projects them to a television audience in situations and circumstances that overexpose our downside.

These shows depict Black people in a fucked-up manner a good deal of the time, which contributes to how we're looked at as a people, and also contributes to how we look at ourselves. If a person on a farm in the middle of Iowa turns on his TV and watches daytime talk shows, he'd swear the United States is fifty percent Black, which develops in him the attitude that we're all fools. It's almost like Stepin Fetchit, Mantan Moreland, Sambo, and *Uncle Tom's Cabin* rolled into one all over again. Ricki Lake, Jenny Jones, and the other hosts, producers, and station groups are getting paid well off our mistakes and bad breaks. Everybody has problems. Do they have to be magnified?

The media's biased and unbalanced portrayal of Black images has helped create the impression that Black people commit the overwhelming majority of crime in America. I'm not objecting to the truth being told. On the contrary, I'm imploring the media to tell the truth and present all the facts about crime. The ridiculous disparity in sentencing laws for crack offenses versus cocaine offenses is a case in point. Congress rejected the concept of parity

FIGHT THE POWER

1 1

in sentencing laws. A person caught with five grams of crack will serve more time if caught than a person caught with five hundred grams of powder cocaine. That's insane. The person with crack is wrong, and the person with the cocaine is one hundred times more wrong, but the reality is the person with the five hundred grams of cocaine is one hundred times more likely to be white.

A person knows when he's done something wrong. If a person steals something she knows what she's doing. It didn't grow out of her arm. If you see a dollar lying on the ground next to someone, you can pick it up and tell yourself that you found it, but you can also tell yourself that it belongs to someone else. It's not yours. A person selling drugs has to put it in the back of his mind. He'll say to himself, "I have to survive," but in the back of his mind he knows he's doing something wrong. "It's a jungle out there. It's about survival of the fittest." It's not really that at all. A lot of people use the excuse, "I have to eat," but there's mad ways to get something to eat.

The *1991 Statistical Record of Black America* obtained information from the U.S. Department of Justice revealing that whites commit more crimes in the following areas: forcible rape, aggravated assault, burglary, larceny, automobile theft, arson, forgery and counterfeiting, fraud, embezzlement, stolen property (buying, receiving, possessing), vandalism, weapons carrying and possession, prostitution, drug-abuse violations, offenses against family and children, driving under the influence, drunkenness, disorderly conduct, vagrancy, and a few others. The three categories in which Blacks were arrested more often than whites were murder, which is, statistically speaking, more than likely an alcohol-influenced person in a spur-of-the-moment rage over money or sex, killing another Black person; robbery, which is also more than likely Blacks robbing other Blacks; and SUSPICION. Even though whites are arrested more frequently in all of the above categories, Blacks are arrested as suspects of committing crimes more than twice as often as whites. It's true that Blacks make up a disproportionate amount of the crime statistics for only representing twelve to fifteen percent of the American

BLACKS ARE ARRESTED AS SUSPECTS OF COMMITTING CRIMES MORE THAN TWICE AS OFTEN AS WHITES.

population, but the cold, hard truth is if a person were to be raped, burglarized, have his car stolen, or if any of the criminal acts listed above were to happen to him, contrary to popular belief, statistics prove that it would be a white perpetrator more often than a Black one. That's not the perception you'd get living in America.

I've written a couple of jams that address the issue of crime and its stereotype, and at the same time shoot a question back for people to think about. One song, "Hazy Shade of Criminal," raises the question of who the real criminal is. On the cover of the single I used a powerful picture to help get my point across. It was a picture of two Black men hanging from a tree in Marion, Indiana, with a mob of white people standing around smiling. My mother had a book in our house called *The Movement,* and that picture was on the third page. I was always shocked when I would look through that book as a child. It's an image that has stuck with me ever since. On the back of the single I wrote, "This photograph is not from the South, it's from Marion, Indiana, the same state where they hung a good friend of mine, Mike Tyson." To me Mike Tyson's case was unclear, and there's an unclear picture of who the *real* criminals are in America. America was founded on a criminal act, but they still want to say we're the criminals. A brother will get locked up for "robbery," for taking two hundred and fifty dollars from a victim, but Michael Milken and other "white-collar" criminals seem to get lax sentences for much heavier shit.

Another song from the *Muse Sick-N-Hour Mess Age* album, whose title is a play on words from the Persuaders' song, "It's a Thin Line between Love and Hate," deals with the fact that the image of rape and crime has been thrust upon Black symbols here in America and throughout the world. America and the Western world have raped entire races of people of their name, God, re-

ligion, culture, and language, have raped continents of their resources and their progeny, and have raped our women, which is the main reason Black people are so many different shades today. The laws of America allowed it, so I titled the song there's a "Thin Line between Law and Rape." The law of the land in America is full of shit. Increasingly people are recognizing the United States of America as being something like an unkempt bathroom.

> YO BLACK SPEND 288 MILLION
> SITTIN' THERE WAITIN' FOR THE FIZZ
> AND DON'T KNOW WHAT THE FUCK IT IS
> BESIDE WHAT'S INSIDE AIN'T ON THE LABEL
> THEY DRINK IT THINKIN' IT'S GOOD
> BUT THEY DON'T SELL THAT SHIT IN THE WHITE NEIGHBORHOOD
>
> OUT THE BOTTLE IN A CUP
> HE CALL IT GETTIN' FUCKED UP
> LIKE WE AIN'T FUCKED UP ALREADY
>
> —"1 Million Bottlebags"

I attack drugs, including alcohol, because it's a scourge that attacks the human family. As an artist I can just look at the musicians whose lives and talent were taken away in a three-year period in the late sixties: Jimi Hendrix, Janis Joplin, Baby Huey, Jim Morrison, and Brian Jones of The Rolling Stones. Those were great losses. The effects on the Black community have been even more deadly and devastating. I won't even get into how it has fucked up the Native Americans. Every Black person in the United States who's in touch with his or her family has someone in his or her family who's been affected by the products of genocide that have taken us down as a people,

I ATTACK DRUGS, INCLUDING ALCOHOL, BECAUSE IT'S A SCOURGE THAT ATTACKS THE HUMAN FAMILY.

even if he or she is personally free of drugs. That's why I take such a strong antidrug stance. That's why I try to change the environment. Looking at junkies on the corner nodding from heroin use in the early seventies is what caused me to say, "I'm not doing any drugs. I'm not trying to look like them." I've never used any drugs or even had a drink of alcohol in my life. I've always been antidrugs.

When Flavor had his problems with drugs and the police, some said, "Why are you talking against drugs and you can't even keep Flavor off of drugs. Public Enemy is a contradiction." That's bullshit. That's a dumb-ass statement. Public Enemy is real. We've never tried to hide that fact, but what we tried to do is say, "We are definitely antidrugs and antianything that destroys our community, and we try to do the most that we can to change the environment." We've stuck to that.

I've never seen Flavor using drugs, and Flavor is such a character that it's damn near impossible for me to tell if he was high on something, because the effects are foreign to me. I can only tell if a person has a problem if he admits the problem. At the same time I do understand that cleaning yourself up, especially with all of the traps that are set, is a lifelong process. We're all human beings. God did not create any perfect human being. We're all men and women, and we're in the entertainment business trying to fight against the things that affect people every day, and can affect any one of us. Flavor's bout with drugs is even more of a reason for us to fight against them. Any news that comes out about humans should not be totally surprising. It would be different if you found out that the Pope was running a prostitution ring, now that would be shocking.

In the 1960s the cheeba movement led to the cocaine wars and heroin addictions of the early 1970s. In the 1990s the cycle is repeating itself. There's a level of acceptance for weed that is setting the youth up for the next level, which may be heroin again, or some other drug, because people are looking for the next high. It's set up like that. Right now on the Hip-Hop scene alcohol consumption and weed smoking have been accepted by

many as part of the culture. That shit is not a part of our culture to be proud of, it's part of the reason for our stagnation as an art form.

Sometimes I feel like I'm a rock in the middle of the ocean, and I realize that sometimes people will not swim to the rock, but that doesn't mean that I shouldn't be there. A person may be like, "Yo Chuck, I'm not really trying to hear that right now. You've been consistent, and that's good looking out. But straight up, if you flipped, I'd be disappointed." I'm not looking for props, I'm just doing my thing. Somebody has got to be the uncool rock there to keep individuals from drowning. I think people appreciate it even if they're cast in dire, fucked-up circumstances such as addiction. I'm not saying that I have full direction on all things, but I know that I can hold my ground and give some kind of advice that may help somebody out. I've accepted the role of being that "uncool motherfucker."

I've heard people say, "I don't want to sound preachy," but I've never heard anyone say, "I don't want to sound stupid." What's the matter with saying something if you know something? If you know better, then say something better. We need to have more people step up and say something of substance. Older people need to get real with young people and tell them, "Your choices are your choices, but I'm letting you know that the choices you're making will lead to a fucked-up dilemma."

People are quick to lose at drugs, because drugs overtake your frame of reference. You may start off with a passion for one thing, and once you mix your passion with drugs, the drugs become your passion. Why? Because drugs will make you feel better than you've ever felt in your life. That's the problem. Drugs don't make you feel fucked-up. In fact, they make people feel fantastic. The problems people can't deal with are the maintenance and the comedown. It's a false high. It takes them to a false level of enjoyment, and many want to stay there, but it costs to stay there.

There are people who have made millions of dollars from the sale of drugs. Doctors, lawyers, politicians, religious figures have all been trapped by the lure of crime and drugs. The drug game is the oldest game in the books. The drug game is older than the music industry. Black people are never going to win at the drug game. We've always been losers. We've never been players, we've all been victims.

In the early part of 1991 I had a title hanging around called "1 Million Body Bags," which was going to talk about the Gulf War conflict. I changed the title to "1 Million Bottlebags" after doing a lecture at Vanderbilt University, and a professor from Vanderbilt gave me some statistics that inspired me to talk about the dangers of malt liquor in the Black community. Black people drink malt liquor like it's going out of style. Malt liquor has a higher alcohol content than beer, but breweries usually won't reveal the ingredients on the label. Malt liquor drinkers don't even know what the hell they're drinking, but buy forty or sixty-four ounces to drink at a time. I also observed that malt liquor was almost entirely marketed and sold in Black, Hispanic, and poor neighborhoods. They don't sell malt liquor in Beverly Hills. Then the companies recruit Rap stars to promote the stuff, helping lead even more young people to the slaughterhouse.

When I finished recording the song "1 Million Bottlebags" a friend of mine from Philadelphia told me about a commercial he heard with my voice on it. He sent me a tape, and I came to find out it was a St. Ides commercial. I couldn't believe it. He told me that people in Philly were surprised to hear my voice on a beer commercial since I've consistently been antidrugs and antialcohol throughout my career.

That summer I filed a lawsuit against San Francisco–based McKenzie River Brewing Co., the manufacturers of St. Ides Malt Liquor. I sued the company because they should have had better quality control. Although St. Ides claimed they didn't know my voice had been used, it's up to the company to make sure that everything is in line. I sued for five million dollars for unauthorized use of my voice in the radio spot. They offered me a settlement of seventy-five thousand dollars and hoped I would shut up. I told my

lawyers they were crazy. They had done mad damage to my image. We eventually settled in 1993 after two years.

Some may think I overreacted, but I'm glad I sued those bastards. There are breweries who may have picked up on our lax attitude and took matters further and attempted to release "M.L.K. malt liquor," or the "St. Malcolm X malt liquor." Some of those companies will do anything to make a buck without conscience. In 1995 a brewing company attempted to use as brand labels for their malt liquor the famous Menominee American Indian leader Chief Oshkosh and the Lakota Sioux leader Crazy Horse who was an outspoken critic of the use of alcohol by his people and renowned for his bravery. It's not enough that Europeans over the last four centuries distributed alcohol to the Natives as a way to get better terms in land deals and better prices in the old fur trade, and profit to this day from sales of alcohol near reservations throughout America, but their actions attempted to desecrate and degrade heroes of the Native American people. I appreciate the persistence of Russell Smith and Lisa Davis, my attorneys on the case, in being diligent over the two years. I brought legal action against St. Ides to make a statement. I feel that we as a community should initiate more lawsuits, class-action suits, and civil complaints against companies and industries that systematically discriminate and devastate underserved and unprotected communities.

It's become blatantly clear that the majority of Black and white people see the world from diametrically opposed points of view, judging by the aftermath of the L.A. rebellion, the Million Man March, and of course O.J. Simpson's criminal and civil trials.

I'm not from L.A. and wasn't out there on April 29, 1992, when the uprisings jumped off, and I definitely don't know what really happened with the O.J. Simpson situation, but I was at the Million Man March, and to hear the reports and commentary on the Million Man March and the negative light that it was presented in makes my blood boil. I get mad anytime I hear someone say something negative about that day, especially if they were not there. Anybody that was there has not forgotten.

The tripped-out thing about that day is I went to DC to be a correspondent for BET, covering the event. I had just arrived in DC and stopped in a drugstore and ran into my father and my sister's boyfriend inside the drugstore. With all of the people that were in Washington, DC, for that day, for us to run into each other was more than a coincidence. It was that kind of a day.

As a correspondent for BET, I was interviewing brothers in the middle of the crowd, shaking hands with the people. Brothers were there from everywhere, from all walks of life. Even Black gay men were there, like Spike Lee depicted in the film *Get on the Bus*, because a Black man who happens to be a homosexual still has to deal with the racist aspects of being a Black man in this society. A Black man is a Black man, not because of his character, but because of his visual characteristics. Homosexuality in the white community is hell, homosexuality in the Black community is double hell. Young Black men and women should first know they're Black men or women and be informed with the bullshit that's going to be thrown at them just on the level of their Blackness.

I know a brother who took his wife and baby to the Million Man March because his wife was carrying their son in her womb, and there were brothers there who were close to a hundred years old.

I've never witnessed a day like that before. I can't even describe the feeling of that day. The only feeling that comes close to the feeling of the Million Man March is when I was in Africa. There was a similar feeling of warmth in both places. Every day in Africa is like the Million Man March. In the United States we get the interpretation of certain aspects of Africa, "They're fighting each other, they're killing each other," but the African principle is like, "Brother what's up? Your land is my land. We come in

> IT'S BECOME BLATANTLY CLEAR THAT THE MAJORITY OF BLACK AND WHITE PEOPLE SEE THE WORLD FROM DIAMETRICALLY OPPOSED POINTS OF VIEW.

peace." That's what I experienced in my travels in Ghana, and briefly in Nigeria. In the United States if you wave, or smile, or hug another brother it's considered some sissy shit. We're so guarded over here. We're always on the defensive and covering our souls, because we feel if we don't cover and protect ourselves we'll get raped again like we did before.

The thing about the Million Man March that I didn't like was all of the side criticism that came to the table. People were saying, "It's not about Farrakhan." Minister Farrakhan never said it was about him. However, the fact can't be overlooked that there must be a catalyst—a straw that stirs the drink. The straw and the drink for that day was the one that Minister Farrakhan actually brought to the table. He mobilized more than a million disciplined, committed, and dedicated Black men to Washington, DC, to show the world another side of Black men. It was so organized and disciplined brothers didn't even take a piss next to a tree. It was like, "We're here and we want to be respected."

All kinds of organizations got a chance to speak and contribute for that event, but it was only right that the man that made it all possible close out the day. I didn't like all of the player hating by envious Black puppets that came out with negative comments after such a beautiful event. When people look back on that day with criticism, I don't see where the criticism comes from because that day was flawless.

Minister Ishmael Muhammad of Chicago was pushing hard to get some rappers up there to speak. During preliminary meetings he was like, "The Hip-Hop Nation has to be represented." But I never did get a chance to present my speech that day, because the time ran over. I was waiting up in the Capitol with my father, Isaac Hayes, Ice Cube, Mack 10, and Ice-T. I remember looking around at the pictures on the Capitol walls. I was blown away and speechless just from sitting in the Capitol and seeing the whole environment being controlled by the Nation of Islam's security. It was a perfect day. I was floating.

One of the best speeches I've ever heard or felt is when Minister Farrakhan's son, Mustafa Farrakhan, introduced his father.

You could tell that he had carried a lot of pressure for a long time, and he had had enough of all the naysayers and doubters. Mustafa's speech rings in my head to this day. I felt him that strong. That was before Minister Farrakhan even came on. Mustafa was like, "On behalf of my family . . . we have been the brunt of a whole bunch of attacks, and those of you who know the plight of my father know that whenever any Black man is in trouble he always comes to your aid. Never be ashamed to stand up and say that Farrakhan is a friend of the Black man. And I challenge all of the leaders that when you are asked by your enemy, and those who oppressed us—my father is not a bigot, he's not a racist, he is not an anti-Semite. . . . From the President on down to everybody that's under him, Farrakhan is in your midst today. . . . Farrakhan is in your midst," and the cameras caught the Minister walking down the Capitol steps. In street language Mustafa was saying, "We're just trying to do the right thing, and we can't even do the right thing without people fucking with us." It was a son's passion and severe love for his father. Mustafa almost made me cry. I watched this from the middle of the Capitol, as I sat next to my father. It was overwhelming. It was over for me right there.

Minister Farrakhan brought all of the previous speakers' comments to a point when he stressed how the perspective of us and our sojourn should be seen from our eyes, instead of the eyes that others are used to. "From this day forward we can never again see ourselves through the narrow eyes of the limitations of the boundaries of our own fraternal, civic, political, religious, street organization or professional organization. We are forced by the magnitude of what we see here today that whenever you return to your cities . . . Know that he is your brother, and if he needs help you are obligated to help your brother, because he is your brother. You must live beyond the narrow restrictions of the divisions that have been imposed upon us."

The Million Man March Day should be observed every year as a Black holiday. America has reminders. Every Fourth of July we're reminded about the people that fought to free America 220

years ago. Every year at Christmas they remind us of the fat Caucasian that supposedly comes down the chimney. At Easter they remind us, not of Christ, but of the Easter eggs and the Easter bunny. At Thanksgiving they don't remind us to thank God, but remind us to be thankful that they stole this land from the Indians, and that there aren't many Indians left.

Dr. King's birthday is a cool holiday because it signifies an era. For Black people to signify another era, we need the Million Man March Day as our reminder, our Holy Day of Atonement, Reconciliation, and Responsibility. A person could be ready to kill somebody, but when they are reminded of the spirit of that day they're like, "Everything is cool."

The American political machine missed a great opportunity, due to fear, ignorance, and arrogance. Instead of giving props where props were due, and paying attention to the focus and theme of the day, they chose to focus their energies on attacking Minister Farrakhan, and distorting the magnitude of the day by drastically underestimating the number of people who participated. If they only listened with open minds to the stated purposes of the march—"to chart the course for our future as responsible heads of our families; to reclaim and build our neighborhoods; to unify our families; to save our children"—and supported the goals of the march, perhaps meaningful dialogue could have taken place afterward. Instead, once the Million Man March was over it became a nonstory, perhaps because they found the self-discipline, unity, and lack of violence disappointing or threatening.

While American political leaders and media attempted to downplay the significance of the Million Man March, countries around the world, especially nonwhite countries, recognized the magnificence of such a feat. Following the Million Man March, Minister Farrakhan could have been on any television news program that he wanted if it was all about him. Instead he decided to go on a World Friendship Tour which included nations throughout Africa and the Middle East. Among the countries visited were:

Ghana, Senegal, Gambia, Algeria, Syria, Liberia, Iran, Iraq, Libya, Nigeria, South Africa, Zaire, Mozambique, Sudan, Turkey, Saudi Arabia, and the United Arab Emirates.

One of the highlights of the tour was the unconditional one-billion-dollar gift offered by Libyan President Mu'ammar Gadhafi to Minister Farrakhan and the Nation of Islam to use for the benefit of Black economic and community development throughout the United States. The Treasury Department of the United States rejected the Nation of Islam's application to accept the money by bringing up some old, crazy law from 1831 called the Logan Act. Libya may be considered a "terrorist" nation by the American government, but Libya and Mu'ammar Gadhafi have never held the Black community down. This government wants the right to define and select our friends, which is a ridiculous concept, especially since the American government itself has not been a friend to Black people in America.

> WHILE AMERICAN POLITICAL LEADERS AND MEDIA ATTEMPTED TO DOWNPLAY THE SIGNIFICANCE OF THE MILLION MAN MARCH, COUNTRIES AROUND THE WORLD, ESPECIALLY NONWHITE COUNTRIES, RECOGNIZED THE MAGNIFICENCE OF SUCH A FEAT.

Public Enemy has always been about one race, the human race. But contrary to popular belief the Western world's philosophy has divided and conquered everyone to think that some other group of people is not a part of the human race. Since that philosophy has been spread across the world, and has led to hatred, murder, and destruction, then I will always stay proBlack as a matter of protection.

The publication of this book, *Fight the Power*, comes at a critical time in America's history, and for the Hip-Hop Nation as well.

FIGHT THE POWER

Hopefully, the issues addressed in this book will generate open and honest communication, understanding, and ultimately respect for Black people's trials, tribulations, victories, and sojourn here in America, and throughout the world.

I GOT A LETTER FROM THE GOVERNMENT
THE OTHER DAY
I OPENED AND READ IT
IT SAID THEY WERE SUCKERS
THEY WANTED ME FOR THEIR ARMY OR
WHATEVER
PICTURE ME GIVIN' A DAMN—I SAID
NEVER
—"Black Steel in the Hour of Chaos"

BLACK COMMUNITY:
Where Ya At?

"**W**hatever you do, don't go to war for this country. Be a conscientious objector." My mother's stern warning to me as a very young man in the mid-sixties is one of my clearest memories of that chaotic period. For many young people who are a part of the Hip-Hop Nation today, the Vietnam War and the turbulent 1960s is a period that they read about in history books—not for me. I actually lived through that and was personally affected and shaped by the pervasive antiwar, civil rights, and Black-Power sentiments as a child.

I remember being at the crib and someone knocking on the door to serve my uncles with draft papers. They were eighteen years old, fresh out of high school and headed to war.

One never came back, killed in the line of duty. My other uncle came back with a Purple Heart, and shrapp in his leg. I remember my brother and I not knowing what a Purple Heart medal was, and using it as a decoration for our GI Joe.

I was born in 1960, and spent the first ten years of my life soaking in what was going on around me. I was surrounded by it: the assassinations, the chaos, the race riots. It was all part of the everyday conversation.

I remember 1963: when Medgar Evers, the field secretary for the NAACP, was slain in front of his home in Jackson, Mississippi, the historic March on Washington by two hundred thousand protesters, the John F. Kennedy assassination in Dallas, Texas, and the mayhem that followed.

I remember 1965 and the solemn mood that permeated my grandparents' house when news of Malcolm X's assassination reached us.

I was in third grade when Dr. Martin Luther King was gunned down. My mother wore all black to work the next day. When she got back home that night she said a lot of white people were paranoid and didn't know how to act because they had never experienced Black people being so profoundly moved by one man, and had never seen Black people mourning en masse.

I had been taught that Dr. King was a man of peace who fought for Black people's rights, and it was real deep to me that he would get killed for that. As a kid, checking all of that out made me ask a lot of questions.

I was just a kid, but all of it was big news, including the massacre of the Black Panthers' Fred Hampton and Mark Clark in Chicago in 1969, and it was not taken lightly in my home.

> I HAD BEEN TAUGHT THAT DR. KING WAS A MAN OF PEACE WHO FOUGHT FOR BLACK PEOPLE'S RIGHTS, AND IT WAS REAL DEEP TO ME THAT HE WOULD GET KILLED FOR THAT.

My parents were young in the 1960s, and had radical ideas. My mother wore an Afro, and I remember wearing an Afro myself, as well as singing the "Free Huey Newton" song. My crucial developmental years took place right smack-dab in the middle of the Black Power movement.

I witnessed my family, and Black people in general, over a five-year span go from using the term "Negro" in 1963–1964, to using the term "colored" in 1966–1967, to using the term "Black" and using it with pride by 1968. By the time the TV shows *Julia* (1968), starring Diahann Carroll, and *The Bill Cosby Show* (1968–1971) hit the air *Black* pride was at an all-time high.

My parents used to play all of the popular jams of the day, and one of my favorites was James Brown's "Black Is Beautiful: Say It Loud, I'm Black and I'm Proud." As a youngster in school we sang that record like there was no tomorrow.

I'm not romanticizing the sixties. I try to make every year something special, but to understand me and the direction of the Rap group I was later to form, Public Enemy, one needs to understand the environment and realities that the majority of the guys in the Public Enemy camp, including myself, grew up facing. We were all born between 1958 and 1961. Most Rap artists today weren't born until 1967 or after. I came through an entirely different era.

I can't even relate to some of the subjects people are talking about today, because they are products of the seventies and eighties, and were influenced by TV shows like *Good Times, The Jeffersons,* and *Sanford and Son.* My influences were the Black Panther Party, the Nation of Islam, Elijah Muhammad and Malcolm X, the Vietnam conflict, and the numerous assassinations. In the 1970s there wasn't any of that. Vietnam was over. It was an era of cocaine, heroin, partying, and having a good time—*Superfly, Shaft,* and the "Blaxploitation" flicks took over.

When I decided to make Rap jams, I could only rap about what was stuck inside of me. As an artist I don't make soft music, I make my music hard and aggressive, which is an extension of the mixture of music I listened to growing up. I didn't just listen to soul and R&B, I had some craziness in the mix. I listened to everything from

Top 40 radio—Sly and the Family Stone, James Brown, The Who, Jimi Hendrix, The Rolling Stones, The Lovin' Spoonful—to Chicago, which wasn't aggressive but had a message. From 1967–1970, the music of the day was protest music, and during the protest music there were rock artists who were dying from overdosing on drugs. They were spaced out on their point of view. As a kid I knew what to fuck with and what not to fuck with. It was a complex time.

My parents always encouraged me to be an independent thinker. I've never tried to think like or follow anybody else. If anyone tried to tell me how to think or act I would purposely do the opposite. Back then I wanted to be an astronaut or a scientist because I used to bug out off of the Apollo Missions and the fact that humans were actually walking on the moon.

All-Time Favorite Groups:

Run-DMC: The songs, videos, show are the best indeed.
Grandmaster Flash and the Furious Five: The supreme; head and shoulders over competition.
Public Enemy: Made a movement; belief in song-video stage.
N.W.A: Reign of terror only could be stopped by themselves.
Salt 'N' Pepa: Overlooked, but why? Millions of sales; strong audience.
Treacherous 3: Innovative rhymers in sync.
EPMD: Dedicated to making you feel it.
Eric B. & Rakim: Blend of rhyme, poetry, and simple selection; Eric is underrated.
Whodini: Showmen; broke the now dormant female audience open in rap.
Stetsasonic: Underrated; hardworking Hip-Hop band and rap scientist.

I didn't watch much TV. My hobbies were reading comic books, drawing, and collecting baseball cards, so I had plenty of time to develop my own imagination and creativity. I definitely marched to my own drummer.

I was born in Flushing, Queens. My family moved to Queensbridge when I was an infant. That's something I have in common with Mobb Deep, Nas, and the whole Queensbridge Crew. When we moved from Queensbridge on the south side of Queens, which was Black as hell, to Roosevelt, Long Island, it was even Blacker. I was eleven years old when we finally moved from Queens to Roosevelt, which was only a ten- to fifteen-minute ride, but my distorted perception was that we were moving out to the "country." When we got there I realized it wasn't like that at all.

Roosevelt, Long Island, in the late 1960s and 1970s was a total Black town, and the people who moved into Roosevelt at that time had a different mind-set. We were a Black *community.* Black fathers were not just fathers to their own children, but they responded and contributed in different ways to the entire community, doing things like running the Boys Club, coaching the Pee Wee football teams, baseball teams, and the junior basketball leagues. Youngsters who didn't have fathers in their homes had their coaches, and there were also more male teachers back then. Roosevelt was going through a transitional period. My parents purchased their home from a white family, so it was Black people moving in and white people jetting out. In 1969 the Black population of Roosevelt was about sixty percent, in 1970 the Black population jumped to around seventy-five percent, and by 1972 Roosevelt was damn near ninety percent Black.

A lot of us young people in Roosevelt attended educational programs during the summer at Hofstra and Adelphi Universities, called the Afro-American Experience. My future Public Enemy partner, Hank Shocklee, participated when he was about eleven years old—as did Professor Griff. The program was developed to supplement the educational experience of young Black kids who weren't getting certain kinds of important information through the regular school system. After participating in the program after our

FIGHT THE POWER

29

fourth-grade year, a lot of us went into the fifth grade challenging our teachers—not just accepting the lies and distortions that they were teaching us. I think that became a threat to the Board of Education on Long Island, and potentially nationally. The program, though it was eventually disbanded, was funded by a grant from the city of Roosevelt, and was being taught and organized by Black college students, members of the Nation of Islam, members of the Black Panther Party on Long Island, and local Black groups. We were a group of ten- and eleven-year-olds on a college campus. We learned Swahili, African drumming, and facts about African culture, history, and the slave trade, as well as partaking in all kinds of physical activities throughout the two months we spent there. We received more useful information in those two months than we got during the entire academic year from September to June in the normal school system.

After completing that program I made up my mind that I was going to go to either Adelphi or Hofstra because of the great experience I had on those campuses in 1970 and 1971, and because they were close to my house. My early years and the supportive environment that I grew up in are my foundation, which is why I feel so strongly about the Black community getting back to where we belong.

DECEMBER 31ST 1999
NEW YEARS EVE OF THE YEAR 2000
AT THE EDGE OF THE 21ST CENTURY
PRESIDENT DUKE
OF THE UNITED WORLD STATES OF EUROPE AMERICA
THE NEW WORLD ORDER
DECLARES WAR ON THE
LAST ATTEMPT
TO UNIFY AFRICAN PEOPLE
AS ONE NATION UNDER A MOVE
YES THERE ARE BLACK FOLKS
AND WHITE FOLKS AMONGST THE PLANET'S COLORS
BUT THE PROGRAMMED
SUBCULTURES
HAVE WREAKED HAVOC ON THE EARTH
CRAKAS AN' DEVILS WHO ARE PROGRAMMED
ON A SUPERIORITY COMPLEX
AIM TO MAKE GAME OF THE RIGHTEOUS
TO TURN THEM INTO NIGGATRONS
IN THE NIGGATRONIC AGE

—"Beginning of the End"

During my years of crisscrossing throughout major and minor cities in America I've developed a theory with regard to the Black community. I call my theory the "Plantation Theory." The Plantation Theory states that Black people don't really have communities; what we have are clusters of plantations. A *community* is an environment that has control over the three E's: education, economics, and enforcement. Without control of these vital aspects of our existence, we're like robots existing in an environment with no real control. In the days of slavery in the South, there weren't any gates around the plantations, but there was a control over the plantation, which told Black people that they were not allowed to educate themselves, employ themselves, or write any laws. As a people we still exist in a similar state to this day.

When someone speaks about a community, they're speaking about a group of commonly identified people who can protect themselves and hold other groups of people in check. The Jewish

FIGHT THE POWER
31

community, the Italian community, the Chinese community, the Korean community, the Irish community all protect themselves. Incredibly, the Black community has not developed to the point where we recognize and unify around our common thread that bonds us; therefore, we have not been able to protect ourselves. We've been open season to other people's attacks and threats for most of this century. We've had a few periods where we've organized against oppressive forces: in the late 1950s and a large part of the 1960s where we organized against discrimination, segregation, and Jim Crowism, and again in the late 1980s. When we had Black Christians and Muslims uniting around Jesse Jackson's run for the Presidency. It's unfortunate that people have to organize themselves in tiny clusters of race to protect themselves, but that's the way it is. White supremacy and racism were thrust upon us—we didn't invent them. We're just by-products of the worst aspects of them. Rebuilding the Black community will involve gaining control of our own education, economics, and law enforcement.

THE KILLING FIELDS

THEY TELL LIES IN THE BOOKS
THAT YOU'RE READIN'
IT'S KNOWLEDGE OF YOURSELF
THAT YOU'RE NEEDIN'
—"Prophets of Rage"

Many people are tricked into believing that an education refers solely to attending the system's schools, but to educate means to prepare and inform people about controlling their community.

The youth of today need to be forced to sit and read something, but they want to read about something that they're into. They'll meet you halfway if you meet them halfway. If a teacher doesn't know anything about current trends and what's going on in society with the youth, then what will she or he teach? Teachers don't have to know Snoop Dogg's lyrics, Grant Hill's stats, or the latest plot on *The Cosby Show* or *Living Single,* but they should be aware of the things that young people are into. How can you teach if you don't know what your students are receptive to? The youth are going right from school to their homes to watch videos. They're learning more from the videos and Rap songs than they're learning from the schools. That's one of the reasons that Rap and other aspects of Black culture have crossed over so successfully into the mainstream, because young whites are able to get a heartfelt perspective through our music, which interprets our situations and expresses our feelings toward what's going on directly into their hearts and minds. It's almost like someone looking in a window from the outside. Hip-Hop culture is an education in a way. The potential danger with that is all someone has to do is come along with a more controlling "Big Brother" type of attitude and say, "We're going to fill Rap, R&B, rock, soul, and Black films with all kinds of negative, degenerative images," and as a people we'll be heading backward. And that's exactly what's been happening. Statistics show who likes to watch TV and videos. Negative is always easy to sell. If you give a fourteen-year-old a choice between a positive video, and a video with tits and ass, or guns and violence, he's going to choose the tits and ass, guns and violence almost every time.

Without proper education from a Black perspective to Black youth we're lost. Our youth are lost and uncontrollable right now because they don't have anything preparing them for their future as Black people. Education gets you out of so much. Education is like boxing: it prepares you to have good self-defense and teaches you to keep your dukes up. Education is not just the ABC's and 123's; those are the basic skills, but it's also learning from other people's experiences, which is a skill of life. As W.E.B. Du Bois stated in his essay *The Talented Tenth,* "A system of education is not one thing, nor does it have a single definite object, nor is it a mere matter of schools. Education is that whole system of human training within and without the schoolhouse walls, which molds and develops men."

Our legacy is not part of our children's curriculum. That's a serious problem. The curriculum doesn't teach how to survive or even function as a Black person in America. The early Black educator/entrepreneur Booker T. Washington said it best in his speech "Industrial Education for the Negro" when he discussed the role education should play in the lives of our people, "No race can be lifted until its mind is awakened and strengthened. . . . Our knowledge must be harnessed to the things of real life. I would encourage the Negro to secure all the mental strength, all the mental culture—whether gleaned from science, mathematics, history, language or literature that his circumstances will allow, but *I believe most earnestly that for years to come the education of the people of my race should be so directed that the greatest proportion of the mental strength of the masses will be brought to bear upon the every-day practical things of life, upon something that is needed to be done . . . in the community in which they reside. . . .*" I clearly remember in the eighth grade having to read *Ethan Frome* and *Great Expectations.* Fuck Ethan Frome, and fuck Ms. Haversham. Why did I have to read that shit instead of some James Baldwin or Zora Neale Hurston? You'd better believe that the publishing company that is putting out *Great Expectations* and *Ethan Frome* is making mad loot.

The schools are not preparing the minds of Black youth on how to function in this war zone that I call cultural one-sidedness. Minister Farrakhan calls the school systems the "killing fields." They're killing the minds of our youth. That's the travesty and the tragedy of the American school system.

I believe that supplementary materials need to be introduced to go along with the basic school texts and curriculum. Everyone must know their basics:

> **I CLEARLY REMEMBER . . . HAVING TO READ *ETHAN FROME* AND *GREAT EXPECTATIONS.***

reading, writing, and arithmetic. I tell kids all the time to master the basics, but at the dawn of the twenty-first century it's not enough to just master the same basics that our parents and grandparents were taught. Due to the Information Age and the tremendous growth of computers and the Internet, computer literacy has become as important as learning how

WHY DID I HAVE TO READ THAT SHIT INSTEAD OF SOME JAMES BALDWIN OR ZORA NEALE HURSTON?

to spell your name. The job market for the computer industry is projected to grow ninety-six percent annually through the year 2005, making it the second-fastest-growing industry. Right along with those basics at early stages in their schooling, especially at schools and school districts with ninety to ninety-five percent Black enrollment, the curriculum should be adjusted in order to reflect more of Black history and culture to better prepare young people for the real world. It would be like the traditional Black colleges, Tuskegee, Howard, Morehouse, or Spelman, but starting at earlier levels. It should be mandatory that Black and white students at all levels of the educational process learn the truth about different cultures and histories of people throughout the world. For example, everyone should be taught about the historic Million Man March, its purpose and its place in history. A lot of times Black students that don't get introduced to knowledge about themselves at earlier stages go into college and have "Black culture shock." They attempt to learn so much about themselves so quickly, and get so excited about what they're learning that they try to cram everything there is to learn about themselves into a two- to three-year period, which sometimes leads to burnout. They overload their circuits with so much that by the time they reach their third or fourth year they have less direction than when they started. If students could learn more about themselves in bits and pieces throughout their educational careers, by the time they got to college they would have learned the basics on every level, and then they could focus on mastering the particular field of study that they choose in college, and they would have more of an idea of what it is they want to major in with the objective of building their own companies to supply goods and services to their own communities upon graduation.

I remember one lecture I did at Memphis State when NBA star Penny Hardaway was still in college, and there was another player there named David Vaughn, who was a seven-foot forward on his way to the NBA. In the lecture I was saying, "If you're in school and fraternize and hang out with each other why not work to build businesses together. Who would you rather use, a man on the outside or one of your own boys who's trying to build a business?" David Vaughn came up to me at the end of my lecture and said, "What you said was interesting." Not too long after that Penny Hardaway went to the NBA, obtained a Black lawyer, and two Black agents, Carl and Kevin Poston. His people were hardcore. I'm using David Vaughn as an example. Maybe he spoke with Hardaway, maybe he didn't, but I know David Vaughn was thinking when he got to the pros to get Black representation, and there *are* qualified Black people out there. We have to encourage young Blacks to understand that level of athletics and entertainment, because it means lots and lots of money, and it can create the opportunity for businesses to be built in the future.

The original purpose of an education wasn't just to prepare for a job, but to prepare young minds to meaningfully contribute to society. Schooling in its original plan was for the white man, *only,* to send their sons, *only,* to school to create a business for the family, or to enhance the business that the father already had. America was so one-sided, sexist, and racist that they didn't even include their women or their daughters in the school program. School was directly tied in to business, and business in America is a family thing.

Shut 'Em Down

Since we've been in America we have never looked at ourselves as being family to each other. The day our people got off those slave ships bound with shackles by neck, hands, and feet, the first brother was like, "Get this shit off of me," and the enslavers cracked that whip on his back, and the others were like, "I don't know that motherfucker." Three hundred years of brutality, and the breeding of fear was so intense that it broke all ties to the concept of family, and made us hate ourselves and each other.

At the historic Million Man March on October 16, 1995, during Minister Farrakhan's speech, he read the text of an address made by a plantation owner from the Caribbean by the name of Willie Lynch, which was delivered at the banks of the James River in Virginia, 284 years ago. The contents of the address touched me, and reminded me of the current state of Black affairs.

In my bag I have a full proof method of controlling Black slaves. I guarantee every one of you, if installed correctly, it will control the slaves for at least three hundred years. My method is simple, any member of your family or your overseer can use it. I have outlined a number of differences among the slaves, and I take these differences and I make them bigger. I use fear, distrust and envy for control purposes. These methods have worked on my modest plantation in the West Indies and they will work throughout the South. Take this simple little list and think about it. On the top of my list is age, but it's only there because it starts with an A. The second is color or shade. There's intelligence, sex, size of plantation, status of plantation, attitude of owners, whether the slaves live in the valley or on a hill, north, east, south or west, have fine hair or coarse hair, or is tall or short. Now that you have a list of differences I shall give you an outline of action. But before that, I shall assure you that distrust is stronger than trust, and envy is stronger than adulation, respect or admiration. The Black slave, after receiving this indoctrination shall carry it on, and will become self refueling

FIGHT THE POWER

and self generating for hundreds of years, maybe thousands of years. Now don't forget, you must pitch the old Black male against the young Black male, and the young Black male against the old Black male. You must use the female against the male, and you must use the male against the female. You must use the dark skinned slave against the light skinned slave, and the light skinned slave against the dark skinned slave. You must also have your white servants and overseers distrust all Blacks, but it is necessary that your slaves trust and depend on us. They must love, respect and trust only us. Gentlemen, these keys are your keys to control. Use them, never miss an opportunity, and if used intensely for one year the slaves themselves will remain perpetually distrustful. Thank you, gentlemen.

The tactics and philosophies expressed in this address are obviously still being implemented today.

When a person from another nationality counters with, "Hey, my people came over as immigrants in the late 1800s and early 1900s and we didn't have anything, and we've progressed," that's a lie, because they did have something. They had a knowledge of who they were. One person from that nationality might say, "I'm going to be the baker," another would say, "I'm going to open a shoe shop," another would say, "I'm going to be a policeman," another would be the fireman, and what they had was a sense of community fostered by their cultural unity because they had a sense of self. They may not have had much financially, but they were able to build from the ground up. Black people didn't come on that same "Love Boat." So the sense of community and the sense that we are part of a larger family is something that was stripped from us. The concept of family is what everything else stems from, and immigrants from other countries recognized themselves as such.

If a man has a business more than likely he's going to put his son or daughter down to run it, or someone who looks like him, or someone who marries into his family, and he's going to take few people from outside of the family to run his business. That's how it's always been in America. With us, we pick up our education to see if we can qualify for a job to be accepted in somebody else's environment, rather than work as hard or harder than anyone else to create a job for ourselves and our future in our own environment.

We have to understand that a Black business has more than an obligation to just call itself a Black business. It has to employ members of our community. It has to build our community. When you have Black businesses out there that think they did it all by themselves, that's like a guy on a basketball team that takes fifty or sixty shots in a game, his team loses, and he brags about how many points he scored.

> YOUNG PEOPLE HAVE TO BE TAUGHT THAT THERE IS PREPARATION INVOLVED IN BECOMING AN ADULT, AND IF YOU DON'T GO THROUGH THE PROPER STEPS YOU'LL BE CUT OFF, FAIL, AND DIE QUICK.

The control over economics is crucial in being able to control the community. If Black businesses can't give opportunities to young people and can't educate them on to how to be prepared as adults, then young people will think they're going to be adults tomorrow. Young people have to be taught that there is preparation involved in becoming an adult, and if you don't go through the proper steps you'll be cut off, fail, and die quick.

Economic integration has truly meant economic disintegration for the Black community. Back in the day Black entrepreneurs had their own successful businesses by default, because we weren't allowed to be included in white businesses. Then in the fifties when a lot of Jim Crow laws began to change, especially down South, and white doors began to open up to Blacks, that marked the beginning of the end for Black economic control and advancement. A clear example is the two-sided effect of Blacks being allowed to play major league baseball. On one side it was just right that Blacks be allowed to compete and participate in this popular

FIGHT THE POWER

sport. On the other side it destroyed the competition and the structure of the Negro Leagues, as many talented players left the league. When the Negro Leagues were destroyed, not only were the teams destroyed, but the whole cycle of Black business surrounding that industry was destroyed. This happened in a lot of different areas: restaurants, hotels, transportation companies. Black ballplayers couldn't go into a city in the South and eat at a white restaurant back then, so they already knew the restaurants in the city they were traveling to. Those successful businesses were in existence for sixty to seventy years out of necessity. When the 1950s and 1960s came along and we knocked on the door of white culture to let us in, it was almost like we went to try to pick up a football, but dropped the basketball that we were holding. They didn't let us pick up the football or get the basketball back so we got stuck without either. That's pretty much what has happened over the last thirty years with our businesses.

In Manning Marable's important book *How Capitalism Underdeveloped Black America* he states, "The 'Golden Years' of Black business occurred in the decade 1919–1929, which not coincidentally was also the period of the most extensive racial segregation. By 1929 the number of Black-owned firms exceeded 70,000. Virtually every Black neighborhood or town in the United States could claim a number of independent Black entrepreneurs providing goods and services to an exclusively Black consumer market: barbers and beauty parlors, laundries, restaurants, grocery stores, newspapers, shoeshine and shoe repair shops, automotive service and repair, funeral parlors, insurance companies and small banks."

When Blacks moved from the South running from Jim Crow, they ran to the North looking to get a job. We abandoned the businesses we had in the South. When Blacks moved into the North there was a "Big American Scam." Allow Blacks to move into the North, stack them on top of each other, put them in small areas, and then have the businesses swoop out of the communities. Which means that for the last thirty years we've had urban decay in the major cities of America. That has been the big picture: Blacks stuck in the cities with no hope, no information, and lacking control of our destiny. Which goes back to the plantation state and shows that freedom isn't based on where you are physically, it's a state of mind and a state of existence.

Top 1990s Terrordome Rhymers:

Snoop Dogg: Changed the flow of the game.
Tupac Shakur: Incredible writer and workhorse.
Scarface: Paints pictures with rhymes.
Redman: Jimi Hendrix all over again with tongue.
Notorious B.I.G.: Ability to simplify and motivate.
Common Sense: Very poetic; true heir to Rakim.
Treach: Sharp; powerful; focused.
Keith Murray: Literally an assassin with rhyme.
Nas: Has survived the hype with adaptable skillz.

I LIKE NIKE BUT WAIT A MINUTE
THE NEIGHBORHOOD SUPPORTS SO PUT SOME
MONEY IN IT
CORPORATIONS OWE
DEY GOTTA GIVE UP THE DOUGH
TO DA TOWN
OR ELSE
WE GOTTA SHUT 'EM DOWN
—"Shut 'Em Down"

On the *Apocalypse '91: The Enemy Strikes Black* album we did the cut "Shut 'Em Down." I got the idea for the title from this brother who walked up to me while I was in the city, and told me that he heard someone on a radio station talking about DJ Red Alert saying, "Yo, Red is shutting 'em down, he's shutting 'em down." I also came up with the title from being a big fan of the

New York Knicks and their good defensive players who are capable of shutting other players down offensively.

After I wrote "Shut 'Em Down" with its famous Nike line at the end of the song, I later did the voice on a Nike commercial and got criticized for it. At the time some Black leaders were organizing a boycott against Nike for its insufficient support for institutions in the community since the Black community buys a disproportionate amount of its merchandise.

Hank Shocklee was contracted to produce the music for the Nike commercial as a Bomb Squad Production, and couldn't find any voice that would fit the commercial, so I did the voice. When people heard my voice on the commercial it was like, "Who's doing the voice on Charles Barkley's commercial? It sounds like Chuck D." "But I thought he doesn't like Nike?" Wrong. I said that I do like Nike but my position has always been that since the neighborhood supports it so heavily, it should put more substantial resources back into the community.

I'll support any sneaker company, but I would prefer to support a Black one. If there are any Black companies out there I'll support them. As a matter of fact I was used in advertisements for MVP sneakers, which was started by a brother from Detroit, Harold Martin. My merchandising company, Rappstyle, had actually developed a line of sneakers in partnership with MVP, then eventually Harold decided to go in a different direction with his company. Since we spend such enormous amounts of money on sneakers, we should at least buy some percentage of them from Black-run, Black-owned companies. That was a dream of mine, to start my own athletic shoe and merchandising company, so I did. Fuck boycotting, build your own.

I don't believe in boycotts. The best way to boycott is to build your own. Forget about having one hundred people wasting

> **I DON'T BELIEVE IN BOYCOTTS. THE BEST WAY TO BOYCOTT IS TO BUILD YOUR OWN.**

their time outside of a Korean grocery store. That's not going to do anything, because after they start picketing, and the boycott is successful in get-

ting the store to close down, then you have people in that community saying, "Where do I get my baby's Pampers from?" The best form of economic pressure would be for those same one hundred people, who were going to spend their time boycotting, to build a store of their own. Build your own, have your own, and support your own. That's better than having a march; that shit is old, played out, and tired. According to statistics Black people extract close to $440 billion a year from the American economy, but most of the money that comes into Black hands goes right out of the community. The only time you see Black people recycling Black dollars where the money goes from Black hand to Black hand more than once is when somebody Black robs another Black person.

Straight up on the real affirmative action, which is being slashed left and right, especially with Proposition 209, the anti-affirmative-action bill recently passed in California. Affirmative action of the 1970s, which came from pressure from the 1960s, has to be adapted to a 1990s formula for economics. Affirmative action in the 1970s was the FCC requiring a radio station be built in a Black community. Affirmative action in the 1990s should require that at least fifteen percent of the businesses in malls be Black owned, whether it's a Black or white mall. We are fifteen percent of the country's makeup so to become an equal part of the economic picture we need to have fifteen percent of the businesses in the malls. That would be affirmative action for the 1990s and beyond. We need new thinkers and new ideas to adapt to new problems, new scenarios, and new solutions.

ANTI-NIGGER MACHINE

THEY GOT ME ROTTIN' IN THE TIME THAT I'M SERVIN'
TELLIN' YOU WHAT HAPPENED THE SAME TIME THEY'RE THROWIN'
4 OF US PACKED IN A CELL LIKE SLAVES—OH WELL
THE SAME MOTHERFUCKER GOT US LIVIN' IN HIS HELL
YOU HAVE TO REALIZE—THAT IT'S A FORM OF SLAVERY
—"Black Steel in the Hour of Chaos"

The third area of control that's lacking among Black people is law enforcement. We're not represented enough in law, either in the creation or enforcement. If we can't make a law in our own environment, then we might as well be living on a plantation. If black leaders can't dictate economic, educational, law-enforcement, and law-making decisions nationwide, then that's not Black leadership, it's an illusion of Black leadership.

One of my all-time favorite PE songs is "Black Steel in the Hour of Chaos," which is one of the original, funk, gangster grooves in Rap about a fantasy jailbreak. Even to this day, hearing that record gives me a chill. In the song we fight for our right to escape from prison because it was the right thing to do. The true message of the jam is don't let anybody try to hold you back from what you believe in. It was a jam that was far ahead of its time.

"Black Steel in the Hour of Chaos" was dedicated to my brothers and sisters in the lockdown, because there's way too many Black people in the prison system. One out of every four Black men between the ages of twenty and twenty-nine is under the supervision of the criminal justice system, either in jail or on probation or parole. There are more Black men in the criminal justice system than there are Black men of all ages enrolled in higher education. Many are locked down as victims of circumstance. Marc Mauer, assistant director of the Sentencing Project, stated in his testimony before a House Subcommittee on the issue, "The evidence for a strong association between inequality and crime is overwhelming. . . . It isn't accidental, then, that among developed countries, the United States is afflicted simultaneously with the worst rates of violent crime, the widest spread of income inequality, and the most severe public policies toward the disadvantaged."

Through Rap music the most negative projection of ourselves becomes the most popular for young people. What develops is a driven hipness to be cool and to be on the side of the criminal. There's a certain level of acceptance to the rebelliousness that's being projected in this country today, and the system is using it to its benefit. Most young people don't understand their environment and the seriousness of the events taking place around them, and there are not enough elders who know what's happening who stop and talk to the young people who are getting caught up and victimized. We have images on television, video, and film talking to us more than we talk to each other. The problem is there's too many children that want to be adults, and too many adults that want to be children.

Nowhere else on the planet are the adults of a culture afraid of their own youth. Anywhere else on the planet people groom their youth so they can take the future positions of leadership. Here in the United States, where the so-called most powerful, educated, gifted, and strongest Black people are, we're afraid of our own youth because we're constantly dealing with the madness and anarchy within. There's been a severe trick in there somewhere, and the bottom line is that we have a culture that is currently unable to control its offspring. The older generations don't reach out enough to the younger generations, and the younger generations are rebelling against the same old ways.

WE HAVE IMAGES ON TELEVISION, VIDEO, AND FILM TALKING TO US MORE THAN WE TALK TO EACH OTHER.

I believe in organized vigilantism when necessary. If it comes down to our women and children getting

slaughtered from the stupidity of brothers who have yet to act like men, then what we need is organized vigilantism. Look at the Nation of Islam. If you do something really crazy in the Nation of Islam, you'll be running to the police to save your ass. I believe the community should pass the real law, but you have to have a community full of people that are organized in one unit. There's a lot more hardworking, law-abiding people in our neighborhoods than criminals, and I don't care how mighty a person thinks he is, a gang of thirty people won't beat one hundred men.

At a recent lecture at Morgan State University, I was explaining how Black and white youth who are buying "Black styles" more than ever don't know that some of those looks being marketed by Tommy Hilfiger and other designers, particularly sagging jeans, started in prison. Jails stopped issuing belts in the 1970s, because inmates were hanging themselves with them. So if an inmate who was 140 pounds was issued a pair of extra large pants, there was no choice but to let them sag. The same thing with Run-DMC and their Adidas sneakers with no shoelaces. That style also started in the jails. Shoelaces were not issued for the same reason as belts. So brothers in jail wouldn't have either. Today you have companies getting rich off of that style, selling it in the malls and shops of mainstream America, with a white guy taking in the profits. That style was created by a circumstance our people had to deal with while locked up in a system that held us back.

The United States is like one big cage for Black people. The places that we call home are ghettos, and projects, which are experiments. The mentality is another cage, because *we're locked into a mentality and a mind-set that limit our potential.* There are people right now headed to jail thinking it's the norm. It's an unbelievable, crazy concept when people embrace slavery. It's almost like the United States is a big laboratory for Black people; they're experimenting and "Black Steel in the Hour of Chaos" says to do what you have to do in order to be free, no matter what.

What's happening in the 1990s is corporations are shutting down their plants and investing in prisons, which have become their legalized slave-labor force for the year 2000 and up. There will be more corporations investing in prisons, and having their workforce operate from prison where an inmate is happy to be working for less than half a buck a day. Our youth looking at jail life as being glamorous is taking us right back into slavery.

The unemployment problem in the Black community will be resolved, but how we're going to be working and who we're going to be working for will be the big questions. This is all going down by the design of big businesses and corporations, working in conjunction with the government of America, and once again they'll be looking at record profit margins, built on the workforce of the close to one million people in prison, helped by harsher sentencing laws, parole release policies that have become tighter, and mandatory minimum drug-sentencing laws. That's a crystal ball that a lot of people see. Slave labor in the near future.

Another song I did dealing with law enforcement and the policing system is called "Anti-Nigger Machine." To me the whole government and the entire policing system is an antinigger machine. As long as the police claim to protect and serve, they mean that they come to protect and serve property owners, and in America we own very little property. They treat us like niggers and act as a machine with the cops at the bottom rung of the ladder carrying out the orders from above.

The funny thing about "Anti-Nigger Machine" is in the second verse, where I say, "Peace the police just wanna wreck and flex, on the kid what I did was try to be the best, so they fingered the trigger figured I was a bigger nigger and they started to search me so I headed west. Went to Cali a rally was for a brother's death, it was the fuzz who shot him an' not da Bloods or Cuzz." Actually Ice Cube helped me by correcting a line in there, because originally the lyrics were, "It was the fuzz who shot him not the Crip or Cuzz," then Ice Cube told me that Crip and Cuzz was the same thing. So I changed that lyric.

Not long after that a brother named Oliver X Beasley was shot and killed by the police in L.A. That was just a sad coincidence, and it's one of the many things I've done in records that turned out to happen after I've written and rhymed about it. My friend Harry

Allen says I'm prophetic in some of the things I rap about. That was a strange twist to that song. When that killing happened it fit right in. Later on when we put a version on a twelve-inch, I put a middle verse in the song talking about the Boston situation with Stewart, the white guy who alleged that his wife was killed by Black guys and the truth was he killed her himself.

"Anti-Nigger Machine" definitely dealt with the issue of whose side the police are on, and the fact that we need our own police. The jam, which was part one of a two-part record ends, "Wondered why I was like so I just held my mic, so I stayed in the crib until I got a buzz." Then Flavor gives me a call at the beginning of the next song on the album, "Burn Hollywood Burn."

It's like there's a game taking place and we're not being taught the rules of the game. Education teaches the rules of the game, and lets you know there's a game being played. Economics teaches how to play the game at some level, and stay away from being victimized. Enforcement gives you a referee. We're in the game where the referee is calling all kinds of calls on us, but nobody schooled us on the playbook.

In this game there's players and victims. Black people have never been the players, we've always been the victims. We've been pimped, whored, played, and macked for the last five hundred years in this land. In order to be a player you have to know the full game, and you have to understand that in order not to continue to lose we need a level of teamwork. We have to learn how to spread the word and pass the ball.

If we don't have control over those three E's—education, economics, and enforcement—we're on a

> BLACK PEOPLE HAVE NEVER BEEN THE PLAYERS, WE'VE ALWAYS BEEN THE VICTIMS. WE'VE BEEN PIMPED, WHORED, PLAYED, AND MACKED FOR THE LAST FIVE HUNDRED YEARS IN THIS LAND.

plantation. That's the serious level we're at right now. We can't say that we live in communities, we don't. We live in plantation systems that are still governed by a legal and subtle apartheid in the United States of America.

Burn Hollywood Burn

As I walk the streets of Hollywood Boulevard
Thinkin' how hard it was to those that starred
In the movies portrayin' the roles
Of butlers and maids slaves and hoes
Many intelligent Black men seem to look uncivilized
When on the screen
Like a guess I figure you play some jigaboo
On the plantation, what else can a nigger do
—Big Daddy Kane in "Burn Hollywood Burn"

The development of the song "Burn Hollywood Burn" was a situation where I just threw the concept out there, and it took on a life of its own. I was doing an interview with a reporter for a magazine, and I jumped the gun and said, "Big Daddy Kane and I are working on a project that will be out soon, it's called 'Burn Hollywood Burn.' " The interesting thing was that I hadn't written the jam, I didn't have a track, I hadn't talked to Kane about it, I just went off the top of my head, the same way I did previously with the title of the album *Fear of a Black Planet.*

Big Daddy Kane was a new Rap phenomenon who came off as a sex symbol, and at the same time would knock your face off. Kane had been saying to me for years, "When are we going to do a record together?" So I figured while doing the interview that it was an appropriate time to make that decision. Little did I know at the time that Ice Cube, who also made a guest appearance on the cut, would be involved. During that time Cube was traveling back and forth to New York, checking out different producers. The night that Kane and I went in to cut the record in the Greene Street Studios, Cube was sitting on the couch, and

FIGHT THE POWER
49

within minutes he wrote his lyrics, and before I knew it Cube was on the record talking about, "Ice Cube is down with the PE, Now every single bitch want to see me." I didn't know how I was going to fit all Cube's "bitch" and "shoot the motherfucker" lyrics into the record, but fuck it, that was Ice Cube. I really thank Ice Cube and Big Daddy Kane for their efforts on that important record.

When it came time for me to write my lyrics for "Burn Hollywood Burn" I had my topic ready. I was dealing with the messed-up side of the film industry, which I had studied from seeing all of the pressure Spike Lee got with his films.

"Burn Hollywood Burn" was challenging the industry about the portrayal of Black people on the "Silver Screen." Who was behind it? And who is behind it still? It's not Black people behind that industry. In the 1930s and 1940s when people saw an image of us on the screen, they were looking at an image that depicted us in a totally derogatory manner and they've never gotten checked on it. They've made millions upon billions of dollars off an industry that makes us look like fools.

Some people say that Hollywood has been and still is controlled by Jews. Others will argue that you can't say Jewish people as a majority run Hollywood. An example is the controversy that surrounded Marlon Brando's remarks on CNN's *Larry King Live*. Brando said among other things that "Hollywood is run by Jews . . . and they should have a greater sensitivity about the issue of people who are suffering because they've [been] exploited." The immediate response by the Jewish Defense League and other Jewish organizations made it clear that those comments were not appreciated.

The people at the helm of the major studios never really identified themselves on that level, they just identified themselves as an industry or as companies. To me the way that you make people accountable is you take the protection away from the term "an industry" or the protection away from the term "company" and break it down to the actual individuals. I wouldn't be cross enough to say Jewish people as a cluster led to our demise as a people based on our exploitation in the movie industry. I will say, however, that there were individuals from backgrounds that were Jewish and individuals of other ethnicities who didn't have any of our concerns in their pictures. Or to be more direct they gave less than a fuck about us, or maybe they were just ill informed that we were people too.

My whole thing is, fuck industry talk. People say, "It's the industry." Fuck that, it was individuals. Fuck companies. Fuck even the point where people say, "Jewish people did it." Fuck that. Let's talk to the individuals, and fuck the religion, and all of the other bullshit. An individual, a person was responsible. Yes, he may have made a business move, but the same argument came to be used to attempt to defend slavery. Individuals made business decisions in slavery. We can't say it was so-and-so company. The legal structure of a company is designed to protect itself. Fuck the protection when it comes down to a company doing wrong. You break that shit down to the accountability of the individuals, and that's what we have to do with Hollywood or anything else that's derogatory. Break Hollywood down to an industry, break the industry down to a company, break the company down to individuals, and you'll see people running like roaches.

Everybody in this country has a first and last name, an address, and a social security number, so there's a way to identify them, and if they're dead, there's a way to identify their descendants.

The pioneers/founders of the following major Hollywood studios have heirs to the fortunes and estates built off of our suffering and they need to be confronted with the facts.

> BREAK HOLLYWOOD DOWN TO AN INDUSTRY, BREAK THE INDUSTRY DOWN TO A COMPANY, BREAK THE COMPANY DOWN TO INDIVIDUALS, AND YOU'LL SEE PEOPLE RUNNING LIKE ROACHES.

Metro-Goldwyn-Mayer (MGM)	**Marcus Loew**
	Louis B. Mayer
Paramount	**Adolph Zukor**
	Jesse L. Lasky
20th Century-Fox	**William Fox**
	Joseph Schenck
Universal	**Carl Laemmle**
Warner Bros.	**Harry M. Warner and his three brothers Sam, Albert, and Jack**
Columbia Pictures	**Harry and Jack Cohn, and Joe Brandt**

If we can determine that these individuals were responsible for the injurious images that came through, then the people that inherited their fortunes need to kick back some dough. According to *Black's Law Dictionary,* the definition of defamation of character is "that which tends to injure reputation; to diminish the esteem, respect, goodwill or confidence in which the plaintiff [Black people] is held, or to excite adverse, derogatory or unpleasant feelings or opinions against him. Statement which exposes person to contempt, hatred, ridicule, or obloquy." You tell me! Somebody's related to those motherfuckers. Somebody is related to them, and is living fat off the riches that were partially earned at the expense of defaming the character of a whole race of people.

Hollywood's dishonesty, distortions, myths, and misconceptions about Black people as nothing but watermelon stealin', chicken eatin', knee knockin', eye poppin', lazy, crazy, dancin', submissive, "Toms, Coons, Mulattoes, Mammies, and Bucks," ever since D. W. Griffith's *Birth of a Nation* (1915), all the way up to the 1950s—which is a forty-year period of straight-up lies, propaganda, derogatory images, and bullshit—have been spread across, not only the United States, but the entire world. That has had a major effect, not only on how society looks at us, but how we look at ourselves. A lot of Blacks in Hollywood right now are controlled by certain foolish stereotypes that they feel they must perpetuate in order to be accepted and keep steady work.

I'm looking for some answers. I'm looking for someone to hold accountable for those actions. It doesn't help matters that a couple of Black actors and actresses get paid well. Fuck that. Reparations are due from the industry all the way across the board. Whether or not it will be a reality is another issue, but one thing that has to be done is it has to be said.

A LOT OF BLACKS IN HOLLYWOOD RIGHT NOW ARE CONTROLLED BY CERTAIN FOOLISH STEREOTYPES THAT THEY FEEL THEY MUST CONTINUE TO PERPETUATE IN ORDER TO BE ACCEPTED AND KEEP STEADY WORK.

BUT SOME THINGS I'LL NEVER FORGET YEAH
SO STEP AND FETCH THIS SHIT
FOR ALL THE YEARS WE LOOKED LIKE CLOWNS
THE JOKE IS OVER SMELL THE SMOKE FROM ALL AROUND
BURN HOLLYWOOD BURN
—Chuck D "Burn Hollywood Burn"

Stepin Fetchit, whose real name was Lincoln Perry, was a very gifted and talented brother, but he was branded with the name Stepin Fetchit as in, "Go in the big house and fetch me something." Bill "Bojangles" Robinson, who was one of the greatest dancers in the world, always had to act like a "Tom" in the movies. The racism in the industry allowed them such a small loophole, either they took the part or somebody else would. Who do you point that finger at? I point the finger at whoever created that small loophole and allowed such a small margin of opportunity that would have people that are so talented stoop to that level.

Hollywood had a chance to help put an end to prejudice, and reverse the tide of racism in America, but they just weren't bold and brave enough to take the stand.

Many people are not aware that there were independent black filmmakers in the 1930s, like Oscar Micheaux, a strong brother who laid the groundwork for Blacks today and attempted to bring honor, dignity, and respect to the images of Black people on the screen. Those early Black pioneers had to handle every aspect of their productions from finance to the final cut, then travel from town to town, theater to theater, showing the film in the few places in America that would play Black films. Those brothers were quadruple-teamed because they were some of the few exceptions to the rule. Spike Lee doesn't get credit for the incredible vision that he put together ten years ago with *She's Gotta Have It*. The industry has opened up to Black people a little since they've found out that we can sell shit, and they've found out that we're commercially viable. People say, "Well, you have to play the game." I believe you can have a foot in the game and do your shit with the other foot. Based on the advantage of having a head start by everybody else, I truly don't believe that exclusivity works in our favor. We need to have the double advantage of building our own and still work in the game.

Public Enemy has been involved on the periphery of Hollywood early on in our careers when Rick Rubin used the song "Bring the Noise" in the *Less Than Zero* sound track. There seemed to be a natural connection with Public Enemy and film. In 1988 we had "Terminator X to the Edge of Panic" in the *Tougher Than Leather* sound track. In 1989 our third sound track cut "Fight the Power," which was probably the most well known, was in Spike Lee's *Do the Right Thing.* In 1991 the Bomb Squad did the score behind the movie *Juice,* which was supervised by Hank Shocklee and Gary G Wiz.

It's been a natural progression for me to become more involved with film scoring, music supervision, sound track advising, commercial voice-overs, children's programming, and television scoring. I've worked hard to get into the nontraditional areas behind the scenes where there are very few Blacks, because we always jump for what's thrown in front of our face.

On a recent film that I was trying to get the composing job for, the music supervisor asked if I would play one of the parts in the film. I never thought I would end up acting, but one night while I was visiting the set of the Alan Smithee film, Whoopi Goldberg, Sylvester Stallone, and Jackie Chan all told me in the same night, "Just try it. You have nothing to lose." I figured it couldn't hurt, especially since I was also going to be working in the background on the music score. The producers asked me if I would have a problem with Coolio. I said, "Hell no, I don't have a problem with anybody, especially another rapper." Incidentally, Coolio and I were born on the same day. In the film Coolio and I play two brothers who are filmmakers who get back at Hollywood. So in my first Hollywood role I figuratively get a chance to "burn Hollywood."

PRELUDE TO PUBLIC ENEMY

Since my first world tour ten years ago I've been to forty countries, performing to sold-out audiences in the United States and countries around the world including Canada, Mexico, Bermuda, the Virgin Islands, Ireland, Scotland, Holland, Belgium, Norway, Sweden, Denmark, France, Switzerland, Italy, China, Japan, Australia, New Zealand, Ghana, Egypt, Nigeria, Croatia, Spain, Brazil, Germany, Finland, Hungary, Austria, Puerto Rico, and Greece. In my travels around the planet, I've continually heard stories of oppression and stories of the rich trying to beat down the poor. Black people suffer globally from white supremacy because we're easily identifiable, so we're used as pawns in the game. But I've witnessed other pawns in the game. In countries where there's not a large population of Black people, they find a way to make people the scapegoat based on religious, ethnic, or cultural differences. During our European tour in December of 1994, one PE/Rap fan in Zagreb, Croatia, named Benjamin said about Rap music and its potential positive impact, "Public Enemy showed us that Rap music is not afraid of subjects connected with national and race issues. We started to see how powerful Rap could be if it were used in expressing our attitudes. The kind of lyrics and consciousness that reveals the whole process of civilization, which is the story of dominance: the dominance of white people over Black people, the dominance of male over female, the dominance of man over nature, and the dominance of majorities over minorities. For some, Public Enemy is just a very good group, for good fun, but for me they have a powerful political statement, especially when we connected what they were saying with the war in Bosnia, Herzegovina, and Croatia. We've always felt that the Muslims in Bosnia and the Croats are brothers, real brothers according to the history.

"On the one hand the music of Public Enemy can help to unite, but on the other hand it can help someone to say, 'Fuck off,' to the oppressor. Those things are included in the message for me, and I like it, I like both things. I like the protest or rebel aspect, and I also like the fact that it's stupid to speak about Black racism when you have the civilizational situation of white dominance."

My upbringing and the fact that I actually lived through the turbulent decade of the sixties gave me an advantage in the beginning of Rap. I was actually considered "too old" when I cut my first recording in 1987 at the age of twenty-six, but

> MY UPBRINGING AND THE FACT THAT I ACTUALLY LIVED THROUGH THE TURBULENT DECADE OF THE SIXTIES GAVE ME AN ADVANTAGE IN THE BEGINNING OF RAP.

while my age may have appeared to be a disadvantage to some, it was actually an advantage based on what I knew.

Rappers only rap about what they know, so information is always advantageous. I didn't want to rap about "I'm this or I'm that" all the time. I bragged about myself in my early records, because we've never been taught to talk positively about ourselves, and I thought that was good. My focus, however, was not on boasting about myself or battling brothers on the microphone. I wanted to rap about battling institutions, and bringing the condition of Black people worldwide to a respectable level.

After graduating from Roosevelt High School in the spring of 1979, I was accepted to Adelphi University. The summer of 1979 was berserk. Long Island was Hip-Hop crazy. Everybody was rhyming. People had books of rhymes, nineteen-year-old girls had rhymes, there were rhymes galore. It was a summer of Rap fanaticism, and it began reaching the Black mainstream. During that summer I went to a lot of parties.

In October I went to a party at Adelphi called the "Thursday Night Throwdown." Back then people had what I call "microphonitus," which I define as an acute and intense desire to pick up the microphone anywhere and anytime. That particular night as the deejays played "Ain't No Stopping Us Now," and "Love Is the Message," I stood on line with about ten other guys to get on the mic. I was the last one to get on, and rocked the mic so I stood out from everyone else.

At the time I was trying to get back in school because I had been dismissed for a semester due to all of the incompletes I had received from fooling around as a freshman. I was going to school every day, I just didn't go to class. The whole college environment was like a hang-out spot for me. I would go to the UC and play ball, there were females from the city there, and I was partying my ass off. I fell into the freshman trap, where school was exciting, but I wasn't doing anything. By that next May I got my grades, and I figured if I kept staring at them maybe something would change. It read, "I—I—I—I," I received about seven I's, and at the bottom it said, "No." It took me three semesters to make those incompletes up and get rein- stated in the spring semester of 1981.

I worked during the three semes- ters that I was out, because my moms was like, "If you're not in school you either go to work, or you're out of here." I wanted to work and make some money any- way—but my perspective changed after making $3.15 an hour for a while. To get to work I had to travel to New Hyde Park, which was not too far from Adelphi. When I would get off from work, and something was happening at school I would end up right back there. I wished I was back in school. That was a soul-

> I FELL INTO THE FRESHMAN TRAP, WHERE SCHOOL IS EXCITING, BUT I WASN'T DOING ANYTHING. BY THAT NEXT MAY I GOT MY GRADES, AND I FIGURED IF I KEPT STARING AT THEM MAYBE SOMETHING WOULD CHANGE.

searching period in my life. I wanted to go to school, and was ac- cepted into the school because of my talent, which I was trying to turn into a skill, and I ended up on the outside looking in. That was my first wake-up call. So I really buckled down and worked hard to get reinstated.

Hank Shocklee happened to be there that night in October at the "Thursday Night Throwdown," and heard me rapping. Hank was the founder of Spectrum City, and they had been one of Long Island's biggest deejay operations since 1975. Spectrum City was known as a crew of deejays that played fly music but had no MCs. Growing up in Roosevelt, I was a big fan of theirs. That night after the "Throwdown," Hank asked me if I wanted to be a rapper within Spectrum City. I was the first MC that Hank thought would fit inside his crew.

We had met at a party the previous summer when he was speaking with this deejay named Everett James, who was called "EJ the DJ." I had gone to the party because I'd seen one of the flyers they had distributed. For a person like me who is artistically inclined, the flyer seemed sloppy because it was drawn up in pencil, and whoever designed it spelled the word "Spectrum" wrong. Hank and EJ were sitting on a car outside of the party, apparently disappointed by the lack of turnout. I wanted to design flyers at the time, so I went up to them and told them that if they had had a more captivating flyer, they might have attracted more people. Then I added that I was an artist who did design work. They looked at me like, "Who is this motherfucker? We're not trying to hear that shit right about now."

From 1979–1982 I worked inside the organization as an MC. Spectrum City would often be hired to deejay parties and different events by the colleges in the area, C.W. Post, Hofstra, and Adelphi, which were the center points for Black entertainment on Long Island at that time.

Through 1982, we were involved in all kinds of things: mobile deejaying, club and party promotions, producing tapes, and record pools. A record pool consisted of deejays who had to pay a fee to be in the pool, and in return would get promotional records from record companies for clubs and mobile events.

Rap records started in 1979 with the Sugarhill Gang, and the previous summer King Tim III was put out by the Fatback Band. When Rap records came out, especially after the Sugarhill Gang, we searched everywhere for them. We were originally a part of the Disco Den record pool, which was on 125th Street and Park Avenue in Harlem. I remember one freezing-cold day in November of 1979 when Hank and I were walking on 125th Street. At the time the Sugarhill Gang was blowing up, and we heard this beat coming out of a store with somebody rapping over it. We went into the store, looked at the record, and picked up two copies. The record was Spoonie Gee's. We also picked up a copy of Woody Wood's *Woody's Rap*. Back then 125th Street was full of Hip-Hop activity. Paul Winley Records, and Peter Brown's The Sound of New York Records were both on 125th Street.

We later became part of the Intermetro record pool, which was predominantly a pool of gay house deejays who were also into Rap. As part of the Intermetro record pool, each deejay would

CHUCK D

> IT'S FUNNY THAT DEF JAM SOLD FOR THIRTY-THREE MILLION DOLLARS A FEW YEARS BACK. IT STARTED OUT WITH AN ARTICLE IN *BILLBOARD* THE SIZE OF A STAMP.

have to select their top twenty records and report them. Then the record pool would compile their list and ship it to the radio stations and record companies. Our top twenty selections were filled with Rap from one to twenty, plus the two bonus cuts we had to select. We would also advertise on our tip sheets any events we had going on, and any new things that were happening in Hip-Hop. I remember one time cutting a small article out of *Billboard* magazine and attaching it to the one-page tip sheet we submitted, which read, "Russell Simmons starts new label with Rick Rubin called Def Jam." It's funny that Def Jam sold for thirty-three million dollars a few years back. It started out with an article in *Billboard* the size of a stamp.

I remember one day in March when Hank's brother, Keith Shocklee, came back to Long Island after taking that long trip from Intermetro's offices at Centre and Spring streets in the Soho district of New York with this record from Profile Records. Keith brought the record back to the studio, and when he played it I was like "Yo, that's the shit." The record was "Sucker MC's" and on the B side was "It's Like That" by Run-DMC. Both songs were thrilling us.

One of the first gigs we threw was in Uniondale, Long Island. It was on the day after New Year's. We invited Jeff Troy, from the newly formed KISS-FM, which was previously WXLO, to host the event. The place was pandemonium. From that we decided we would continue to do our own gigs.

In 1981 and 1982 we tried to sell our mix-tapes, but they were a hard sell for ten dollars, even though people wanted them. Then I started to think about Adelphi's radio station, WBAU, and how it wasn't being facilitated right, especially on the Black end. A lot of Black people from Queens and Long Island listened to that radio station, so I felt that WBAU could compete with KISS-FM, which had just been formed and was *the* station for the Hip-Hop audience. Spectrum City made people identify and bond with us through the flyers we designed, so I thought we could possibly transfer that identification over to the radio station. I wanted to go from making tapes to getting free radio airplay and promotions for Spectrum, and simultaneously advertise the radio station. That way people could record a tape every week on their own. We wouldn't make any money off of it, but we would receive more notoriety.

At that time is when I first met with Rusty J, a popular WBAU deejay, about the possibility of getting a show on the station. I knew Rusty because he had hosted a few of our college gigs. Rusty played garage music and wasn't too keen on the idea of sharing his show with anybody, but he told me about a show that played Hip-Hop on Monday nights hosted by Bill Stephney. I ended up meeting Bill one day. He had heard of Spectrum City so he invited us to come by WBAU to check out his radio show. When we went to see him we brought some of our mix-tapes for him to listen to. The chemistry was right, and we hit it off immediately.

Since Bill's show came after *Monday Night Football*, we figured we could get a lot of people to listen to the show. As far as I can remember Monday nights have always been the center point of all activity on Long Island. We figured people would be like, "Spectrum is on the radio? I can get my tape for free off of the radio."

Bill Stephney and Russell Simmons were instrumental in bringing Run-DMC to the station to do their first interview ever. We couldn't get them to say much at all, but when they came back from doing a couple of tours and their record was red-hot, we interviewed them again and they were real open. They were like different people, telling us about shows they did with the Bar-Kays, George Clinton, and their travels to different cities. The thing that really made us happy was when they told us that wher-

ever they went they would take their WBAU tapes with them. As a matter of fact, on the second Fresh Fest tour we did with Run-DMC, they used to bring their WBAU tapes and play them on that tour, which was flattering because we were a radio station that helped inspire them to do their music, and their music helped inspire us to do better radio.

Pound for Pound Greatest Rhymers of All Time:

L.L. Cool J: In this game, purely the best.
Ice Cube: Best word for word rapper/songwriter workhorse.
Big Daddy Kane: Pound for pound the most talented, dynamic I've seen.
KRS One : Committed and devastating; strong-willed.
Rakim: Most poetic; able to make the music move to him.
Melle Mel: Power; the first to do this right.
Kool Moe Dee: Most tactical; calculating executioner.
Ice-T: The Deion Sanders; the story teller; the real deal.
Kurtis Blow . . .

WBAU had a method that they used to determine how many people listened to each show. Every five phone calls meant that five hundred people were listening. There were a lot of white programs on the air at BAU, many of whose hosts looked down on the Black programs, of which there were only three: JB Walker's, Rusty J's, and Bill Stephney's show on Monday night. Some of the guys that worked on one of the white shows called "Who Knows What," ended up working with the infamous Howard Stern. That show had the record number of phone calls with thirty-four callers during the program. After a few weeks of heavy promoting in the

Hempstead, Freeport, and Roosevelt areas, that Spectrum City would be on the air on Monday nights, we received twenty-three phone calls, which was the second best of any show, and the calls kept coming in. The next week we broke the record by getting thirty-six calls, then it went up to seventy-six, and eventually reached the point where we were receiving ninety calls a night. After about a year, all three phone lines would stay lit all night long with callers, to the point where the number of callers was up in the hundreds. Our numbers blew *all* the white shows out, and set new records for listenership.

We were running a nightclub, we were on the radio weekly, and we were doing mobile gigs. Many times I would finish doing the radio show, be out of there at 1 A.M. and then drive to Bay Shore, which was about fifteen to twenty-five miles away to manage the nightclub we were running.

In those days there was no real Long Island pride. When we threw parties and the MC would ask, "Is Brooklyn in the house?" the crowd would go off. If the MC asked, "Is Queens in the house?" the crowd would go off. The majority of the people actually lived on Long Island, but Long Island was the place where everybody had come to from somewhere else, so they would represent where they were originally from. We worked to shoot all of that down. What we did through our music and through the radio station was try to jell all the areas together, and give Long Island some pride.

One night while we were on the radio, this guy called up and said that he was from Strong Island. That term, "Strong Island," which is very popular now, came to us from over the phone lines at WBAU. What I would do to build some Long Island pride is give each town its own nickname. Hempstead had three areas that were known. There was "The Terrace," which was called "Termiteville," "The Hills," and "The Heights." We called Roosevelt "The Velt," and Freeport, "The Port." Uniondale had the derogatory nickname of "The Onion." I wanted towns that were considered wack to have some pride as well, so I began to call Uniondale "Chill City," Lakeview we called "Sunken City." Uniondale and Lakeview were two towns that were best known for their good-looking girls. Since the listening audience was predominantly high school kids, the nicknames stuck and worked really well.

Eventually Bill Stephney became BAU's program director, and gave us our own show on Saturday nights from 12 A.M. to 1 A.M. We called it the "Super Spectrum Mix Hour," and my cohost was Butch Cassidy, who is now with the group 5ive-O, and the DJ was Keith Shocklee. Not long after that our show was extended to an hour and a half (11:30 P.M.–1 A.M.).

We would make original tapes with local artists and play them on the air, because there wasn't enough Rap records at the time to play throughout the entire show. We would have local artists come to our studio and headquarters, which we established in 1982 at 510 S. Franklin, to make the tapes that we would broadcast on the air. Keith would charge five dollars to make a tape, and then would present the tapes to Mr. Bill to see if they could get played. A lot of the guys that are with us today are back from those early days.

We had groups like the Classy Three, Choice Five MC's, Townhouse Three, The Deadly Three. The people out there used to like the groups with the tapes almost as much as the groups with records. People swore I had records out in 1983. What really made our radio show so popular was that we were playing a lot of the unrecordeds. There was some real good talent coming across the airwaves.

Some of the best material coming out at that time was made by the Townhouse Three, a crew that

THAT WAS THE FIRST DAY I SAW FLAVOR AND HE WAS WEARING A BLACK HAT, BLACK PANTS, BLACK SHADES, A BLACK JHERI CURL, AND HAD A BLACK PACK OF CIGARETTES.

later became known as Sons of Bazerk. I invited T.A., from the Townhouse Three, to the studio one day to do a tape, and he brought a guest. Initially I was a little pissed, because I couldn't understand why he would bring somebody. His guest was none other than the world-famous Flavor Flav. That was the first day I saw Flavor and he was wearing a black hat, black jacket, black pants, black shades, a black Jheri curl, and had a black pack of cigarettes. He had bought some Player cigarettes the first day they came out, and scraped the front off to make it look like he had his own brand of cigarettes. Then he kept fucking with my black keyboard. So here was this Black person, with a black Jheri curl, black clothes, a black pack of cigarettes, fucking with my black keyboard. At least we knew he was Black.

My first words to Flavor were "You can't smoke up here. You have to go outside." Eventually he started hanging out up at the station, and people would crack on him all the time. Flavor would be the target of many, many snaps. One day a few of us were up in the station and someone who was snapping on Flavor started unbuttoning Flavor's clothes, talking about, "Here's a layer," unbuttoned another one, "here's another layer," unbuttoned another one, "here's another layer," unbuttoned another one, "here's another layer." Under that he had about four sweatshirts. He had this leather Sherlock Holmes hat, and goggles. He would wear four or five spring jackets in the wintertime instead of getting one winter coat.

Flavor was on the periphery of the Townhouse Three, so he would hang with them when they would come to WBAU. Townhouse Three made four or five hits in 1983. Flavor started spending more time up at the station, and everybody had

> FLAVOR WOULD DO CRAZY SHIT. AT THE BEGINNING OF HIS SHOW HE WOULD PLAY A TAPE OF THE ACTUAL SOUNDS OF PENN STATION.

to have some function to justify being up there, so his function became answering the phones, writing the messages down as neatly as possible, and getting them to Mr. Bill.

One day we were in the station snapping and Flavor was sitting in Bill's seat behind the glass. Then Bill was like, "I'm going to give Flavor a show." We thought he was joking. To our surprise Bill was serious, and eventually gave Flavor his own show from ten to eleven-thirty. He was MC DJ Flavor. On Saturday nights from ten to one, beginning with Flavor and ending up with us, we were knocking WBLS and KISS-FM out of the box.

Flavor would do crazy shit. At the beginning of his show he would play a tape of the actual sounds of Penn Station. He went to Penn Station and recorded the guy making the announcement, "Attention please, all trains going to Patchogue and Lindenhurst have been cancelled. We're sorry for this inconvenience, thank you." He put that on the radio and people bugged out. He used to record everything. Everywhere he went he took his big boom box and would record. He just wanted to do something different, and bring out something different. He was always one of those out-of-the-ordinary type of brothers, so the shit that he played on the radio was original. He used to go around town taping everybody.

Many of the people who are a part of Public Enemy to this day I met during my college days at Adelphi. I met Harry Allen while we were taking an animation class together. When I reenrolled in school I started back with the school newspaper *The Delphian*. I had a weekly cartoon strip in the paper called "Tales of the Sky," and I would write stories about the Spectrum City crew being an outfit from outer space.

As freshmen at Adelphi, Jeff Thomas, who was from Uniondale, and myself were two Black graphic artists who occupied a whole page in the school newspaper, we both had cartoons. My first year I had one called "College Madness," and Jeff had a strip called "The Guardians of the Galaxy." So when I first met Harry Allen he was like, "You're Carlton Ridenhour? I read your cartoon strip every week." We began working together doing projects in animation class. Harry was a journalism and communications major, and was also into taking photos. My major was graphic design and my minor was communications. We used to call Harry "Harry-O Vicious Video," and he started hanging around the whole WBAU scene.

I also met Andre Brown that semester. His right-hand man was Tyrone Kelsie, who went to New York Tech at the time. Together they became Dr. Dre and T-Money of the famous WBAU *Operating Room* show, and later became the Black Costello of the Abbott and Costello team with Ed Lover. Together they went on to cohost *Yo! MTV Raps,* star in the movie *Who's the Man?,* and are now the hosts of the popular early morning talk show on HOT 97 in New York.

By 1984 we were blowing up every single Rap record that came out because we were hungry for it. For one gig we planned to bring a group from Brooklyn out to do a show. Known as the Disco Three, the group had a record out called "Fat Boys." Hank, who was ingenious at conceptualizing flyers, said, "If we put Disco Three on the flyer, nobody's going to come out because people won't know who they are." So we put the Fat Boys on the flyer, bigger than life. We kept telling them that night that they should call themselves the Fat Boys, and eventually they did. I'm not positive if it was because of us, but that's another group we helped to blow up in our area. We held Bill's farewell party the same night we brought the Fat Boys to Adelphi University.

Another record we helped to blow up was this record we picked up in Queens by T La Rock called "It's Yours." Hank and Harry Allen had made arrangements to do an interview and take photos with T La Rock, who was getting down at the Manhattan Center, which was then called Ben Franklin High School, in Manhattan. I couldn't make the meeting because I was doing a gig. We were running a club at the end of Long Island called Twilight, that we turned into Entourage. That same night there was another rapper getting down who had recently been signed. All I know is when Harry and Hank came back to the Island, I asked them, "How was T La Rock? Did he rip shit?" All they kept saying was,

FIGHT THE POWER

69

"L.L., L.L. He's on some other shit." He had excited them. L.L. had brought Rap to a whole other level. That was all they would say.

As promoters we built up everybody, either through flyers or the radio station, but mainly through the radio station. People from all over New York, New Jersey, and Connecticut were trying to get tapes of WBAU. The signal for the station was only one hundred watts, but people outside of that radius would hear so much about us that by 1984 people were making tapes for people who couldn't receive the signal on their radio.

One night we were throwing a gig at this roller rink on the borderline of Nassau County and Queens. I originally had this group called the Masterdon Committee scheduled to be on the show, but we couldn't get in touch with them the night of the gig. Then someone suggested, "You have L.L.'s number—why don't you give him a call?" Hank and Harry had gotten L.L.'s telephone number from him earlier that year when they checked out his performance, but I didn't know if I should call him because he didn't know me from a can of paint. After a while I called his house and he actually answered the phone. I said, "Do you think you could come down to this roller rink and perform?" He said, "Yeah, I'll be there." I was amazed that I was talking to him. I was thinking, "Damn, is it that easy to get to him?"

The people were waiting for the Masterdon Committee to come on, because we had built them up through the flyers. They never showed, but this seventeen-year-old kid walked in with his blue jacket, the same blue jacket that he wore on the back of his album cover. It was L.L. Cool J and he asked, "So what

THIS SEVENTEEN-YEAR-OLD KID WALKED IN WITH HIS BLUE JACKET, THE SAME BLUE JACKET THAT HE WORE ON THE BACK OF HIS ALBUM COVER. IT WAS L.L. COOL J AND HE ASKED, "SO WHAT DO YOU WANT ME TO DO?"

do you want me to do?" I said, "Just get on the stage and just be here." He went on the stage and we had him be a judge of the Rap contest. Just the fact of him being there wiped away all the other shit about the Masterdon Committee not being there. Dre was on the turntables, and after the Rap contest L.L. went in the DJ booth and started freestyling. He ripped into this unbelievable freestyle that defied all gravity, put his hand on the turntable, stopped the record and said, "We don't need music." Everybody looked in shock and amazement. Everybody. Flavor was like, "Get this boy a cold rag, he's having a seizure." He was losing it. He was just killing it. He saved the gig, and saved my promotional life. I promoted the gig and went out the back door with the money and my girl. I said to myself, "I don't know how I'm going to pay him back," but L.L. I owe you one.

I was first influenced to start writing by guys like Hollywood and Eddie Cheeba, but after a while I stopped writing Rap lyrics, and wrote more freestyle for an MC. Once I got into MC'ing, which is different from rapping, I stopped my quest for making a record. I would write things like, "That's right never relax while the needle is playing on the wax, we guarantee to give you what you got, it's hot." Speaking fast and fly. Guys like Hollywood and Cheeba specialized in that. The first guy I heard really do rapping right, straight up Hip-Hop style Rap, was Melle Mel. He came to the Roosevelt Rollerskating Rink in the summer of 1979 with Flash, and he was so clear. I could understand every word. They ripped shit.

When records started coming out I noticed that with records someone could use a word in a song and within the span of a week everybody would know the word, but if a story came out in a newspaper it would take about six months for people to know about it, and still a lot of people wouldn't know about it. The recorded word was a powerful medium. Hank used to say back in 1979 when we first hooked up, "Yo, we have to make a record."

What inspired me to do lyrics specifically for records was when we had the radio show, and I wanted to do a record once in a while to show my rapping skills, and also to promote the radio

show. I did both the low-tempo record "Check Out the Radio," and another song called "It's Working" to promote the radio station WBAU, but I didn't want to do a record with a record company because we had interviewed too many people who told us nightmare stories about their experiences in the music industry, and how they were not getting paid properly.

Eventually in 1984 we released a record as Spectrum City called "Lies." The B side was "Check Out the Radio." We knocked out "Check Out the Radio" in about five hours, and that turned out to be the jam. "Check Out the Radio" was originally called "Low Tempo," which was a slow-tempo record. Run-DMC loved "Check Out the Radio." Rush Productions actually based two of their future jams off of that song. The Beastie Boys had a B side called "Slow and Low," and Run-DMC did "Together Forever"; both records were based on that same low-tempo vibe.

Then one day I was in Joe Halls Barbershop on Nassau Road in Roosevelt getting a haircut, and Steve Drayton, Flavor's brother, was cutting my hair. Flavor came in the barbershop and said, "Yo Chuck, they say you're losing it man. What's up with that man?" He said this local rapper wanted to battle me. I wasn't into battling or any of that, I was into making tapes to put on the radio. I was trying to help MCs, not battle them. I couldn't understand why someone would want to battle me, because I hadn't done any of that for a while. So I decided I would write a jam that could serve dual purposes: promote the radio show and let people know that I still had rapping skills.

Back then my father had a furniture shop in Laurelton, Queens. He used to move furniture for fabric companies in Manhattan. They would have surplus furniture that they would want to get rid of so my father used to store it in his shop in Laurelton. Flavor and I were working for a little income with my pops. One of us would drive, most of the time it would be me, because I wasn't going to sit in the passenger seat while that crazy motherfucker drove. So while we would be driving in the truck, we would practice routines. I would be the rapper and Flavor would do what he does.

Those were the days of the most fun because it used to be crazy cold, and we would be riding around town in my father's U-Haul truck, putting up flyers on the poles to promote our next gig, until our hands froze. People would drive by looking at us, splashing slush on us, but when the gigs rolled around people wanted to get in. Then there would be times after we'd finish where I would be driving, and Flavor and Keith would be in the back, and I'd turn the corners real fast and crazy to make them fly all over the back of the truck with refrigerators, desks, and chairs that were back there.

One day Flavor figured he would get me back. He got behind the wheel and told Keith and me to get in the back, but we never got in. We went to the back of the truck, shut the back door, and left. He sped off and was driving like a madman, laughing, hitting bumps, turning the corners real fast and wild, hitting curbs, thinking he was giving us the ride of our lives. When he stopped the truck to check and see if we were all right, we weren't in there.

In the beginning of the song "Public Enemy #1" Flavor says, "Yo, tell them that stuff you was talking about in LA Laurelton Queens. Let them know what goes on." That came from when Flavor and I were riding together while working for my pops. It was true. I was telling Flavor to say on the record what he was telling me earlier in the truck, and he was telling me to Rap the routine I was doing in the truck.

Flavor made it onto the tape I was making for the station, because one night I was up at the studio at 510, and I always wanted to rock this record called "Blow Your Head" by the JB's. It was a roller-skating record, and every time they would play it at the Roosevelt Rollerskating Rink I loved it. It was a crazy record. I was in the studio making a pause tape of the instrumental beginning of that song. That night Flavor happened to be in the other room, and I didn't have a beginning or end for the song, I just had my lyrics for it, and I didn't know how to open the song up, or close it out. I called Flavor in and asked him if he would help me complete the tape. He said, "What do you want me to say?" I said, "Just kick some shit in the beginning, then I'll come in with my verses, then at the end you close it out."

The Flavor idea was influenced by the James Brown/Bobby Bird technique, and was also influenced later on by Philly rappers Schoolly D and Cold Money who in 1984 had "PSK What Does It Mean?" and "Gucci Time," which were big records. We played the hell out of those records, and they both had Cold Money opening up the song like, "Yo Schoolly, tell them what time it is." Then Schoolly would go into the jam. Schoolly D was a big influence on my vocal application, rhyming style, and delivery.

When we finished we had the tape "Public Enemy #1." I called it "Public Enemy #1" because Flavor told me that a local rapper wanted to take me out. I was paranoid that people were after me, so I had to fend them off with some skills. They were treating me like I was a public enemy. Once I put that tape on BAU they left me alone, because it was mad hard and it was dope. No one could compete against a tape back then. That was the first song I did that said anything about Public Enemy.

As we went into 1985 and 1986 we hit roadblocks. It got to a point where the club and the radio show were very popular, but it wasn't translating into anything for us financially. We didn't know what we were doing would lead to. We stopped our radio show in 1985 because we felt we had been spinning our wheels without being properly compensated. It seemed like we were treading in the same areas without going forward.

Def Jam's Rick Rubin had signed Original Concept, the Beastie Boys, and L.L. Cool J, three totally different artistic concepts, and Rick wanted to sign me bad, because he thought I sounded different. He must have thought that I was a missing piece in the puzzle. He had L.L., the most devastating young rapper out, so he didn't need that, and he had the white group that he was planting seeds with. He was looking for

> RICK RUBIN WANTED TO SIGN ME BAD, BECAUSE HE THOUGHT I SOUNDED DIFFERENT. HE MUST HAVE THOUGHT THAT I WAS A MISSING PIECE IN THE PUZZLE.

something in the middle. Def Jam's early releases were proving to be big successes, so for all the other major labels it looked like there was something brewing that was worth keeping an eye on.

In 1986 Hank and I were falling behind in our rent for the studio, and everybody had basically gone their separate ways. We decided we would try to throw some more gigs, and see if we could get a record deal out of the buzz we'd create. Hank would go to the city and take our demo tapes around while I was working. When I was working I would supplement the income for him to go into the city, and vice versa.

I had finished school and got a job processing film at a photo lab that I absolutely hated. I was trying to write lyrics at night, but with this job I usually came home tired from working on the processing machine all day, I had to be at work on time, and I had to literally run across town to get there. I was ready to quit that job, but before I did I took a week off by calling in sick. One day while I was looking in the classified section of the paper I saw an ad that sounded like the company I worked for. I thought they were trying to replace me. I told my girl at the time, who later became my wife, "Look at this ad, they're replacing me." It was in the summer so I walked down there, and told them that I just came to pick up my check.

When I got back home I called the phone number from the classified ad just to play a joke, thinking it was the company I worked for. It wasn't. There was another company also named EPD, which was a photo lab located right across the street from the EPD I worked for, and they had an opening for the same position. When I called them up I found out they also had a messenger opening, and I found out that the messenger job paid more money than the big title job I had of Processing Artroom Assistant. The messenger job paid more money hourly, and paid 50 cents per mile for traveling expenses, so I could end up clocking $320 a week. At the time I was bringing home $176 a week after taxes, and I was busting my ass.

I came to find out that the new EPD was a Black company. So I accepted the messenger job. It was the easiest job in the world.

I was on my own time, I just had to make my deliveries. Mr. and Mrs. White, who was the Black family that owned the company, handled photo work for government contracts and major companies. While driving around as a messenger, I would have a tape of a track and I would write to it. I actually composed most of my songs in 1986 while driving in the car at work, or listening to radio station WLIB. I religiously listened to Gary Byrd in the mornings, and Mark Riley in the afternoons. WLIB was a gigantic influence on opening up my mind on who we are as a people. New York's WLIB is the greatest station ever in my book. I was working for a Black company, listening to Black radio, so I really felt a great deal of Black pride.

During the last year of doing gigs we hooked up with different people in different areas. We would hire Dre to do the music. Unity Force, which was a security organization in Roosevelt, with Mike, James, and Griff, would be brought in to do security at the gigs. Hank and I both knew Griff the best, so we would tell Griff, "Bring Unity Force to the gig, and if we make any money, we'll pay you something." We never really came off, but it was a fun place to be at the end of the night. I would put up my money to get the spot, and at the end of the night there might be enough money to go around. If not, everybody at least got some food, and had a great time. Unity Force later turned into the S1Ws inside the group.

Unity Force would be at the parties with their black uniforms and black berets. The funniest thing was when somebody from Brooklyn would come out to Long Island tripping, thinking everybody was a punk, but they didn't know what they were stepping into. The 98 Posse, who were the street brothers from the area, had a little static with the S1Ws, but that was a standoff. So they both decided to be cool with each other. The rule of thumb was as long as they were in the back of the party doing whatever they did to make their money, as long as they didn't mess up the gig and make the females feel unsafe, there would be no problems. Eventually, a bond developed between the 98 Posse and the S1Ws. If somebody came to the gig from Brooklyn tripping, they didn't just have the security to deal with, but there were hard-core brothers inside from the 98 Posse who would handle them also. It got to a point where if somebody came from Brooklyn to start some shit, not only would they get toughed up by Unity Force, but they might catch a beat down from the 98 Posse, then they might get picked up by the Hempstead Police who we knew, and they would get locked down with more brothers we knew. So while they were locked down inside the joint they were still getting beat up, because they tried to mess with a Spectrum party.

By 1986 I was thoroughly convinced that Rap was big-time based on Run-DMC's success. When Run-DMC debuted with their album in May or June of that year with the "Peter Piper" and "My Adidas" singles I was stunned. I was flabbergasted. I saw their album in Record World at the Green Acres mall in Valley Stream. I noticed on one album they wore New York Mets colors, orange and blue, and I noticed on another album they were wearing green and yellow. On the cover Run looked like he was counting money, DMC was in the room, and JMJ was sneaking out of the back. I stared at that album for about half an hour. I kept turning it to the back and then to the front, that album looked big-time. It looked like something you would see in the rock world. It looked legitimate, and it was a total package. I said to myself, "This shit is incredible." That was just from looking at the packaging and design of the album on the outside. The actual album was incredible. Their singles "Peter Piper" and "My Adidas" were awesome, and were blazing. I had never heard such a diversity in Rap, cuts that were hard-hitting on all angles. The beats were strong, and the rhymes were strong. I was amazed.

Not long after the release of their album, Run-DMC did a concert at Madison Square Garden. That's the concert when Run said to the audience, "Put all the Adidas in the air," and over half of the audience held up their Adidas. I was invited to the concert by the people that were trying to sign me, and I was very impressed with the warmth of the whole Rush family. After the concert was over I was backstage, and Run-DMC was still very humble. When

they first came up to BAU for their first interview they were humble, then when they came back to BAU they were humble, and after they had just finished rocking nineteen thousand people at Madison Square Garden they were still humble as ever. I was very impressed, and it made me think, "Damn, and they want me to get down with them?" That was one of the things that helped me make the decision to go for it.

Another motivating factor was when Bill Stephney said to me, "Rap needs somebody that can bring a higher level of thinking to it. Someone who can deal with the people on the level that you're on. I think you can be the one." Bill offered me a challenge. He felt I could do some of the things that weren't already being done.

Another challenge came during Run-DMC's tour when the media was ripping and blaming Run-DMC for an incident that occurred in Long Beach, California. The next day the headlines for the story read, "Rappers cause violent outbreak." What really happened was the Run-DMC concert had gotten caught up in the middle of a gang war in Southern California. The media blew it up like Rap was the cause of the incident. The media was dragging Run-DMC through the mud, and asking Run-DMC to explain themselves after an incident that they had no knowledge of. I felt I could be a person who, if the media wanted to fuck with me, could fuck with them just as much, because I would deal with the media at a higher level.

I was older than most rappers, had more sense about myself, and I wasn't interested in the business just for the sake of making a record. I was also concerned with the way Rap was being exploited and interpreted. I had been involved with Rap for a long time, and I felt I could explain what Rap was about. Reporters could ask me questions in front of the camera, and I'd be able to turn it around without having a publicist speak for me. Bill Adler, who was the publicist for Rush at the time, tried to lessen the media outbreak on Run-DMC by being a spokesperson for them, but the cameras were still coming to Run-DMC, and Run-DMC—oblivious to a lot of the facts of what was actually going on—were unprepared, and rightfully so. Why should they be expected to explain something that they didn't know anything about? Those three things helped give me the spark to develop Public Enemy into what it eventually turned into.

By 1986 Bill and Dre were both part of the Def Jam camp, and both were encouraging me to get down with them. Bill was working at Def Jam, and Dre had his group Original Concept on the label, and had released another record called "Pump that Bass," which turned out to be a big record. They were both telling us, "It's not that bad here. It's a situation where you can build. Rick wants to hook up." Def Jam's deal with Columbia was heavily contingent on them being able to sign new acts to fulfill their end of the deal, but they wanted to sign a diverse number of groups. They felt that we had a unique situation because we were a self-contained operation from Long Island.

Hank and I were hesitant about signing with any record labels, because we didn't want to be sucked into a situation that we couldn't get out of. We had chips on our shoulders and felt we could run our own record company. Then one day Bill said that Rick wanted to set up a meeting between us. Hank and I figured we had nothing to lose. Since the meeting was scheduled to be at Rick's apartment, Hank felt we should have a few songs prepared. We prepared four songs for the demo: "Public Enemy #1," "The Return of Public Enemy"—whose lyrics became the lyrics for "My Uzi Weighs a Ton"—"Sophisticated Bitch," and "You're Gonna Get Yours."

We played the four songs for Rick to check out. After hearing the demo tape Rick said, "Let's do this, let's go. It's great, let's cut these things." Originally he was interested in a single, but after he

heard the tape he wanted to do an album. Public Enemy was under way.

We came up with the name *Yo! Bum Rush the Show* for the album because that was pretty much the momentum we had as an operation. Harry Allen eventually went into Hip-Hop journalism. Dr. Dre went into radio, then into TV. Hank went into production. Bill became a record executive. Eric Sadler went into production. I went into being an artist and using my graphic skills. So we all moved forward but diversified ourselves in different angles and different aspects of the music business. We *bum rushed the show.*

I wanted to continue to call the group Spectrum City, but Hank felt that we should come up with something new. Since two of the songs on the demo contained the words "Public Enemy" Hank suggested, "let's just call the group Public Enemy." Ding-ding-ding-ding, just like that.

Originally, I wanted to be the creative person behind the scenes, because I had been a behind-the-scenes person for the previous five years with Spectrum City. I wanted to control the direction of the group on the management end where I could simultaneously help develop other groups. Obie, who was one of the high school guys we recorded on WBAU and who is now Sgt. Black Terror in the group 5ive-O, had the closest voice to mine, so we tried to get him to be the lead vocalist for Public Enemy. I felt I would be a better director than artist, but Rick Rubin was adamant about me being the vocalist in the group. I was in a situation where I received an offer that I couldn't refuse, and I had to do it. It handicapped me in one way, because I had to be this guy that I really didn't want to be at that time.

> ORIGINALLY, I WANTED TO BE THE CREATIVE PERSON BEHIND THE SCENES, BECAUSE I HAD BEEN A BEHIND-THE-SCENES PERSON FOR THE PREVIOUS FIVE YEARS WITH SPECTRUM CITY.

Once we decided on a name for the group I used my graphic design skills to design the logo for Public Enemy. The silhouette is of E Love, who was L.L. Cool J's sidekick at the time. Then I drew a target around the silhouette. I did the stencil letters, and put a crossbar in between them, and bam, it looked like they were made for each other.

Def Jam wanted me as a soloist, but I didn't want to be out there rapping by myself. At the time there were several groups with three members: the Fat Boys, Run-DMC, Whodini, and others, so I wanted to create more of a posse concept that would give the same impact of Grandmaster Flash and the Furious Five in terms of numbers.

Harry Allen, Dr. Dre, and myself had first seen Grandmaster Flash and the Furious Five in all their glory at the Ritz in 1984. Their show was awesome. They had six MCs *all* ripping shit like I had never seen anybody rip a show before. I wanted to recreate that powerful posse feel, but with each component having different duties, and coming out like something that people had never seen before. Even though I was doing the majority of the rapping, I thought everything else around me would give the appearance of six people, each with identifiable qualities.

The first person that we worked on building was Flavor. Flavor Flav was originally known as MC DJ Flavor on WBAU. One day Hank suggested, "You should throw a name on your name like Melle Mel, Flavor Flav." When we performed the first record he would move back and forth onstage, and I remember Hank said, "Whatever you do, just wear white and keep moving, because if you wear white and keep moving people will definitely pick you up."

Butch who was down with Spectrum and my cohost on the radio show, said he knew someone named Norman who could make some fly mix tapes. I knew Norman's brother because we had gone to the same high school. At the time Norman was doing some things on his own, then he began making tapes for BAU, and became one of Spectrum's deejays at the club. Norman ac-

tually quit working with Spectrum to go to work for the music retailer Crazy Eddie right before the Public Enemy opportunity presented itself.

I asked Norman if he wanted to be down because I appreciated the work he had done when he was with Spectrum. He was a hard worker and never caused many problems, which were two ingredients that were very hard to find. At the time he was known as DJ Mellow D. In "Public Enemy #1" I refer to him as that. I gave him the name Terminator X, which meant that he was terminating all the nonsense, and the X symbolized the unknown, a mystery. He's terminating all the things we think we believe, that we really don't know about. The first day I told Norman that his new name would be Terminator X he didn't like it.

Terminator X became the next person to get built up. He got built up in the same way that Run-DMC built Jam Master Jay, off of the hook line in the song "Jam Master Jay." When we did "Rebel without a Pause" we mention Terminator X. If "Terminator X Speaks with His Hands" did not do it, "Rebel without a Pause" was the record that really made him known. People wanted to know "Who is Terminator X?" It just sounds fly so we used it in the hook.

Griff was the next stage, and after Griff each one of the S1Ws was to develop an identity. The S1Ws meant Security of the First World. We wanted Unity Force to come along with the Public Enemy project because we liked their look. Initially, we called ourselves the Black Panthers of Rap, so Unity Force's look fit the concept. Unity Force was an organization where a few of the brothers were in the Nation of Islam, a couple of the brothers were dedicated to martial arts, and everybody was dedicated to a sense of culture, so that became the symbolic look of the group.

Security of the First World represents that the Black man can be just as intelligent as he is strong. It stands for the fact that we're not Third World people, we're First World people, we're the Original people. A lot of people misconstrued the S1W's use of Uzis onstage. The Uzis were stating the fact that the white man went into Africa with the gun and controlled us with the threat of the

1. Chuckie D back at 90.3 WBAU col chillin' in a B-boy stance. The beginnings of Run-DMC, the greatest Rap group of all time. (1983)

2. We call this the great surrender. Signing with Def Jam, June 1986. *l. to r.* Rick Rubin, Steve Ralbovsky of CBS, me, Hank Shocklee, Ron Skoler (our lawyer), Flavor Flav, Terminator X, Brother James Norman, and Brother Roger Chillious.

3. All over the world together we've traveled, east–west coast brothers. This man I respect above all in the game. The immortal Ice-T. (UCLA campus, 1988)

4. Indiana Black Expo. At yet another panel representing the Rap game with the hard-core legend, Parrish Smith of EPMD. (1989)

5. Me and Ice Cube at Greene Street Studio in early 1990. Probably the best Rap lyric writer ever. Here we are posin' the peace signs during production of his album, *America's Most Wanted*.

7 & 8. Damn right it's hard rhymin' indeed, similar to Dizzy Gillespie blowin' his thing. Blowin' over 105 bpm in 1990. Lookin' over my shoulder backed by a million at a peace rally at Harlem State Office Building, New York City 1989.

9. Me and Flav bring the noise during PE-Anthrax tour, 1991.

gun, and, therefore, we were saying if we needed to we would use guns in our defense. Europeans used the gun, and we would too to defend our rights to be men and women, to defend our rights to be equal, and to defend our rights to hold on to our culture, language, and our God. That was heavily influenced by the powerful stance taken by the Black Panther Party for Self-Defense in 1967, when thirty brothers and sisters registered their grievance with the way things were going by storming into the California State Capitol in Sacramento with loaded guns, and read a statement by their Minister of Defense, Huey P. Newton.

Top All-Time Deejays:

Jam Master Jay: The best show deejay of all time.
Grandmaster Flash: The first to do this the right way.
Terminator X: Over a thousand shows; very few mistakes.
Jazzy Jeff: Hand and eye coordination unbelievable.
Cash Money: Inventor of the transformer; the master of tricki.
Cut Creator: Perfect complement for Cool J.
Ali Shaheed: Perfect piece to tribes rhyme volleys.
Mr. Mixx: Speed and bass and able to fit in.
Mase: Another innovative cog to the Dela machine.
Dr. Dre: Underrated but always on point; knows records.

We signed with Def Jam in June of 1986. I said, "You can't have me unless you bring Flavor." So Rick's big question was, "What does Flavor do? I'm not going to sign anybody that's not

a vocalist." We really couldn't explain what Flavor did, he did his own unique thing. All I knew was I didn't want to do it alone, and, secondly, I wanted to do something similar to the James Brown/Bobby Bird approach, "Everybody over here. Get on up. Everybody right there. Get into it." I needed someone I could bounce off of, and Flavor was the perfect person for that. After some convincing by Bill, Hank, and myself, and also by splitting the contract, we made the provision that Flavor would be written in. Record companies usually only sign vocalists, so we said Flavor would be a vocalist. He had very limited vocals on the first album, but he was there just enough to justify a contract. That was something that we pushed hard for.

Initially our contract with Def Jam called for Flavor and me to split five points, and we received a five-thousand-dollar advance. It must be understood that Def Jam was basically an experiment by CBS. CBS was cutting Def Jam's throat, so you know we were getting our throats sliced by Def Jam. We were just looking for an opportunity so that we could get ahead and renegotiate in the near future. We looked upon that first signing as an opportunity, but also as a compromise, because we surrendered the full control of ourselves by getting into a world where you need strong business minds to back you up.

Our attorney at the time was Ron Skoler, and we decided to create our own management company with him. We didn't want to be signed to the Def Jam label, and be managed by Rush Artist Management, and have to answer to both situations without having some kind of autonomy for ourselves. Our attorney wanted to bring in another attorney, that he looked upon as a mentor, by the name of Ed Chalpin. Ed Chalpin was supposedly a big deal maker who was "guaranteed" to propel our situation forward. We put our full trust in our lawyer, and together started a management company with both of them called Rhythm Method. Rhythm Method started to manage other acts like Red Alert, Ultramagnetic MC's, Original Concept, and other artists who were not as well known. Hank and I didn't really know too much about the management aspect of the business, but we knew we could handle the creative end and left it to the attorneys to handle the legal and business end. We later had some differences with both of them. I felt that instead of being in control of our own situation, we were on the losing side.

Initially we controlled thirty percent of the management of Public Enemy under Rhythm Method. Then Rush Productions wanted to manage us so they purchased fifteen percent of the management from Rhythm Method. As a group we still had to pay a thirty-percent commission. We were experienced with Rap music on a small scale as far as our deejaying operation, yet we were rookies in the major operations of music. There's no way to get trained on the seamier elements of the music business being on the street—that element is reserved for the boardrooms. You have to have somebody that's able to teach you the rights and wrongs of the business, tell you what to look out for, and coach you through.

After the signing we spent the month of July 1986 rerecording "Public Enemy #1." We had to figure out how to keep the original loop, and keep the raw sound. Back then they didn't have samplers that would create a loop. What Steve Ett, the engineer at Chung King who engineered L.L. Cool J's and the Beastie Boys' album, did was take the two-inch tape and cut it into a ten- or twenty-foot piece of tape, which he ran through a two-inch stutter machine wrapped around a microphone stand in the middle of the room. Then we recorded the DMX drum machine beat over the loop. Hank and Eric suggested that, instead of using the programmed drum machine over the loop, Eric play the drums by hand, which gave the recording the rawness and imperfection of the original.

We completed "Public Enemy #1" in August of 1986, and were originally slated to come out in October, but our album got pushed back into February/March of 1987.

When the single "Public Enemy #1" came out it was four or five months after it should have. Our music was fly, and Flavor's input saved the record, because he was doing things that were totally new. I recorded our album from being influenced the previous year by Run-DMC and Schoolly D. My vocal application seemed

FIGHT THE POWER
85

outdated with the release of KRS's and Eric B. and Rakim's albums. Our album would have been received a lot better if it had been released five months earlier when it was slated to, but being at a major label we had to wait. Major record companies move big-time, but they move like dinosaurs.

In 1986 Rakim came out with "Eric B. for President" and "My Melody." The groups of three had dropped down to groups of two: Eric B. and Rakim, Jazzy Jeff and the Fresh Prince, and another team that had just come out and was phenomenal, Blastmaster KRS One and DJ Scott La Rock. At the end of the summer of 1986, their record came out called "South Bronx." The combination of Rakim and KRS One changed the face of Rap forever. Rap had forged into its next era. The first era was the old-school era with Grandmaster Flash, Kurtis Blow, Afrika Bambaattaa, and the whole Bronx/Uptown scene. The next era was in 1984 with L.L. Cool J, Run-DMC, Schoolly D, and the whole environment from 1984 to 1986. Eric B. and Rakim and KRS One brought in the next era. They introduced a whole new vocal application. The thing that was amazing about Rakim and KRS One was that they were able to take a faster beat and slow it down with their vocals. Their vocalization was splendid. If "South Bronx" and "Eric B. for President" didn't change the Hip-Hop flavor at the time, Eric B. and Rakim's "I Know You Got Soul" flipped it for good. The style from 1985 and 1986 was out of there, and our first album *Yo! Bum Rush the Show* was created in the old 1986 style.

The sociopolitical meaning of Public Enemy came *after* we decided the group would be called that, because the meanings and the connections of what we were about fit right in. The Black man and woman was considered three-fifths of a human being in the Constitution of the United States. Since the government and the general public follow the Constitution, then we *must* be the enemy.

We represented a combination of self-empowerment, nationalism, and militancy from the combined influences of the Black Panther Party and the Nation of Islam.

In the early part of 1987 Dre brought Scott La Rock and KRS One up to WBAU. There was some static between Mr. Magic and the Juice Crew and Scott La Rock, KRS One and Boogie Down Productions at the time. When BDP came up to BAU we happened to be there. Scott La Rock and KRS One laced into Magic and the Juice Crew.

By that time the Juice Crew/Bronx tension was on. MC Shan had done "The Bridge," which was wrecking somebody. As a follow-up Scott La Rock and KRS did "The Bridge Is Over."

"Public Enemy #1" came out in February of 1987, and when Magic debuted it his boys must have tipped him off that the record was from the same camp that had dissed him. Marley played the record and at the end of the record Mr. Magic said, the beat was dope but the Rap was whack, and turned it off. He didn't want any more music from us. It seemed like our first record got dissed on WBLS because we were caught up in the middle of the Bronx-Queens riff.

When the album was released in March of 1987 we were making promotional appearances. We were one of the first Rap groups to come out with an album without having lead singles. We came out with a single in February and our album dropped in March, with everybody asking the question, "Who are these motherfuckers to come out with an album? They must be some kind of gimmick." We went through the whole month of March trying to prove that we weren't a gimmick.

Our first gig in New York City took place at the popular Latin Quarters. I told Griff and the S1Ws, "Yo, I need a bunch of y'all, we're going to the Latin Quarters." I had my father's van, which was a rickety, old, yellow-and-white Chevy that smoked a lot, and it was questionable if it would make it from Long Island to the city. It made it though, and we pulled up right in front of Latin Quarters, opened the door of the van, and about twenty of us got out and rolled up in there.

As we were getting down on our first show, Melle Mel, who was quite bitter about what was going on in the industry, started lashing out while we were performing. In the background I could hear him shouting, "Y'all suck, get the fuck off the stage." I just had to keep going forward. It was part of the breaking-in process.

CHUCK D
88

> AS WE WERE GETTING DOWN ON OUR FIRST SHOW . . . I COULD HEAR MELLE MEL SHOUTING, "Y'ALL SUCK, GET THE FUCK OFF THE STAGE."

I didn't take it personal, I felt it was something we needed to go through. We knew we weren't going to get our props right away. New York City has never been a place that gives up props to another city. That's just the personality of the city. As a matter of fact, it was the best thing that could have happened to us, because it showed us that we had to earn our props. All that we had done in Long Island was known out there, but if we wanted to conquer other places we would have to go to each place and make ourselves known. Melle Mel let us have it that night. Guys like KG from the Cold Crush Brothers was more accepting. He was like, "Keep doing what you're doing."

The Beastie Boys' Licensed to Ill tour began in January of 1987, and since Rush had invested in buying fifteen percent of Public Enemy's management they tried to find a way to get some of their money back. Since they were comanaging us it was worth their while to put us on the tour. We were invited at the end of March to go to Detroit and check out the show. It was the Beastie Boys, Fishbone, and Murphy's Law. What I saw that night at the Fox Theater in Detroit bugged me out. I was stunned. I was amazed at their whole show. It had happened to me before with L.L., it happened when I first saw Whodini in 1984, and Run-DMC had overwhelmed me on a few occasions.

I loved my job as a messenger, because I liked having my freedom, and I enjoyed getting a regular paycheck. I didn't want to leave my job, but I had to make a decision: either stay on the job or go on tour. After that show we agreed that we would go on the Licensed to Ill tour.

I don't know how much Fishbone was getting, but they told us we were going to get one thousand dollars a show. Out of the one thousand dollars, thirty percent came off the top for management and another ten percent went to the booking company. That left us with six hundred dollars.

Three people stayed in a room with double beds, one person slept on the mattress, one person slept on the box spring, and Terminator usually slept on his own bed because he was the biggest. Griff and the other two guys slept in the other room. We just kamikazied our way through that tour. Everybody got paid, and people got paid better than their jobs. I came out of there with about four hundred dollars a week, and on my job I was getting paid three hundred dollars a week.

Our first show on that tour was April 1, 1987, at the Capital Theater in Passaic, New Jersey. Rush Management said, "We'll get you a limo," so they sent two limos to pick us up and take us to do the show. Later when we got the bill we were being charged seven hundred dollars for two limo rides to New Jersey. That's when we said, "Nix that, we're going to rent our own vehicle and drive from city to city."

Then Rush said they would give us credit to get a tour bus, but we would have to pay them back. We said, "Screw that." I borrowed my father's credit card to rent a van, and we took turns driving to each of the remaining fifteen cities on that tour.

The first two S1Ws to come out on that tour were Ben Ransome and Dwayne Crusant. They were stationary and had big, heavy, S1W steel plates on their chests. The S1Ws would stand on two towers—one on the left and one on the right side of the stage—with their Uzis. Griff would be in the middle, moving from front to back. The idea of mobile S1Ws came later from Doug E Fresh. Doug suggested that they move around onstage.

On the first few shows I wore a clock. At first I wore a little stopwatch, which was the style back then, then TA had bought a clock from a furniture store named Fortunoff that I decided to wear. I went to Fortunoff and purchased three clocks and gave Flavor one. I said, "You should wear the same thing I'm wearing." Flavor wore the clock the first and second tour to signify what time it was.

We were finding that people weren't impressed unless they saw

you onstage with something expensive, so when the tour hit Richmond, Virginia, we went into one of the department stores and
bought eighty dollars' worth of fake gold chains. The people
onstage couldn't tell. In our early pictures we look like we have
gold around our necks, but none of that shit is real.

I remember during our second tour, which was the Def Jam tour
with L.L. headlining, L.L. went home one weekend and got a fat
gold rope chain. The chain cost close to one thousand dollars.
Rakim looked at that shit and went home the next weekend and
came back with some shit twice the size. Then L.L. went home the
following weekend and came back with something even bigger.
L.L. and Rakim were always trying to outdo each other on pur-
chases.

In 1987 Eric B. and Rakim dropped "I Know You Got Soul,"
which was the most incredible Rap record I ever heard. I was fanatical being a Rap fan, and pissed by being a competitor, because I knew we didn't have anything to go up against that. And
it was coming from the same camp that was dissing me, saying I
sounded old. Hank and I got together and said, "We have to do
some wild shit." We went into 510 S. Franklin and started fucking around with some records and came up with a combination
track, which became "Rebel without a Pause." Three young high
school guys were there the night we developed the track: Charlie
Brown, Dinco D, and Buster Rhymes, who later became the group
Leaders of the New School. We played the song for them at 510,
and I remember they started dancing *real* crazy. They were losing
their minds. I thought to myself, "We have something here."

We cut "Rebel" at the end of April 1987. Our other songs were
dying down and we were getting ready for the second single release. Hank and I went to Bill and said, "We have this jam that's
the bomb and we have to go with it." Bill suggested that we take
it to Rick and Russell. Russell immediately vetoed the idea saying,
"No. I don't want y'all to put out B sides, because it would ruin
the album sales." We were looking at each other like, "What album sales?" At the time we had sold approximately 82,000
copies, which, back then, was a low number because Run-DMC

had sold three million and L.L. had sold a million. We said, "Fuck that," and went over their heads.

We went to Jeff Jones who was the product manager, and Steve Raboski who was the A&R person at Columbia. We told them, "We have this shit that's the bomb, we don't know what Def Jam is doing, but we have to sneak this cut on the B side." The slated single for us to release was "You're Gonna Get Yours," which was the A side, and "My Uzi Weighs a Ton" on the B side. We told them, "Rebel is the shit we want to go with." We tried to ask Russell one more time. Russell was going over to London with Run and DMC. We followed them all the way to JFK airport trying to get his approval. They were ready to get on the plane, and we said, "Russell, let us get this jam on there." He was like, "I don't know, I'll talk to y'all about it when I get back," turned and went to get on the plane. Then Run turned around, looked at us, and said, "Go ahead and do it." That's all we needed was somebody to give us the go-ahead. We went to CBS, filed all the information, and rushed the process through the system. It actually came out on wax before Def Jam knew anything about it. They were surprised when they found out about it.

When we got the acetate from the plant we immediately took it to KISS-FM deejay Chuck Chillout. Chuck Chillout knew us from some parties we did with him in the past. We drove up and he was standing on Broadway outside the offices for KISS. We walked up to him and handed him the record. When we got back in the car we were driving for about two minutes, and when Chuck Chillout came back on the air the first record he played was "Rebel without a Pause."

We started the record off the same way that KRS's "South Bronx" started off with the "Get Up Off of That Thing" by James Brown. The introduction, "Brothers and Sisters, I don't know what this world is coming to" is Jesse Jackson as he was about to introduce the Soul Children on the Stax record "Save the Children."

Chuck played that record off of the acetate for about fifteen minutes straight. By that time we knew we had some shit. That was one of the few records where after we cut I said, "I know it's a hit.

FIGHT THE POWER
91

It's going to come out and smack everybody." There was no doubt about it. The major labels slow the process up with all the formalities, and we had been burned once before like that. If "Public Enemy #1" and "Timebomb" would have come out in the fall of 1986, we would have had some competitive shit out there, but the lag time made them come out damn near the spring of 1987, and that hurt us. So we did "Rebel without a Pause" in one week, and had it out two weeks later.

When Russell heard the record came out there was nothing he could say, because the cut was the bomb and people were screaming and yelling about it.

During our first year we set a goal to conquer a territory that nobody else cared about—the international market. The album *Yo! Bum Rush the Show* was immediately a big hit in London. When we came out with the concept of being "the Black Panthers" of Rap, we set ourselves apart from any other Rap group, and that generated great interest in the European market and press. Not only did our records strike people as being different, but we had set up a strong European base through massive press interviews. I was saying things in interviews that they had never heard from a rapper before. They were like, "Damn. This is Rap? He sounds like Gil Scott-Heron." By the time "Rebel" hit overseas it was over. Other artists had a negative attitude about going overseas. They would complain about the lack of good food, the lack of what they felt was fine females, and the cold weather. We went overseas with an attitude like we were going to boot camp with the army. We all pur-

> WHEN WE CAME OUT WITH THE CONCEPT OF BEING "THE BLACK PANTHERS" OF RAP, WE SET OURSELVES APART FROM ANY OTHER RAP GROUP, AND THAT GENERATED GREAT INTEREST IN THE EUROPEAN MARKET AND PRESS.

chased heavy black jackets fit for wintertime, hats, boots, and trooped over there with L.L. Cool J and Eric B. and Rakim.

Our first performance in London was on November 1 at the Hammersmith Odeon. We stepped in there and it was pandemonium. London is known for whistles, and people were blowing their whistles like mad. L.L. and Eric B. and Rakim had seniority over us, but we were getting a chance to boost our show time to twenty-five minutes a night. The first night when we opened up people were like, "The headliner is getting down now?" It was pandemonium from minute one. Every cut was known over there. We were getting the same response that Eric B. and Rakim got on their records. By the latter half of the tour Eric B. and Rakim's "Paid in Full" came out. Since we had an even number of recognizable jams, the rest was up to the visual presentation and the attitude of the artist. From jam number one it was on. We opened the show up with sirens. We recorded that first show, which was hosted by Dave Pearces for Fresh Start of the Week, to open up our second album *It Takes a Nation of Millions to Hold Us Back.* "Ladies and gentlemen, welcome to the Def Jam tour." The sirens would go off, then Griff came out, "London, England, Armageddon has been in effect. . . . Consider yourselves warned." *Yo! Bum Rush the Show* was the first jam, the shit was on. Rap fans in the United Kingdom say that *It Takes a Nation of Millions to Hold Us Back* was the greatest Rap album of all times, but they also rank *Yo! Bum Rush the Show* in their top ten. It was like playing in Philly, the American city where we received our greatest response, all over again. The crowd was getting wrecked hard by us, and we were the first group. We were so hungry on the stage that we were out to take everything. We were like, "Fuck that, the show ends now!" That first night in London, England, was the hottest we *ever* left the stage. That stage was like nitroglycerin. It was like, "Shut this motherfucker down and everybody go on home." That's how intense we were. After a whole summer of being treated like little motherfuckers on the American tour we were like, "No, naw." Our confidence came from our Philly and New York shows during the Def Jam tour, where we received a really

strong response. We knew we were going into a country that knew all of our jams, and we had the number-one album in the country.

Eric B. and Rakim got off, they did their thing, but their songs were more melodic so they didn't seem to move much. L.L.'s show started off well, but that was the gig where, L.L. was on the couch performing "I Need Love," and people started throwing money at him. Not throwing money in the good sense, they were pelting him with coins, booing him. London wasn't into soft music. They wanted their music rock hard.

I remember going into the back room and telling L.L., "Don't worry about it, we're all in this shit together." We played a couple more dates, but Eric B. and Rakim finally got fed up with the food and the conditions. They left the tour and went back home. L.L. wasn't too happy about the food and the conditions either, but this was the Def Jam tour, and he was headlining.

Our attitude was like Mr. T and Rocky downstairs in the basement listening to a radio with a hanger sticking out of it, doing push-ups. L.L. was staying in suites in the hotel. It wasn't like that back then for us. It was freezing cold over there, and we were sleeping on the bus. It was like being in the service. We weren't getting much food, so all we had to look forward to was the next show. It didn't matter to us, because we had the eye of the tiger.

Outside of the United States you have to earn your respect through performances, you're not going to get over by just having a popular jam. In Europe, if you perform your ass off, fans will continue to check your jams out. That's what we did.

We went from ripping London to Amsterdam, Norway, Sweden, and Denmark, all through Germany. It was a great experience for us. That's when we realized that if we never dominated the U.S. market, we would take the markets that nobody else wanted—the rest of the world.

ATHLETES AND ENTERTAINERS

The athletics and entertainment industries have both had a tremendous impact on the mind-set of today's youth to the point where many young people grow up idolizing athletes and entertainers, yet the only time these "idols" are seen is if they're playing ball, singing, rapping, or dancing. The only time somebody Black, especially Black and male, gets the spotlight or accepted into American culture on the high economic end is if we're athletes or entertainers. People in other areas don't get highlighted. Black youth, especially young Black men, gravitated to Rap when it first came out, because it's a vocal expression, whereas in athletics you'd see somebody do incredible athletic things on the court or field, but you'd never hear anything from their mind. The travesty is that both athletes and

entertainers could be, and should be, more visual and vocal sources of hope for young children in the ghetto and throughout the world. Regrettably, athletes and entertainers have become nothing more than "high-priced slaves."

Black tennis star Arthur Ashe wrote in his book *A Hard Road to Glory,* "Contemporary black athletes' exploits are well known, but few fully appreciate their Hard Road to Glory. Discrimination, vilification, incarceration, dissipation, ruination, and ultimate despair have dogged the steps of the mightiest of these heroes. And, only a handful in the last 179 years have been able to live out their post-athletic lives in peace and prosperity." In the 1960s several high-profile Black athletes were actively involved in the struggle for equal rights and justice in America. Among them, heavyweight champion of the world, Muhammad Ali, gold and bronze medal winners in the 1968 Olympics, Tommy Smith and John Carlos, basketball Hall of Famers Bill Russell and Kareem Abdul-Jabbar, and football Hall of Famer Jim Brown. Athletes in the 1960s took a stand because they knew they were thrust into the mainstream arena as pieces of meat. They went beyond the call of duty. Back then most of them didn't get the microphone time athletes do today, so what some did in defiance is change their names. Where they may not have been respected as Black men, others had to respect their demands to be called by their new Muslim and African names. I remember when Lew Alcindor changed his name to Kareem Abdul-Jabbar and announcers continued to call him Kareem Jabbar, and he had to correct them over and over. He was like, "I'm not going to give you the proper day or time if you don't call me by my full name, it's Kareem Abdul-Jabbar." The same thing happened with Cassius Clay when he changed his name to Muhammad Ali. He had to check people all the time. That was defiance.

Today's athletes are pacified by what they're paid. An unfortunate reality is most athletes don't have a historical understanding and appreciation for some of those who came before them and paved the way. Recently, Curt Flood, who was a National League all-star baseball player in the 1960s, passed away. His opposition against the "reserve clause" in major-league contracts is a big reason athletes get the millions of dollars they get on the "free agent" market. Flood took a stand against the reserve clause, which meant the complete and infinite ownership of a ballplayer's rights until *the player got traded or sold by the original owner*, or in other words the equivalent of slavery in sports. What he sacrificed his career to achieve was a player's right to sign a contract with any team after the first contract expired. Athletes of today don't even know Curt Flood's name.

TODAY'S ATHLETES ARE PACIFIED BY WHAT THEY'RE PAID. . . . [THEY] DON'T HAVE A HISTORICAL UNDERSTANDING AND APPRECIATION FOR SOME OF THOSE WHO CAME BEFORE THEM AND PAVED THE WAY.

Other Black athletes who sacrificed themselves without getting the honor and respect they rightfully deserve include Bill Russell, whose book *Go Up for Glory* depicts the sacrifices professional Black athletes endured in the fifties and sixties; the indignity of being denied hotel and restaurant accommodations with the rest of his white teammates, and constantly being called derogatory and racist names by fans. Russell writes: "The American Negro has attempted to make it better 'for your people' by playing the game of life with bigots by maintaining the status quo. It never worked. The only way to gain rights is to fight for them. Regardless of whether I was suspended, fined, or whatever, I was going to fight." For his honest work he was lambasted by the nation's sports critics, and accused of being egotistical and ungrateful. The critics' attacks on Bill Russell and other athletes who spoke their minds were based on the erroneous and racist view that if it were not for professional sports these Black men would not have been anything in life. Harry Edwards's book *The Revolt of the Black Athlete*, quotes a former director of intercollegiate athletics at a major university expressing his views on Black athletes' ungratefulness this way: "It's beyond me why these people would allow them-

FIGHT THE POWER

selves to be misled by fanatics like Harry Edwards and H. Rap Brown. These athletes are seen by millions of people on nationwide and world-wide television. . . . Why our niggers right here at the University have never had it so good." Bill Russell adamantly refuted the claim that basketball is what made him, by reversing the charge and saying if it wasn't for him basketball would not be what it is today. Russell was one of the greatest basketball players the NBA has ever known, leading the Boston Celtics to an unprecedented eleven world championships in thirteen seasons.

Jim Brown is another brother that sacrificed greatly as he gave up his cleats at the pinnacle of his professional career. Nobody could touch him. He was breaking all kinds of rushing records, and at the same time he fought and organized for Black people. He was able to encourage the Cleveland Browns to contribute resources to the poorer areas of Cleveland, and also worked with Black MBAs and students to develop economic structures and opportunities for the underdeveloped Cleveland community. Jim Brown hasn't stopped. He is still very active in Los Angeles with his Amer-I-Can Program for Social Change, which has now spread to several major cities, teaching former gang members the responsibility of self-determination and positive change. My vote for President in 1992 went to Jim Brown as a write-in candidate.

Muhammad Ali's bold stand while heavyweight champ of the world had severe consequences: it cost him his prestige, his income, and his title, but he did it for the cause of Black dignity. Muhammad Ali was so great because when he *did* get on the mic, he talked about what *he* wanted to talk about. That's where his respect came in. He was proud to say that he was Black and worshipped Allah. He got that through all the time. Sportscasters would

MUHAMMAD ALI WAS SO GREAT BECAUSE WHEN HE DID GET ON THE MIC, HE TALKED ABOUT WHAT HE WANTED TO TALK ABOUT.

grab the microphone from him and tell him that he shouldn't brag so much. He wasn't bragging, he was talking about the untalked-about.

We all saw what happened after the Washington Redskins, led by Black quarterback Doug Williams, won the 1988 Super Bowl. The mood in the country was like something was wrong—things just didn't fit. He wrecked all kinds of previous Super Bowl records, throwing for 340 yards and 4 touchdowns. When it was over it was like, "We can't wait till next year." John Elway is an incredible player, but it was almost like just about everyone was holding him up and trying to buy him a championship. In the book *Quarterblack: Shattering the NFL Myth*, Doug Williams says that after winning the Super Bowl he didn't get *any* calls from major corporations for endorsements and appearances. The year before, Phil Simms, quarterback for the Super Bowl Champion New York Giants, made close to two million dollars in corporate endorsements and appearances. Doug says he was lucky if he made two hundred thousand dollars. That's not even three fifths. Maybe the country was in shock that after sixty years of organized, de facto discrimination in professional football by NFL coaches, general managers, and owners not wanting Black men in leadership roles such as quarterbacks, middle linebackers, or centers, the first Black quarterback to ever appear in a league championship game shattered many records.

Gross injustices are still taking place in modern times. Former Chicago Bull, Craig Hodges, who was one of the best three-point shooters in basketball and helped the Chicago Bulls win back-to-back World Championships in 1991 and 1992, has taken an official step and filed a federal lawsuit against the NBA alleging violation of his civil rights and destruction of his career. After the Bulls released him in 1992, he wasn't even offered a tryout with another team. Although the NBA denies any wrongdoing, Michael Jordan and Phil Jackson both said it surprised them that no one was interested in Hodges. The problems reportedly started when Hodges, after the 1990–1991 championship season, wore traditional African garments to the White House when they went to

meet then-President George Bush. What kind of shit is that? A Black man, a descendant of Africa, being "white-balled" because he wore traditional African garments. African heads of state going to the White House wear their national dress to the White House all the time. My guess is that it wasn't the clothes people had a problem with, but that in their eyes he was being an uppity slave.

Hodges once told me that when he was playing for the Milwaukee Bucks, Minister Farrakhan came and spoke in Milwaukee, and he attended the lecture. The next day in the local newspaper they had pictures of him in the front row at the speech. The day after that he was traded to the Chicago Bulls.

I've noticed that in 1997 there has been a reduced amount of Hip-Hop in the NBA arenas. I can tell it's not being played as much as it once was. That's some bullshit. The only reason I can think of is that they probably feel it's derogatory to their marketing. The ballplayers are all largely between the ages of twenty and twenty-eight, and Hip-Hop artists are between the ages of twenty and twenty-eight. They're the same brothers. Once again this is a divisionary tactic. Allen Iverson of the Philadelphia 76ers won the MVP award at the NBA's rookie all-star game, but all sorts of voices have criticized him for not fitting the NBA's created image. He's twenty-one, loves Rap, and travels with a group of his homeys that he grew up with in Hampton, Virginia, and that's bad for the league's image. Why? I think because it's too Black. What does Hip-Hop have to do with the NBA's image? It's an image that they want to be able to protect and conserve. Reducing Hip-Hop music in NBA arenas is racist, I believe. Especially since almost every little white kid in America can relate to the Hip-Hop vibe. Professional sports franchises and the leagues will tolerate the Black player as long as he fits the "goody-two-shoes" Negro, Hertz Rent-A-Car jumping in airports image once held by O.J. Simpson. Everybody jumped off the O.J. bandwagon quick, even after he was found not guilty. America said, "Fuck it, he is guilty." O.J. rocked their world.

It is my opinion that MTV has done the same thing by de-emphasizing Hip-Hop. It became too powerful and too many white kids were getting a taste of what it's like to be Black. When *Yo! MTV Raps* was the highest-rated program on MTV in 1990, they seemed to withdraw support from it and decreased its attraction to the wider audience. When they say the NBA is Fan-Tastic, they want their Negroes formulated in their own form, and we know who's running the NBA—white boys in suits. They're full of shit, trying to turn the NBA into the Niggatronic Basketball Association.

I did a record called "Air Hoodlum" on the "Greatest Misses" project, which talks about athletes that get caught up and believe in the system, then the system disses them. The majority of Black athletes that have the hope and dream of becoming a professional athlete don't make it. College athletes need to realize that these motherfuckers don't give a fuck about them unless they can be the best at dunking, running touchdowns, or hitting home runs. College athletes should be focused on getting an education while the opportunity is there for them to get it for free. *The Revolt of the Black Athlete* reveals, "a Black athlete finds that his equals are not his white teammates, but the basketballs, baseballs, jock straps, and other forms of property and equipment—all of which, like him, are important and vital to sports."

I've developed an attitude where I question Black athletes and their commitment to Black life. It's more than just saying, "I'm not a criminal or contributing to a criminal element that should be good enough." It's not enough. It's not an issue of donating money to Black causes. What makes me pissed off is that they are not saying much of anything. Their words and their time could help steer a lot of young people out of the traps that are set for them. Black professional athletes have tremendous potential for power, but are in fact powerless, because they're not unified. They're unified by one white cord that holds them together, yet individualizes them. Michael Jordan or Emmitt

> I'VE DEVELOPED AN ATTITUDE WHERE I QUESTION BLACK ATHLETES AND THEIR COMMITMENT TO BLACK LIFE.

Smith could make big changes in society with just five or six spoken words in one direction.

All of the millionaires in professional athletics who have white agents, white accountants, white lawyers, and white wives, and at the same time are not doing anything for the Black community, need to get their asses checked. They should at least understand that the privileges white America is giving them are temporary, and that they're Black and their words of encouragement could help somebody else come up. Not just the kids who see them on the playing field, or at the United Way events that the league escorts them to. That doesn't mean shit. Along with that they need to do some things in the neighborhoods and communities that they came up out of.

Athletes are afraid to speak on anything significant or controversial because their agents will advise them not to. It's all about money. If an athlete is making seventy million dollars over a period of time, why should it be about money? Like they have to get *all* the money.

The same thing with entertainers. Rappers get checked and knocked for saying rebellious things, but what the fuck is the average R&B singer saying? It's cool to have "Live Aid," and other benefit concerts, but these concepts are devised by whites who say, "I think something should be done." A lot of Blacks in the entertainment ranks, especially in R&B, are full of shit, they're not saying anything. At least rappers will come out and say *something*. Whatever we feel we'll come out and say it, whether it's regarding police brutality with N.W.A's "Fuck Tha Police," or giving our mothers their respect with Tupac's "Dear Mama." In April 1992 when the rebellion took place in South-Central Los Angeles, the voices of rappers were heard coming out and expressing an opinion, but the voices of spineless ass singers and Black athletes were silent.

They say Spike Lee is a crazy man, because Spike says what he has to say and doesn't hold his tongue. Denzel Washington said he knows he's a role model and he comes out and says what he has to say. Wesley Snipes comes out and kicks what he has to kick. They know that they're worth "x" amount, but they don't give in to being a puppet for the white man. They're in charge of their own destinies.

Initially I wondered about Arsenio Hall. Arsenio had his own show, and was clearly the most talented talk show host on TV. When Arsenio got more "radical" with his show by allowing strong Black viewpoints to come across to the millions of his viewers, the forces that are in control forced him off the air. The loss of *The Arsenio Hall Show* affected Rap greatly because that was the only vehicle Rap artists had in order to be seen in front of a national audience. What's messed up is there was not enough Black people to stand up and say, "Look, you're going to leave that show on the air or fuck you."

If we don't recognize and take advantage of being in these key positions and areas, what we'll have is a situation where, without a public voice, a lot of people will get swept into a vacuum of athletics and entertainment being a dream for a few, but a nightmare for most.

THE MUSIC INDUSTRY

I'm part of the first generation that turned eighteen and nineteen when the first Rap records were coming out. Rap music in its current state is similar to the rock world prior to its being structured and organized back in the 1960s with people like The Rolling Stones, The Beatles, Eric Clapton, Led Zeppelin, The Who, and Jimi Hendrix. They had artists and others around the art form who said, "Yeah, this is rebel music, but we're going to organize and structure it. We're not going to infringe upon the music, but we'll build a world around it." That has yet to be done in Rap and Hip-Hop. Right now there's a whole bunch of white boys salivating at the mouth to put a structure around Rap. Many come in the guise of being acceptable headz, homeboys, and allies, but it's only a matter of time for some of them to go from wearing Tommy Hilfiger to Giorgio Armani. Hip-Hop's a universal circle, but I want

to make sure that our people don't get locked out. When referring to the "power brokers" of Hip-Hop, right now the majority of them are white.

The only reason I believe that older people have strayed from supporting and listening to Rap is because it hasn't been organized. People are not going to flock to something that's half-assed and unorganized. Rock 'n' roll lives on because it has organization in all phases: it's newsworthy, historical, and its historical achievements are documented via books.

Favorite Nineties Groups:

Wu Tang Clan: A swarm from all directions.
Cypress Hill: Took it and marched their beliefs
back and forth across the world.
Naughty by Nature: Always hungry and
aggressive anthemers.
Arrested Development: Speech took
combinations; never seen or heard in Rap.
Bone Thugs N Harmony: A religious cult?
Outkast: Laid-back approach easy for the soul.
Fugees: Revolution; international overview built
to last.
A Tribe Called Quest: Rhymes, rhymes, rhymes;
gotem for days.
Das EFX: Changed the Rap flow drastically;
resped up the East Coast flow.
Gang Starr: Great combinations and music
selection.

The Rap industry is in total chaos right about now. Rap could be likened to Africa, which has been a refrigerator for the world's resources for hundreds of years without any payback. Rap music has been a refrigerator for today's musical culture without any payback. Rap is waiting to be seized and organized, but is it going to take white boys to come in to organize and put a structure around it?

Professional basketball today is the same game they were playing in the 1970s—players dunked, and did all that fancy shit, but the NBA was in serious trouble in the late 1970s. It's the same NBA, but they got reorganized and marketed correctly; agents, marketing specialists, and organizers came in and reformed the image. The same thing happened with rock 'n' roll.

Historically, the entertainment business has been a one-sided rip-off deal. The entertainment industry, like any other industry that depends heavily on a community, has an accountability to that community. I'm tired of seeing record company executives, lawyers, and accountants in the business go through long tenures and million-dollar bank accounts while the artists, because of a lack of schooling and a lack of concern for the art form, end up broke and penniless most of the time, misdirected, and dependent upon foundations for their existence. There are guys who've been behind the scenes of the music business for forty or fifty years, living fat the whole time by exploiting Black creativity.

There needs to be a concerted effort in the music business to contribute to fixing aspects of the society that it cannibalizes and feasts on like a buzzard. Then when it gets full it keeps circling looking for its next prey, and a lot of times drops shit on the remains that it chewed upon. That's the music and the entertainment industry as a whole. If these record company executives continue in the direction they've been going without trying to institute programs and organizations that will help artists and the communities from which the art derives, they're going to be identified.

I see way too many artists from the "Old School" who have contributed immeasurably to Rap but are out of the game and out of a job. Since Rap is a billion-dollar industry, there should not be so many poor and broke people on the Black side, while the same white faces make more and more money. A few years ago one of the larger Hip-Hop record labels ran an ad that read, "This is how

we go from the old to the new." *No, that's how you take from the old all the way up to the new.*

I run into people like KG of the Cold Crush Brothers, Kool Herc, Grandmaster Flash, and other Hip-Hop pioneers who had to rely on doing concerts to make a living, and when they did gigs they would get paid three to five thousand dollars while the use of their names would pull close to ten thousand people in those days, and the promoters made all the dough.

Music artists are always getting exploited by somebody who claims they are in it for the business, but business only. I know this is show business—five percent is a show and ninety-five percent is business—but fair business is fifty-fifty. The music business doesn't operate fairly. It's a game run by hustlers and gangsters. My theory is if they want to deal on that level, artists need to develop their own "gangsters" to protect their interests. With all the gang-bangers we have out there some need to be trained to secure the structures that we build for economic empowerment. Once they're taught how to get money in a "legalized" gangster business, we can go head-to-head into the music business and approach these people behind the desks. Brothers have killed each other for much less. Every business needs a threat team.

If we don't step up and realize that we have a vested interest in seizing control of this industry and take advantage of what we have to do right now, we will be relegated to just being artists, en-tertainers, and actors. If you're in the Rap game you should want to see the game elevate. I'd like to see the Rap game elevate to a level like the NBA. The NBA is organized. Rappers should get or-ganized, because this is the perfect chance for Black people, es-pecially young Black people, to organize and control it.

There's not many people that have a sincere love for the art. There's far too many people in this business that have more love for money than the art, and are in it just for that. But they shouldn't be allowed to do a half-assed job, and nobody tests their sincerity. The record industry has been underexposing Rap. They've been carrying out orders to do what they've always done, and since the

Rap community is in a total mess, capable Black people are afraid to take the necessary steps to get involved with taking it to the next level.

I've developed a philosophy about the music industry called the DOAM Theory. The DOAM theory deals with what I find to be the essential elements for the survival of the Hip-Hop genre: discipline, organization, administration, and management.

In the past I've been misunderstood by people who think that because I say what I say, I think other rappers should say what I say. Rappers should say whatever they feel. Every story has to be told. Personally, I just try to take Hip-Hop and raise the understandability of it to another level. Here's the double-edged sword—when something Black is disciplined, organized, administered, and managed properly, and begins to rise to another level, it will be accepted by a mass audience. Unfortunately, all kinds of roadblocks will be placed in the path, because others will feel threatened that it's too Black and too strong. Especially when they start to see young white kids coming up and Redman or Method Man happens to be his hero instead of Spider-Man or Superman. That causes problems for the white structure, because young white kids start to realize that their race shouldn't count. "Redman is my hero." His father has a problem with that, because it's not him.

Discipline means that there are certain professional standards that must be strictly adhered to. If an artist is on the road, he can't be out there throwing couches off of hotel balconies or smoking weed in the middle of public places. The law would rather make a negative example out of a rapper and Rap music, which makes it more difficult for everybody else down the road. A lot of times artists attempt to make the whole world their stage, when we need to just let the stage be the stage. When there's no discipline, and no union of sorts, then you're open to be attacked from all sides by structures that make it impossible for any business to survive.

Organization in the industry exists in the form of recording contracts. Every single recording artist at one time or another has

signed a recording contract. We can step up the level of organization from the point of signatures on contracts to doing a lot of other things for the protection of the art form. I don't care if it's Luke, Redman, Speech from Arrested Development, or M.O.P., we all have some things in common and should be organized around our common goals and interests, regardless of the style of music.

We've had different attempts at unions and unifying organizations in the past, but my plan is to join all of the unifying efforts together so people won't be able to say, "I didn't know that was taking place. I got beat out of my loot." Record companies are searching for answers to organize what they already have. They are looking for and would welcome something like this to take place. When it takes place a lot of the traditional game playing will get checked at the door.

Administration is making the world of Rap and Hip-Hop recognized through certain legalities that can protect artists and the art form. Proper administration would have people assigned to follow up and implement ideas that are introduced at industry conferences, and compile lists of entertainment lawyers, reputable accountants, and information on different aspects of the business.

Management ties all the areas up in Rap and Hip-Hop together, from merchandising down to who negotiates getting Rap shows into venues. Right now the buildings aren't allowing Rap shows because they believe the stigma that's attached to Rap. Insurance companies aren't insuring Rap shows, because they also believe the stigma that comes through a lot of the media.

There's no such thing as *real* Rap management. I'm not talking about a company that has a stable of artists who happen to be hitting at a particular moment because of name recognition. I mean a stable of artists who are developed, know what they have to do, and know how to facilitate the public. Good management teaches the artist what it takes to build, then preserve, a career. There's a couple of situations trickling around like the Flavor Unit Management with Shakim and Queen Latifah in New Jersey; Ice-T and Charlie Jam have a management situation that's solid, and Malik Entertainment has a management situation that's becoming solid. We're going into the full development of artists, and if one of our artists is not down to do the basic things, then they have to go. Our artists have to do one hundred percent of what we say or they're not worth messing with. We must run the ship damn near like Coach Bobby Knight runs his college basketball team. There's no if's, and's, or but's, no excuses. We don't consider ourselves experts in Rap, but we do consider ourselves higher students of learning. Unless you have your basics down or have a successful record behind you, you won't be in the game long. And just because you've sold records doesn't mean that you know what you're doing. You can find a player on a basketball team who scores thirty points per game, but he can be dumb as shit, and his team constantly loses. He has the talent to score baskets, but he doesn't have the skill to play the game. That's what happens a lot of times in Rap. Artists have the talent to come up with nice verses and flows, but may not have the skill to write a song. Or they may have the skill to write a song, but not the skill to stay in the business. There are a lot of management situations in Rap that are undetermined, "He's my man so he's my manager." A lot of the management relationships are on a trial-by-error basis, where the manager knows a little more than the artist herself. Therefore, the artist receives very little development. Proper management develops artists' talent into a skill, and gives them a proper understanding of the total environment around their art. Management should also make sure that the artist is always interacting with the public. If the public is all around the world, then the task is that much bigger. A career is built on four points: the music, objective, video or visuals, and entertainment or performance. That's what I call the MOVE principle. A group must hold all four categories up to stay afloat. Most artists are only fulfilling, at the most, three dimensions, because the violent stigma attached to Rap has nullified any Rap tours.

In order to expand Rap's horizons and break down some

doors, we need people who understand that Rap goes beyond the limited view of what its realities are: Philly, Los Angeles, New York. We have to understand that people are into Rap all over the planet. Public Enemy has performed to loyal audiences on every continent all over the planet. Originally rappers wanted to go to as many places as possible to prove themselves, but now the business tells us, "It's wild out there. Do your song and video and call it a day."

> THERE'S A MORE RECEPTIVE AND LEARNED HIP-HOP AUDIENCE IN EUROPE THAN THERE IS IN THE UNITED STATES.

There's a more receptive and learned Hip-Hop audience in Europe than there is in the United States, but a lot of artists do not travel to Europe to experience it for themselves. They're trained to think locally. There are a lot of groups that the world would like to see, but may never because the groups don't want to explore, or they just don't know enough about it to investigate.

Now that the Eastern Bloc of Europe is opening up, there are people in places like Romania and the Russian, Czech, and Slav Republics that want to check out Hip-Hop. Most people in the United States can't comprehend the world power of Rap, and don't care to believe it. In 1994 when Public Enemy did our latest European tour in Budapest, Hungary, and Zagreb, Croatia, people were traveling by the busloads from former Eastern Bloc countries to check out the show and invite us to their countries to perform. We've spent years being one of the biggest Rap groups in the world because we went and sought out the world. You can't get there if you just sit on your ass and stay at home. You also can't determine how big a group is just from record sales. Snoop Doggy Dogg does music that is very popular. There are lots of Black kids who buy his music, but white kids are buying his music just as much if not more. So the next level for somebody like Snoop is to go out and perform in a lot of different places, and let the people see him. If the people never see him then his audience will shrink-wrap right back.

To expand your career you have to be open to traveling to different places and learning more about other people. When I was in Brazil I swore I was in Oakland. It's like a tropical Oakland.

In other parts of the world young Blacks are confused by Black people in the United States. They're like, "Why are they calling themselves bitches and hoes? What does that mean? Why do they call each other nigger?" Their consciousness is higher, they are not into a lot of frivolous things. They don't get as much bullshit as we get on TV, so they're a lot more open and sharp, and they know what they're up against because they see it on a daily basis.

RAP TOURING

Black people don't control the music business, so therefore it has no rules. *No rules.* We don't own venues, so Rap groups hardly get to travel anywhere. A few acts have the basics of touring down, and actually go around the world performing for the people that buy their records: Ice-T, Ice Cube, Cypress Hill, Gang Starr, and Public Enemy. But what needs to be incorporated into the younger groups coming up is an understanding of the basics. They have to go out and prove their records, and get down. That's what we've always been about. Even if you're sick the show must go on. To sell yourself you have to go above and beyond the call of duty. I've been sick more than a few times, but I've never missed a gig because of it. You have to take care of yourself while on tour. If you don't you'll be fucked up. If you're fucked up you can't operate.

Public Enemy always did our best teaching by example. During the heyday of touring we would be at a show, and people would have their doubts about us. They'd be like, "Public Enemy, they're a bunch of old guys on their way down." But when we'd go around to different cities and new artists would play in front of an audience for fifteen minutes and make no impression, and we'd be dropping bombs, then they'd say, "Damn." Then they would

FIGHT THE POWER
111

listen to what we had to say because their once-limited view of us expanded. Then they'd start asking us to help them with their show. "What am I doing wrong?" They may go around the way and say, "Public Enemy haven't been hitting for four or five years," but if they're actually with us on the road and see us perform, it's a different story. In the last few years there haven't been any Rap tours. Rap groups hardly go anywhere. If anything they've been doing small, limited engagements. A few years back I tried to put together a group of new artists to put on Terminator's record: and none of them would get down, because their whole perception of us was that we were over with. Their view of us is a small, limited one. We can't even show them by example, because we can't even put them on a tour with us. We'd be doing them a favor by adding them to the package, but they're not checking for any advice that we have.

The same thing happened in the NBA. When Magic Johnson came out of retirement to become the coach of the L.A. Lakers, he had problems with the attitude of some of his players. In a recent *Newsweek* article Magic said, "I came in the league with the attitude of winning, with nothing else mattering. . . . These new players want the glory without the pain." Magic had just played two years before. He has the basics down. A lot of the young guys coming up from college see the NBA commercials, and just because they can do fancy dunks they become beneficiaries of a marketing program, but because of their lack of basics they never really master the game. Magic Johnson's and Michael Jordan's basics are solid. The same thing with Public Enemy and Ice-T—the basics are solid. This white group of teenagers from L.A. came

> MAGIC JOHNSON'S AND MICHAEL JORDAN'S BASICS ARE SOLID. THE SAME THING WITH PUBLIC ENEMY AND ICE-T—THE BASICS ARE SOLID.

out in an international magazine saying, "Ice-T can't rap, he's whack." They needed their asses checked for saying something like that. They have no historical documentation or reference points as young people, which means that they're open to being exploited to the highest degree.

I question the drive of a lot of artists, because they're in the game just so they can make money and get girls. Those things will be there regardless. Artists should do it for the competitive spirit. Artists should be doing it to enhance the art. Artists should be doing it to win. Some people do it for the money because they say that getting the money is winning, so they'll do anything to get it. I won't do just anything. I think you have to hold on to what you believe in.

Record companies seek young artists that have skills and sign them, they sell a whole bunch of records the first time around, they get a second chance, don't sell any records and then they're cut loose. Frustrated at twenty-one. A record company would make crazy money and continue to do that same thing over and over again for a hundred years if they could keep that pattern flowing. That's why historical information and documentation are so important. It gives you perspective and a realization of the necessity to learn the basics. The basics are the key.

In the state that we're in today there are very few Rap shows, because a lot of people believe the stigmas about violence and are afraid to go. In the early days of Rap there were promoters who just wanted to make money—fuck the show, fuck security for the show. "I'm gettin' twenty thousand people in this spot, and I'm up and out of here." There were a lot of people that got involved in the game with that attitude. There were booking agencies that were only concerned with getting their money, therefore the price for a Rap artist was way off scale. The public wound up paying top-notch for tickets because the promoter had to pay an inflated price for the artist. The promoter also had to pay inflated insurance rates for the venue, whose management was saying, "We don't want to get our building torn up so we're going to raise the insurance," and they raise the insurance so high the promoter has

FIGHT THE POWER
113

to have a high ticket price to cover costs and make a slight profit. A heavy-metal band could play a venue and the insurance would be like twenty-five to thirty cents a ticket in the United States, despite the fact that at previous shows a similar audience tore up all the seats.

On our 1990 Def Jam tour our insurance was damn near two dollars per person. At the end of the night if ten thousand people came to the show the insurance was twenty thousand dollars off the top. It got to the point where live performances in Rap were complete dirt. Shady characters started to see Rap as an opportunity to be parasitic. People today are still taking out of Rap what others have sacrificed to put in to it. I've seen promoters lose their homes trying to make money, and at the same time do the right thing by the artist. I've also seen artists abuse promoters; promoters abuse cities; promoters abuse artists; booking agencies abuse artists and promoters; promoters go bankrupt; artists get caught up with the drug trade; drug dealers hang around promoters and artists; drug dealers as promoters; artists go in front of the public and burn the public. The whole aura of live performances in Rap has disappeared.

Videos became more important than live shows in the 1990s, because with a video you can get a film producer and make yourself loom larger than life. Also when *Yo! MTV Raps* went national, it opened the market up tremendously. A lot of white kids living in suburban areas wouldn't come to a Hip-Hop show. When we would play at the 10,000-seat Pavillion Arena on the campus of the University of Illinois, which is smack in the middle of the hood on the West Side of Chicago, white kids weren't coming from the suburbs to a show in the middle of an all-Black neighborhood. There were some who didn't care and came anyway, but most of them were afraid. They saw it as being easier to go to the mall and pick up a tape and learn about the culture that way, or they could just watch *Yo! MTV Raps* in the comfort of their living rooms and copy the culture that way. Another factor that has hurt live Rap performance turnout has been that artists have burned the public by not giving the public worthy shows.

> Ten Emcees That Make Me Say Damn!:
>
> Supernatural: Unconscious skill at finding the right phrase in quicktime.
> Mad Skillz: Smoother, flowing, and sharp with wit.
> CL Smooth: Elaborate phrasing style; nice.
> Volume 10: Pistol grip pump, he was in a zone.
> Zack Delarocha: Committed energy styled to rage beats.
> Hyenas in the Desert: Kendu power and cleverness.
> Sonslawta Melquan: Hopefully this wordsmith will be heard.
> Tung Twista: Chitown speed rhymer.
> Shaquille O'Neal: Rhymes that are realistic; good flow.
> Rampage: Busta rhyme protégé got 1990s power.

When the modern generation of R&B artists started becoming more popular, the female audience started to go see Jodeci, Boyz II Men, Al B. Sure!, Bobby Brown, and Johnny Gill concerts, because they knew it would be a safer environment. Even though Rap was becoming softer and more melodic, the shows were still heavily populated by males. Since there were not as many females in the audience, there was bound to be drama. Shit was bound to go up in gunshots and smoke, because a brother who was drunk or high would look up at the stage at artists he spent money on doing a bullshit show, look around and see very few females, and with the slightest mishap could jump off into some drama. That whole scene developed to the point where the last *all Rap* tour Public Enemy did was in December 1991 with Al Haymon. Public Enemy can always tour because we've built a following, and had as our number-one mission to expand to a world audience, and also to expand to more audiences than just one. A

lot of people say, "You have more of a white audience now." That's not true. There's a Black audience out there, but will they want to pay the ticket price? Probably not. If there was a situation where eight or nine groups were in a theater for ten dollars then Blacks would be there. But they're not paying twenty-five or thirty dollars for a show to see two groups. A white audience has more expendable income, and if it's in their area they won't be afraid to go to the show.

Ice-T and I have discussed starting our own booking agency to handle Rap acts. I feel like right now the William Morrises, the ICMs, and the CAAs of the world are looking at Rap as being headache money. R&B has become safer, softer, surer money, so they're looking at Rap as being something to keep on their roster, but not something that they should actively push as options for tours.

The booking agent is an artist's contact point for promoters for shows and engagements. To build an independent booking agency is going to take a solid union between the artists. The process of building a booking agency will involve a fight, because once we make a power move, those same booking agencies undoubtedly will double back and give an, "Oh, we love Rap. We're doing a fantastic job," spiel as an end to cover their means. These agencies can't be in two places trying to catch rain at the same time. We will have to get real troopers, and build a Dream Team of artists, then everybody else will follow. The basketball Dream Team is twelve all-stars. How many people wanted to get on the U.S. Basketball Dream Team once it was rolling? How many people felt left out when they didn't make the team? When developing a Dream Team you don't worry about getting a hundred people. You pick twelve and call it a day. Then people will want to get on. That's the best way to build with people, especially Black people. Don't ask everybody. Do it and then say, "This is what's going on. Do you want to be down? Yes or no, because it's already rolling without you." Once people know something is rolling without them, they want to be a part of it. It's sad to say but that's a fact of reality.

Walt F. Goodridge in his books *This Game of Artist Manage-ment* and *Rap: This Game of Exposure* names all the areas that need to be covered in the music business. He not only names all twenty-five areas, but he also tells you what keeps you in business if you're in one of those areas. If you don't build anything, then you have nothing. If you don't build anything you always have to be a part of somebody else's shit. To be a part of white people's structures is whack, especially when it comes down to Rap, be-cause they're not fully down with it.

One thing I've learned in this business is to go with your heart-felt decision. Make your move and don't look back. When you overanalyze situations, they call it "analysis to the point of paral-ysis," you go back and forth to where you make no decision, which is the worst decision. There's only a small percentage of people that have a genuine concern for Hip-Hop. There may be apprehension about making a move, but if you don't, someone else will.

That's one of the reasons why in 1990, I decided to start my own merchandising company, RappStyle, because I felt that mer-chandising companies like Winterland were not adequately ser-vicing my needs, and the needs of the Hip-Hop community on the retail and mail-order levels.

I saw that Rap artists were inspiring the public to buy the clothes that we wore. I'd wear a hat and start to see a whole lot of people all over wearing the same type of hat, or an artist may wear a jacket and a whole lot of people will buy and wear the same type of jacket. Lucrative contracts abound in the sports world for that same marketing power. Athletes have major en-dorsement contracts with sneaker and merchandising companies. People are not going out and buying clothes based on athletes they see wearing them. When you see an athlete, he's usually wearing a uniform and some sneakers. I can understand athletes and sneaker contracts, but in a video, especially a Rap video, people see what clothes the artists are wearing, and actually go out to buy what they see. I told Winterland I had a problem with them not having enough of our style of clothes in the stores. People

can go to Foot Locker and buy all kinds of sports gear. If sports apparel has international sales potential, how come Hip-Hop apparel doesn't have that same global market when it exists worldwide? The common response questions the world power of Rap. I've been in too many countries, and everywhere I've gone people bought the shirts and hats at the shows, because they evidently felt it was the only place they could buy them. You mean to tell me that someone can't facilitate that need and fill that void as far as people wanting to buy clothes associated with Rap?

I worked with my father and Joe and Sal Girgenti to put together a RappStyle to work with retail outlets. Joe and Sal Girgenti are Italian-American, but at the same time my father is involved and I'm involved. At least it's a joint venture. It's a joint venture that works well because they know the merchandising and manufacturing end of the business, and since there's racism in the clothing business we have a team that can handle that. Don't have a situation where a big corporation is making all the decisions and there's no Black faces in there. That's bullshit.

Rap is being raped. There should be at least one franchise or store in malls that specifically sells Hip-Hop merchandise. If statistics show that eighty to eighty-five percent of Rap music and Hip-Hop merchandise are being purchased by white kids, then there must be a way to make those two ends meet. It will get done, but what we must prevent from happening is it getting done by two white corporate heads that really don't give a damn about the music or the community from which the music comes. That's something we have to fight against. We have to do it ourselves.

> RAP IS BEING RAPED. THERE SHOULD AT LEAST BE ONE FRANCHISE OR STORE IN MALLS THAT SPECIFICALLY SELLS HIP-HOP MERCHANDISE.

LAWYERS, NO LOYALTIES;
ACCOUNTANTS, NO ROYALTIES

Here's a saying: lawyers, no loyalties; accountants, no royalties. Over ninety-five of all Black entertainers in the music business, especially in the hyper-critical R&B world, have white lawyers and accountants. When are we going to turn the ball around? I detest the system of white lawyers, agents, and accountants dominating the music and sports industry. I see so many people kiss up to that shit. I don't detest the people who use them, I detest the systematic process and the way it works. I understand the process, but as much as I'll work with it, I'll work against it. That's why sometimes I rebel against it. Someone may say, "Well Chuck, you make money off of that process." Yes, and as a matter of fact I want to make much more money off of that operation.

Entertainment law is not like real law. Real law is more stable and the environment is built around it. Entertainment law can shift at any time. One and two don't always add up to three; one and two may add up to six tomorrow in the entertainment industry. At the same time entertainment companies and lawyers don't make amendments to contracts, they keep making money off of whatever new comes up until you catch it out there, then it's amended.

In 1983, the Compact Disc Group, a coalition of record labels, hardware manufacturers, retailers, packaging manufacturers, and other divisions of the music industry, formed to promote the transition from vinyl to CD. Back in 1983 if you were to tell the average person there wouldn't be any more vinyl records he would have told you that you were crazy because everything was set up for vinyl: jukeboxes, turntables, etc. Even though they knew in 1983 that CDs were the next major recording format, the contracts that were being drafted by their lawyers weren't changed regarding CDs unless you specifically asked for it to be changed. I signed my contract on our low-point scale in 1986, and CDs weren't written into the contract. They used the term "sides," which was referring to vinyl. I didn't get my contract renegotiated on CDs until I got a new lawyer. I had to get a lawyer to just check my old lawyer's ass.

It doesn't make sense for me to have to pay three different lawyers to all check each other. Or to obtain two accountants, one to check the next one. Maybe I'm in the wrong business, maybe I should have been a lawyer. Your whole career you're paying lawyers and accountants for checking each other. That's the biggest crack that Black people fall into. The screening of people. We have to develop many more of our own professionals in those areas, who are competent and have integrity. If an artist is using a white firm and paying their high fees, and if they're really as important to the firm as they say, an artist should be able to take a person that just got out of college up there and say, "I want you to train this college student as an intern at your firm."

We need to develop our own firms. Especially in the 1990s, because one lawyer ain't saying shit. If you have one lawyer, he's going up against firms, teams, and leagues. Even trying to get into the game of building your own law firm is difficult, because the established law firms have the game of bait and hook. The larger law firms, which are historically nonBlack, will wave a ninety-thousand-dollar-a-year job at the top Black recruits, bring them in, train them, and have them as "pseudo partners." They're not really partners. The partners are the ones saying, "I have mad stock in this firm and I know that I'm responsible for the rent on the triplex we have on Madison Ave." I feel that white accountants and white lawyers are maintaining a fucked-up tradition that goes back to the plantation and the slave/slave master days. *I can't stand them for that.* This tradition needs to change.

They have so many tricks in this business, like when a kid wants to record and the record company refers the same

> MAYBE I'M IN THE WRONG BUSINESS, MAYBE I SHOULD HAVE BEEN A LAWYER. YOUR WHOLE CAREER YOU'RE PAYING LAWYERS AND ACCOUNTANTS FOR CHECKING EACH OTHER.

legal counsel that they sometimes use, which is clearly a conflict of interest. It's a crazy game.

In my next five years I want to become a union head. As union head I'm going to develop a threat team. These crackers in the business have been running such a complete game on Black people, and as many Black faces as there are in the industry, they're nothing but chocolate icing on a fucking vanilla cake. None of them are getting to the core. As long as I'm in the music business I'm definitely going to fight against exploitation, and I'm not afraid of losing. I'd be losing if I didn't fight.

BLACK LAWYERS AND ACCOUNTANTS

There have been a few star athletes who have bucked the system and obtained Black professional representation like Penny Hardaway, Jason Kidd, Glenn Robinson, and Chris Webber, but the numbers are still crazy unbalanced. As one Black agent stated, "It's not about excluding them [white agents] as much as it is about including Black, competent professionals for Black economic developmental reasons."

There's a lot of Black artists today who want their own Black lawyer and accountant, but it's a difficult searching and screening process because there's only a handful of them.

The problem is when a young artist gets a Black lawyer or accountant they fail to realize their lawyer or accountant, in this day and age when there's so many Black artists in music, film, books, etc., may have a large roster of artists that they represent. "Who's your lawyer?" Everybody wants to say, "Kendall Minter, Ron Sweeney, or Stephen Barnes." It becomes a trend.

Black lawyers and accountants in general have to be forthright with young artists and let them know when they cannot adequately handle them because they wouldn't be a priority on their list. I've been burned myself by a lawyer who wanted to handle me, but I came to find out I wasn't even cracking his top ten. He wanted to handle everybody. For example, I would call my lawyer

and wouldn't get calls back. With Black professionals there's a serious traffic jam. They may be good-hearted, but it messes things up when they're not forthright enough to let artists know when they can't really handle them.

I suggest that the popular Black lawyers and accountants get more Black lawyers and Black accountants in their business and make it grow, and train them as they come along. I know that may seem like an uphill battle, but it's all an uphill battle across the board. Black artists should seek out Black professionals first, but need help in screening and selecting the right one for the job. Wendy Day and the Rap Coalition has done a good job of compiling information on lawyers and accountants, and the more databases we build, the stronger a foothold we'll have in the industry. The easiest thing is to direct artists to the Rap Coalition and they'll help the artists find someone reputable for them instead of searching on their own, because artists will search and find eight bad apples out of twelve. I've been burned several times. Whether it's an accountant not taking care of taxes or a lawyer not handling phone calls, it's a big paper chase all over the game. Everybody is trying to stack as many chips up as they can, and that's fucking the whole game up for Black folks who happen to be in it.

BLACK RECORD EXECUTIVES

The pioneering efforts for Black executives and record companies that set the standard of measurement are those established by Stax Records with Al Bell, and Philly International Records with Kenny Gamble. In Nelson George's informative book, *The Death of Rhythm and Blues*, Nelson documents the socioeconomic statement made by Stax in 1972 with a concert they called Wattstax. "On August 20, 1972 [Al] Bell and [Jesse] Jackson stood side by side in the middle of the cavernous Los Angeles Coliseum, chanted 'I am somebody,' and then raised their fists in the Black Power salute before a hundred thousand [100,000] music fans. . . . It was a symbol of Black self-sufficiency." One hundred thousand music fans all brought together by a Black music company with its roots firmly grounded in Black culture *and* the Black community. *The Death of Rhythm and Blues* is a must-read for anyone who wants to get a historical perspective on the Black side of the music business, and make themselves aware of the battle that lies ahead for the future of Hip-Hop.

The majority of men in the music business are not straightforward enough, especially Black men. They're subservient to a structure and an industry where they think they can't look a white guy in the eye and say, "We need a different set of rules. I know the important thing is the bottom line, but we have to make amends, because as a company and as an industry we have a responsibility to the community." There are so many of these fuckin' fools that are just trying to stack chips. That's their whole thing—stacking chips. "I want to get mine now, because I don't know how long the shit is going to last. I don't know how long I'm going to live. It's about now." That's Black people's apocalyptic lack of vision to begin with. We're always into getting four years of excitement and sixty years of bullshit. Black folks live a long time even when we're living foul. Black people live to be seventy-five years old, but their last forty years may be whack. The shit in the music business is insane. Sylvia Rhone of Elektra Records has the most balls of any Black executive in the industry because she's honest about what the relationship should be between the companies and the artists, and the companies and the communities, and she's a woman. She has more balls than every single Black executive in the industry who's afraid to look a white person in the eye and say, "Yo, this is what's going down."

I remember one very painful incident that occurred on the Def

Jam tour in 1990. That's the infamous tour where Heavy D's dancer Troy "Trouble T Roy," had a fatal accident while playing backstage during one of the shows at Market Square Arena in Indianapolis. I took that death real hard because I felt that if we had been more persistent about the tour rules that we set at the beginning of the tour, of no playing backstage, that accident would probably not have happened. We were at the hospital all night. I saw Heavy D and Eddie turn from boys into men that night. The next night in Detroit we dedicated the show to him.

After that incident Heavy was going back and forth over whether he should finish the tour. Emotionally it was just too much. I remember we played the Louisiana Superdome and Heavy came to me with tears in his eyes. He said, "You know, Chuck, I don't know if this is right. I lost my best friend I had my whole life." He was really struggling to deal with that serious, real-life issue.

In one of my most pissed-off moments, Andre Harrell, who was the head of Uptown Records, Heavy D's record company, and also the head of Heavy's management, and I were talking in Jacksonville, and I was saying, I really enjoyed the pleasure of working with him, and enjoyed the experience of having his artists on the tour. Then I explained the sympathy I had for what was going on within their camp and the drama that took place with Troy, and Andre started asking me about our record sales. He attempted to take a serious issue and sidestep it into a business discussion about record sales. I was like, "It's whatever it is." Then I was talking about the Heavy situation and he basically said that the only thing Heavy should worry about was his career. I stared at his face and questioned my respect for him at that point.

It's situations like that which make

I WAS TALKING ABOUT THE HEAVY SITUATION AND HE BASICALLY SAID THAT THE ONLY THING HEAVY SHOULD WORRY ABOUT WAS HIS CAREER.

me question the integrity of people in this business. If a person doesn't have integrity for the art form and it's just about business, then anything can be business. There's a lot of people like that in the music industry. That's one of the reasons I'm not part of that clique. I don't go to late nightclubs to be among all these phony motherfuckers working the scene. I don't hang in the middle of that clique that just goes, "ra-ra," hooping and hollering just because they're down. I think that's bullshit. That's one of the reasons I was happy when West Coast artists started coming up and asserting themselves, because the West Coast artists came up outside of that clique. They didn't come up in the middle of the bullshit where a person would get a record deal because he knows somebody. Or a person would get on a tour because they're down with the clique. I respect the West Coast artists and people like Sir Mix-A-Lot out of Seattle; Luke Skywalker from Miami; the Geto Boys and the Rapp-A-Lot situation with James Smith in Houston, Texas; Too Short's operation, which is now running out of Atlanta; Hammer's operation, which ran out of Oakland, California; the situations with Ice-T, Ice Cube, and Dr. Dre; the Atlanta situations that are jumping off with Dallas Austin, Jermaine Dupri, and Organized Noize with Outkast and the Goodie Mob. I respect them highly because they ignored that clique. The white media structure is in New York, the white record company structure is in New York, and they believe that New York is where everybody should magnetize themselves to. I think that's bullshit. I came up out of that clique. I'm from Long Island, and I still hold to those roots.

My original dissatisfaction with the whole Def Jam camp stems from my disdain for the trendiness, cliquishness, and bullshit we had to deal with on the "Greatest Misses" project. Everyone thought we should do a concept record, and I was like, "fuck a concept, this is anticoncept." I wanted to do some creative shit. Russell Simmons and Lyor Cohen started to take more of a commanding role over Def Jam in decision making, where before they wouldn't question our camp situation.

FIGHT THE POWER
125

That was the beginning of my drama and problems with Def Jam, because it was once a company that was innovative and transcended the form of Hip-Hop. When they started following other trends is when I started not wanting to be a part of that camp anymore.

I'm a supporter of both Russell Simmons and Andre Harrell to a degree. They've done some remarkable things in this industry. At the same time when you rub your nose with the white boys, and you're in a position to make things happen, especially if you're the figurehead of an industry, you should do whatever it takes to make waves and force changes. I don't believe they've done enough of that.

Too many times the philosophy of today's executives in general is how many chips can they end up with. There's no value in going off to Tahiti and settling on an island. Anybody can do that. There's value in fighting and keeping the road paved for everybody else in the industry and making them understand what kind of battle we're in.

We have a level of Black executives in the business who are silent, and don't say anything to the white boys that made them responsible for the music going out to the community. It's not about flossing or flaunting your check. Rap is supposed to be about coming out and attacking the status quo. You can't go out and purchase your acceptance.

always looked at playing in different places and in front of different
audiences like waving the flag of Rap.
My goal was to go around the world
and stick the flag in the ground. I
don't understand people not wanting
to travel, explore, and see different
cultures and lifestyles. If you believe in
something, you should fight for it and
fight to make it known. I've never
been afraid to go places, that's what
it's about. If this planet is to be ex-
plored and I only have so many years
on it, I could never be satisfied by just
being in one spot. I'm not saying that
everybody has to go skydiving, but
you haven't fully lived if you're only
living in a limited way.

In 1991 we went on three entirely
different tours, playing in front of three
entirely different audiences in order to
expand our audience without alienat-

ROCKRAP

ing any of them. In the span of six months we knocked out an Alternative tour with the Sisters of Mercy, a Thrash Metal tour with Anthrax and Primus, and from December to January we did "The World's Greatest Rap Tour," which featured Queen Latifah, Naughty By Nature, Geto Boys, A Tribe Called Quest, Jazzy Jeff and the Fresh Prince, and the Leaders of the New School. Ice-T opened up the first week, but because he was shooting a movie he couldn't continue. The first night on tours we headlined, we would have a meeting amongst all the groups in

ANDREW ELDRITCH, THE LEAD SINGER OF SISTERS OF MERCY, WANTED US ON THE TOUR BECAUSE WE WERE SAYING THINGS THAT NEEDED TO BE SAID REGARDLESS OF THE CONSEQUENCES.

the arena and lay down the "family rules." We'd let everybody know that we have to look out for each other and work together because customers are paying to see one good show. We had learned an important lesson from some of the earlier tours we did where the headliners would treat the other acts like peons, and we knew that undoubtedly caused friction between people, so we tried to create more of a family atmosphere.

The first tour, which was probably the oddest combination you could find, paired us with the British alternative rock band Sisters of Mercy. Also on the tour was Gang of Four, the hard-rock band Warrior Soul, and the white Rap group I had a hand in putting out, Young Black Teenagers.

We were not the first Rap group to perform with rock bands. At the same time, Ice-T was touring on Lollapalooza with Jane's Addiction. Prior to that back in 1981 Kurtis Blow played with The Clash at Bonds. Kurtis wore a white disco suit and kids in the audience threw tomatoes at him while he was performing. Not long after that Grandmaster Flash opened for The Clash at the Pier, and the audience tossed bottles onto the stage. And people wondered why the S1Ws used to carry Uzis onstage with them. We weren't playing that shit.

Andrew Eldritch, the lead singer of Sisters of Mercy, wanted us on the tour because we were saying things that needed to be said regardless of the consequences. I agreed to be on the tour because to me concert tours, whether they were all-rock bills or all-Rap bills, were becoming too predictable. Everything was sectioned off into neat categories and the audience already knew what they were going to get before the show began. As usual, I wanted to be a part of something different, where the audience wouldn't know what the hell to expect.

In June, Anthrax's tour with Metallica and Slayer concluded, and they invited Flavor and me to their show in Madison Square Garden. We actually came out onstage and performed "Bring the Noise" at the end of the show. The crowd went crazy. There were 20,000 white, rock, head-banging kids, and the crowd went berserk. It was like 130 beats per minute. It was like a whole other world.

Our first night on tour with Anthrax we swaggered into Poughkeepsie. We didn't really practice for the show because we had just finished coming off of the Sisters of Mercy tour. We thought we were ready. The whole day while setting up in the arena we were playing football. We weren't thinking much of it, we were just going to do our thing, so we thought. Primus went on and did their show, then we went on and did our set. First nights are always bad for us. We weren't great, but I felt we were all right. When Anthrax did their set in Poughkeepsie they wrecked us. Anthrax came out with a blistering set. We were like, "Daaaammmn.

> ANTHRAX CAME OUT WITH A BLISTERING SET. WE WERE LIKE, "DAAAAMMMN. THIS IS WHAT THEY DO." WE GOT BLOWN AWAY WITH THEIR ENERGY.

This is what they do." We got blown away with their energy. Which was a lesson for life. All I remember is after that show I got on the tour bus with an attitude, screaming at my guys. I said, "We wasn't shit, we better not ever get blasted like that again." Most of my guys were saying, "They do a totally different thing than we do." I said, "No they don't do a whole different thing." I was impressing upon my guys that we all do music. It's about energy. If they look hard we can't go out there and look soft. They just looked harder. I was like, "Fuck that, we ain't ever having another group give more effort than us when all it takes is to get down and give a little more." It's like being on a basketball court and somebody just outrunning you, outhustling you, and winning all the time. I said, "Don't let another group outhustle us. If you have one verse to go, you take that verse to the last fucking note." Because sometimes in the middle of a verse you may feel like quitting. While you hear me rhyming, sometimes I'm thinking, "Damn this is a long verse. How long before it's over?" Sometimes you may feel like turning around and saying, "Yo, cut it. I don't feel like doing this shit tonight," but you have to. You have to give it your best effort.

My philosophy is if you're onstage performing, you don't need to have a guitar or a drum, but you'd better have the same intensity and energy. I got the point across because the rest of that tour was a learning experience, and we were going hard every night. We wanted to prove that we were the hardest set ever in Rap.

We don't make nice music, we make hard music, and we want to come across hard—indigestibly hard like a brick. There were some memorable shows on that tour.

I remember our show in Houston. It had to be one hundred degrees inside the arena. We ripped that show. It was awesome. I think that was the most together two different groups that do two different types of music could have been in one night. We wore the crowd out. The audiences were mostly white, but it was a different type of white audience, it was a collaborative white audience. It wasn't a straight-metal audience, the audience knew both groups and both groups' songs. Some may have been into Anthrax, others may have been into Public Enemy, but they were checking out both. By the end of the night they were together as one, because we would come back out at the end of their set and perform "Bring the Noise." It was crazy hectic. One of our guys got to play the guitar. It was dope. It was a workout. That one show made our set harder.

Now when you see a Public Enemy show you see energy. I'm telling you that shit came from the Anthrax tour. Earlier in the year when we did the Sisters of Mercy tour we did a normal Rap set, but on that first night of the Anthrax tour they kicked our ass. We looked like we were going in slow motion.

Another memorable occurrence during that tour was when we played at the University of Connecticut in front of about ten thousand students, and that same night we had to be on *Saturday Night Live*. We were coming out with the *Apocalypse '91: The Enemy Strikes Black* album, and the lead single was "Bring the Noise" so Donny Ienner of Sony pulled some strings so we could get some important exposure. We got the invitation from *Saturday Night Live* but the problem was we already had a gig booked. So we rescheduled the University of Connecticut gig to take place at two o'clock in the afternoon. After our performance we went to the NBC Studios. That night Michael Jordan was the host. Spike Lee and Jesse Jackson were guests, and Public Enemy was the musical guest. That was the Blackest show they ever had, and it was also one of the highest rated shows they ever had.

The Anthrax tour is what really taught us the difference of stepping up. A lot of people thought that because we played with Anthrax we were selling out. Thinking we were up there with instruments playing rock I said, "Why don't you bring your ass to the show? We still play the same jams. We do the same exact show. The only thing that's different is we do 'Bring the Noise' with Anthrax at the end. If you're really down with us you'd come to the show and check us out, support us, and represent." Because of the preconceived notion in many heads, Black faces were few and far between. I encourage people to pick up information about

issues and music so they can have facts to back up what they say and not sound ignorant.

We were taught a lot on that tour. One of our guys, Krunch, developed into a light man on that tour. I saw Anthrax's show one night and said, "We need a light man." Krunch volunteered to do the lights. He had to, because everybody in our situation needs a function to justify themselves being on tour. All the ends have to justify the means, so Krunch got his first training on how to do the lights by Rick Downey, the road manager and light man for Anthrax. They had a very tight organization, and it helped us run our ship tighter. Automatically other Rap groups would look at us and say, "We want to be like y'all. Y'all run the tightest Rap ship in the business." Shit, compared to rock groups we're just normal, but we strive to be above normal. It was a very successful tour.

Our last date was in Vancouver. We had one of the craziest food fights ever. Flavor wasn't allowed into Canada because of his previous problems with the law, so I did the last show without him. That tour went all the way from Boston, Massachusetts, to Vancouver, Canada. That's one thing about rock tours: when they say they're going to have a date, that date is there. There's not much pulling dates down.

The important thing to me was that the people who came to the shows were there, not just because of Anthrax and not just because of Public Enemy, but because it was history. It was a history-making collaboration. That's something that the Run-DMC collaboration with Aerosmith did not do. Theirs was a stepping stone, but what we did made it complete. If you're going to do something, complete the job. In my opinion Aerosmith disrespected the power of Run-DMC by not including them on their tour.

That tour with Anthrax made people realize that Rap music is music that's legitimate. We went into Chicago three times during that period. The first time we went into Poplar Creek, way out in the suburbs on the alternative tour, the second time we went into the Aragon Ballroom with Anthrax, and the third time we went into the Rosemont Horizon. People got a chance to see us in three different markets in the same city. In New York City we played Radio City with the Sisters of Mercy tour—we were the first Rap group to go into Radio City Music Hall—and we turned that motherfucker out. We came back into New York and played the Ritz with Anthrax, with a combination head-banging/Rap squad crowd. It was rough up in there. Then we came back in the wintertime and played Madison Square Garden. Unfortunately, a lot of Rap magazines overlook those accomplishments. If they're going to keep stats and facts on history-making events, keep *all* the history-making events so people can weigh them and judge.

I want to be an ambassador for Rap and show that Rap music can be just as exciting visibly and audibly as any other musical format. We fight for people to recognize that fact.

In 1992 we started another European tour. While we were in Europe U2's camp contacted us and asked if we would participate in a protest rally they were cosponsoring. U2, in conjunction with the international organization Greenpeace, were planning this big rally in Manchester, England, to protest the expansion of the Sellafield nuclear plant, which dumped radioactive waste into the Irish sea. The leukemia rate in the areas around the plant was reportedly three times the national average.

I originally met Bono, the lead singer for U2, in 1989 at the A & M Studios in Los Angeles. It was Hank Shocklee, Bill Stephney, Jimmy Iovine, who now runs Interscope, and me, and Bono happened to be in there. So Bono, Hank, and I were talking about doing a cut together. We threw it out there and then we all went our separate ways. Of course, they went their separate way up in the air and we went our way building our thing on the ground.

The rally was being held in this giant arena. We played with B.A.D. II, Kraftwerk, and U2. For all the old-school Hip-Hop

heads, Kraftwerk is the group who did the song "Trans Europe Express." They're a German group, and we found out that they first got into music because they were working on equipment. They're actually computer makers. One of the guys in their group invented the toggle switch, the pit control bender, all kinds of shit like that. They have patents up their ass. They own patents on equipment, patents on computers, patents on software, hardware, gadgets, and boards.

So Bono and U2 had put all of this together and contacted our office to be a participant. We were like, "Cool." We went over there and participated in their videotape and the concert. They had a serious camera crew. Cameras from all over the world were there. It was the biggest setup we had ever seen backstage. The TV screens that they used during their sets had flashing messages like, "RID THE WORLD OF NUCLEAR WAR, FALLOUT, MUTANT, PLUTONIUM, RADIATION SICKNESS."

At the end of the show Bono said, "We saw what you guys have. I've been a fan for a long time, and we're getting ready to embark on a United States tour. I was kicking it around with my guys and we want you to play with us." I immediately was like, "Shit, hell yeah."

Our first gig on the U2 tour was in Madison, Wisconsin. There were close to ninety thousand people. The thing that got me was looking at this football stadium, and looking up at the top tier in the corner and thinking, "What are those people getting out of this show?" They were like two hundred yards away from the stage.

U2 runs their operation like a government. That tour was a learning experience and a half. Prior to that tour we considered ourselves a disciplined operation. They said we would get thirty minutes a night to perform. On the first night we played for thirty-three minutes. As I

> U2 RUNS THEIR OPERATION LIKE A GOVERNMENT. THAT TOUR WAS A LEARNING EXPERIENCE AND A HALF.

walked off the stage, I looked at the sound man with some self-assurance like, "We'll get it down tomorrow." The sound guy looked at me and shook his head yes, like he knew I was going to do it. The next day I looked up at the board and that shit read, "twenty-seven minutes." They took those three minutes back. Those motherfuckers are like the government—they have an economy. As an operation they grossed 279 million dollars that year. That's an economy. That's more than the country of Ghana. There's four members in the band: Bono, The Edge, Larry Mullen, and Adam Clayton, the one who was engaged to Naomi Campbell. They're all from Dublin, Ireland. The Sugarcubes were also on the tour. All of their shows were in the stadiums that football teams and baseball teams play in. No buildings, just arenas. We played The World in Chicago three nights in a row. The thing about that tour that bugged me out was we had Hip-Hop guys come and say, "Why are you playing with them?" I said, "Shit, because I can. I'm happy to. I'm trying to know a level that we're trying to bring Rap to, but we're far off."

One night before the show we were doing at The World I was saying to my guys, "Where's U2's bus?" My answer came from the sky. Buses? Nope. We saw four lights in the motherfucking sky, then the security started clearing out the parking lot. All of a sudden, as the people were moving back, the wind starting coming up. The first helicopter came down. A guy went up to the helicopter and opened the door, and the only thing in that helicopter was suitcases. We were looking for bodies—nothing but suitcases. The next helicopter dropped down and Adam and Larry got out. Mind you, this was not the U2 show, this was the U2 band members coming to the show. The next helicopter came down—Bono jumped out and came over, "Hey Chuck, hey y'all what's up?" and slaps our hands. Then another helicopter came down with The Edge. From that day to this I've never forgotten that image because to me it represents the different levels that the two musical genres are on. It was a clear message to me that we have a lot of development to do in the Rap game. We have U2 stories up the ass.

It took them thirty-six hours to set up their stage. They would set up a transmitter, a TV station, which could transmit signals around the planet. They had cars and big screens on the stage as props. According to Bill Flanagan, author of *U2 at the End of the World* the cars used as props for the stage were called "Trabants," cheap automobiles manufactured in East Germany. The members of U2 had seen lots of the cars abandoned along roadsides after the reunification of Germany, and wanted to include them in their show. As Flanagan says in his book, "Bono's ideas for staging the concerts are ambitious enough to make grown accountants weep. He wants giant TV screens across the stage, broadcasting not just U2 but commercials, CNN, whatever's in the air . . . He wants to erect the illusion of a whole futuristic city. . . ." Backstage they had a satellite dish, a little garage port for their Honda motorcycles, which they rode around inside the stage since they couldn't go out in the street with all the people. They had so much shit under the stage it looked like NASA. TVs, monitors, and computer equipment that registered which way the wind was blowing. You name it, it was down under that stage.

> Favorite All-Producer List:
>
> RZA: How can one guy spread like a virus? RZA knows.
>
> Erick Sermon: Has the right feel; funk is his dog.
>
> Dr. Dre: Sharp, crisp, knows records and music and what not to do.
>
> Bomb Squad: Hank, Eric, Keith, Gary; the first true team; never be another in Rap quite like this.
>
> Larry Smith: Music skills formulative to Rap's big hits.
>
> Marley Marl: Inventor of real sound, sample and noise.
>
> Rick Rubin: Created the aggressive rock approach; hard, 808 driven.
>
> Premier: A workhorse will experiment with sound.
>
> Muggs: Creative with sounds and arrangement.
>
> Pete Rock: Found a blend of soul undeniable to feel.

While on that tour the father of the chef for U2 died, and nobody was able to console her. So Malik Farrakhan, our Chief of Security, who has also done security work with Minister Farrakhan, spoke to her and was able to soothe her. When he would go back to their tent he would tell us how they had lobsters, caviar, ice cream, watermelon, cantaloupe, peanuts, M&M's, round- and thin-headed toothpicks, juice, water. And for the ice cream they didn't have a little spoon to dish out the ice cream, they had a scooper. Waiters would be clearing the table as they finished eating. It was a sight to behold.

U2 respected us because of our word. They said to me, "That's

more important than anything, your word. You fight for your people and you fight for what's right." That's why we were on that tour. Anybody that came and asked me, "Why are you on that tour?" I told them. One thing I can't stand is a motherfucker trying to tell me what to do with my shit. "You don't tell Charles Barkley how to dunk, don't tell me how to tour." For us not to have gone on that tour would have been like declining an invitation by the President of a Superpower country who invites you to the table, out of respect, to show you how things could be.

> U2 RESPECTED US BECAUSE OF OUR WORD. THEY SAID TO ME, "THAT'S MORE IMPORTANT THAN ANYTHING, YOUR WORD. YOU FIGHT FOR YOUR PEOPLE AND YOU FIGHT FOR WHAT'S RIGHT."

Here's another story. We were invited to do a date on *The Arsenio Hall Show,* our first date on *Arsenio* while we were on that tour. In the past we felt that Arsenio's people must have been afraid to have us on the show because they thought we were too controversial. I resented that. It was nothing personal. I thought Arsenio himself was a good guy and all, but I felt anybody as talented as him shouldn't be afraid to have us on his show, especially since he seemed to have had many other Rap groups on his show. Why not put us on? At the time we were the number-one Rap group in the land and people were asking why we weren't on the show. A rift developed in the press when they weren't putting us on. Finally, Arsenio called me and we talked. He was really mad about the way things had escalated, because he had tried to call me earlier but couldn't catch me. When he finally caught up with me he said, "Look, whatever we need to do to squash all of this let's just take care of it because I'll love to have you on my show." Before speaking with him I had made up in my mind that I wasn't going to be on the show, but after he stepped to me the way that he did I agreed to do it. On the day of the show he came up to our dressing room and said, "We're brothers. Here's my hand, it's out in peace. Let's just do this." I said, "Yo, let's just do this." I respected him for being a man and trying to squash whatever difficulties there were and just saying, "Yo, let's just do this." And we did it. I really appreciate his efforts for trying to tie our two situations together.

On the way to *Arsenio,* however, was another experience. We had finished doing a show at the University of Texas at El Paso, and the next night we had to be in L.A. when we finished playing the show in Texas our schedule was to go back to the hotel, catch some shut-eye and catch an early morning flight into Los Angeles. To go from the arena back to the hotel and then get up in the morning to go to the airport to fly to L.A. is a trip. Bono said, "I heard you guys are going to L.A. to do *Arsenio* tomorrow." He said, "We're leaving tonight, why don't you come with us tonight on our plane." Their plane was a rented MGM and it was being serviced, so they had some kind of clause in their contract where Alaska Airlines would lease them a whole fucking jet. So there we were in the middle of the night after the show, we hurried back to the hotel, packed our bags, and got our bus to take us to a real private, dark airport. Their crew waved us over, opened the side doors on the bus, and moved all of our shit out of the bus onto the plane. They said, "Don't worry about it, just go aboard." You know you can't get a 1 A.M. flight anywhere. Here we were at one o'clock in the morning getting on an Alaska Airlines airplane with the Eskimo logo on it and everything. They had the whole plane— stewardesses, food—and this is how they were traveling every damn day on tour. Brother Malik had his son with him, and Bono gave him a first-class bed. It was just their crew of fifteen to twenty people and our crew.

When we got off the plane they had all of our luggage out on the tarmac lined up like the President of the United States was coming. That's how they were rolling. Large limousines, trucks, all facing the same direction to roll out.

After the show their drummer would go straight to a plane and fly home, then fly back in for the next show. They didn't have to pack any bags or anything.

FIGHT THE POWER

139

During the plane trip Bono said, "Sit up with me, Chuck." Bono gave me some advice I'll never forget. He said, "Chuck, I know some of the shit that you might be going through. We heard the same shit when we were coming up. First we were playing clubs, and there were always pessimistic motherfuckers around." The Irish in Europe are treated damn near like Blacks. They're hardcore. So he was like, "We were playing in clubs in Dublin and people were telling us how we need to just be on the street. Then we went and played theaters and slightly bigger clubs, and the people who were playing the clubs said we needed to be playing clubs. Then we played arenas, and the people who were playing theaters said we needed to be playing theaters." I remember him saying specifically, "You just have to make your plan, stick to it, and go forward. Where I come from it's like the crab-in-the-bucket theory. They won't let a crab get out because they'll pull him back down. You have to ignore all that shit and go forward. We wanted to be the biggest band in the world, and here we are ten to twelve years later, and we are, because we wanted it. And that's the same thing you have to do. You have to want it, don't look back, and don't pay attention to what motherfuckers say." We also talked about collaborating and doing a couple of projects in the near future. He said, "Whenever you get the time, cool." I couldn't say he was bullshitting because here I was sitting on an Alaska Airlines jet as we headed into L.A. at two o'clock in the middle of the night.

Throughout the U2 tour our show consisted of thirty minutes of bombs: "Shut 'Em Down," "Can't Truss It," "Hazy Shade of Criminal," "Fight the Power," and "By the Time I Get to Arizona." We were throwing blows with no breathing, and had the crowds rocking. It was a great tour.

People were sleeping out in front of the stadiums for weeks. I couldn't understand it. I was trying to figure out how U2 got their following. I love Rap, and I want to see Rap get to a higher level. Sometimes I get mad because I want to be in business, I want to be about business, and I want to make sure Rap grows and is busting other genres in the ass on an equal par, but there are people holding it back because they're ignorant, stupid, jealous, limited, and shortsighted.

We played in Mile High Stadium in Denver where the Denver Broncos play. It was packed. We shot the video for the "Louder Than a Bomb" remix that night. I wanted to show the magnitude of that shit. We showed a large part of the tour on the "Louder Than a Bomb" video.

We've been through a lot, and we've seen different levels—the Anthrax situation was on our level, but in a different vein of music, which means that their competition makes them more aggressive and more disciplined. In our vein of music, it's loose, open, unorganized, and undisciplined, so we're disciplined in an undisciplined environment. But U2 is a superpower. It changed us to say, "This is where we can take it if we have all the people doing what they're supposed to do in ten to twenty years."

You can always hear about some shit, but being a part of it is altogether different. In 1992 we closed the U2 tour without much acclaim. The rock community respected us because we came from the Hip-Hop realm and we showed that Rap is bigger than how it is usually presented. It's bigger than graffiti and a beat box. My philosophy is that Black music should always evolve and change—do combinations, be exciting and daring, and, when weighed up against other musical genres, bust them in the ass. So the rock audience definitely respected us because they knew that our lyrics meant something. We dealt with different topics, and we also performed well. That's one thing they want to know: is it performable? It happened to be.

Due to a previous commitment to go to Australia we didn't do the last third of the U2 tour. The Disposable Heroes of Hip-Hopracy replaced us on those dates. That was the group that was formerly known as the Beatnigs. Rono Tse, who was an Asian guy, and Michael Franti, who was a towering six-foot-six intelligent, committed brother, had a political Rap record out. So they did the shows in Philadelphia and New York. They sold out three dates at the Meadowlands and the tickets were on sale for two days. I still don't understand how they sold so many tickets so quickly.

FIGHT THE POWER
141

When we went to Australia and New Zealand we played with Ice-T. It was the second time in Australia for both Ice and us. The thing that bugged me out about New Zealand was the beauty of the land. The whole crowd in New Zealand was hip and vibrant, and the location was this island in the middle of the Pacific ocean. We would bug out on the intensity of the Rap audience in New Zealand. They knew every album. Harry Allen went with us on that tour, and we documented the Maori from New Zealand. They were hard-core. After New Zealand we hit Australia.

Australia is a vast country, with some of the most beautiful buildings and beautiful cities I've ever seen. Mad modern—not many Black people though. When I think of Australia I think of the Aborigines, the Black natives from that continent, but I realized that masses of Black people were murdered in the first two hundred years of the settlers' "development" of that country. It used to be a European penal colony.

Over there you find the same bullshit as everywhere else. The Koori people were disproportionately represented in the ranks of the alcoholics, drug addicts, and AIDS victims. It's similar to what's happening to the Native Americans in America. The native people that are indigenous to the land have been killed off for the benefit of white culture. So we performed there on a rebel tip. We invited mad people from the hood to the show. Their hoods are fucked up. Downtown Sydney is the most fucked-up hood you ever want to see. People over there have mad problems from the takeover of European culture. Rap music is the shit down there though. All of the white kids looked at Rap music as being the shit too. They were into the most rebellious music coming out, and at that time that was us, and they were down with it.

We hit Perth, Sydney, Canberra, Melbourne, and Brisbane. We played those dates and showed the Australian people our "Tour of a Black Planet" home video that we put them in from our previous trip there. I remember sitting in Brisbane with Ice-T talking about, "Damn, people say that we don't have shit going on, yet we have careers and we're able to travel the world, but the whole Rap mentality in New York is twisted to the point where they make who they want to make seem important. But there we were in Brisbane, Australia, had just come back from England, and were ready to head to another part of the world. So what's better?" we rhetorically asked.

After we finished those tours I finished them with an attitude because all of my peers respected us, but we noticed that this growing, building Rap press had started to evolve.

> SO MANY PHONY SMILIN' FACES
> TRACES OF SLANDER
> GOT 'EM COMIN' OUTTA FUNNY PLACES
> I HAD IT AN' HEAR 'EM
> TALKIN' LOUD BEHIND MY BACK
> WHAT WAS GOOD FOR THE HOOD
> IS WHAT THEY SAY IS WHACK
> —"I Stand Accused"

As I developed and matured as an artist I wanted to make records that related to everybody's situation around the world. The problem I have with journalists is when someone tries to cover Hip-Hop from afar, and says, "The record was spotty." As if all the records on our album are supposed to sound the same. Then you have a Hip-Hop person come along and say, "They just didn't have those beats." Like everything has to have those beats on an album. If you supply four or five records with "those beats," then you're doing your job. With the other cuts you can experiment. That's why very few Rap albums have been put alongside classic albums by Led Zeppelin, The Who, or The Rolling Stones. The science of making an album is that you have some records that fit the standards of the time to show that you can do it, then you have songs on the album that are experimental or are things that you believe in and are challenging to the listeners. If you do an album and just hope to look for everybody's approval and make sure that everybody is comfortable with it, you're selling your shit out. Have you ever gone up to somebody and said, "Love me, please?" "Give me a reason to like your ass." You don't ask people to love you, either they're going to love you or they're not. The

IF YOU DO AN ALBUM AND JUST HOPE TO LOOK FOR EVERYBODY'S APPROVAL AND MAKE SURE THAT EVERYBODY IS COMFORTABLE WITH IT, YOU'RE SELLING YOUR SHIT OUT.

same thing with making an album. Either they're going to like the album or they're not. My whole thing is if they like it or not doesn't matter, but when they start giving reasons for not liking it like they think you can't do it a hundred times over, that shit is silly. They have to understand that I'm going to do what I feel like doing regardless of what anybody tells me I should do. Unless it's my crew saying, "Yo, Chuck, I think we should do this." I'll take that into consideration. If somebody from the outside that I don't know from a can of Lysol tries to tell me what to do, I'll be like, "Man, you don't know me, you only know of me. What I do should not matter to you." They can take it or leave it. When they start trying to get into my head and classify me like "you fell off," I get on when I want to get on, and I get off when I want to get off. That's artistry.

Ice-T says it best with his statement, "Albums are meant to be put in a time capsule, sealed up, and sent into space so that when you look back you can say that's the total reflection of that time." The *total* reflection, not just the one-dimensional reflection of a trendy art period.

In the Rap industry we have respect amongst our peer group. There's a silent rule that you just can't pop up and talk shit because you're going to run into somebody and have to work with them down the line.

How can someone claim that they follow basketball and the only thing they know about is the three-pointer? They can't make that claim. They definitely can't be a referee. So they would need to shut the fuck up, sit, watch, and learn the game. It's the same thing with Rap. You have a lot of these "Rap experts." I call them "journigalists" and "parasites." My view on Rap criticism is if you can't help to build the situation what are you there for? To help take it down?

My whole thing in questioning these people is how can they be considered Hip-Hop experts when there's no such thing? What are their credentials? Where the fuck do they come from? They get their badges quick. As a matter of fact they put their badges on themselves.

Rap music, and the industry surrounding it, has existed strong without these people. Eventually what they want to become is the judge, jury, and determining factor on what's hot and what's not. That's some typical white-boy divide-and-conquer shit. And they say they're looking out for the consumer, but at the same time who is keeping them in check? Where are the checks and balances for them once their magazine starts selling several hundred thousand issues per month and they start feeling powerful? It takes more than having correspondents in different cities and reading historical facts to become a power broker in the Rap game. That's why I say to make it easier and simplify it they should just concern themselves with building the environment of Rap since Rap is being attacked from all different sides. You have to be humble no matter what you do, whether you're building bridges, sweeping the street, if you're an engineer, an artist, or if you're a writer. Just be humble. Especially in the Rap scene right now where the definition of careers and artistry is in a hazy, gray area. We have to be able to say, "This is what it should be and this is where we should take it."

The Source calls itself the "Bible of Hip-Hop Culture and Politics," but *The Source* came out in 1989, ten years after the first Rap record. So when those guys actually assumed the position of being "Hip-Hop headz," it was a typical white aggression. During the period of 1979–1989 the opportunity to start a Hip-Hop magazine was open to any Black person that chose to do it. These guys at Harvard decided to take the first step in this area. From that point on they've made their bold statement of saying that they would be the center point of Rap and Hip-Hop culture and poli-

tics. Of course being a service to the industry I work with the program. I tip my hat to the creators because they filled a void that people really didn't think was glamorous at the time. The only question I had early on was why is it them all of the time?

So they started their magazine and people started reading it for facts and information, although limited at the particular time, and considered themselves headz. Eventually, they were able to Siskel & Ebert themselves into saying what was fly and what was not. How many Black people do we have that could have done that? I went to school with Harry Allen who was taking up journalism. I was the spark that told Harry Allen he should do something with his journalistic skills, especially since he loves Hip-Hop, put the two together. Harry was whiteballed when he first started writing for *The Village Voice,* by being an advocate for Rap and Hip-Hop music, and he was vilified for being too radical. I encouraged Harry years ago, before there were any Rap magazines, to put his two passions, writing and Rap, together and start a magazine.

Now *The Source* reportedly has a circulation base of eight hundred thousand; their advertisers are huge companies such as Nike, Converse, Adidas, and clothing companies like Levi's, and Foot Locker. So white mainstream corporations have recognized the potential selling audience and buying audience of Rap music, and have jumped into the picture. Dollars are being spent in Hip-Hop culture, but how much is being triggered back into the hands of Black entrepreneurs?

In 1989 I saw it coming, and for every heap of praise they give you, it's almost like "God giveth, God taketh away." Critics are like that. My opinion about the Hip-Hop magazines is that I like the service that they are giving but not every writer is qualified to write. Even if they're able to put together two or three sentences, they still have to be well informed on the music, not just Hip-Hop, but music in general.

The dilemma is many Hip-Hop magazines shoot down an artist's quest to get as widespread an appeal as they can possibly get, yet at the same time the magazines are constantly trying to achieve that same widespread appeal they criticize the artists for.

My man Hank described it as being similar to a situation where you're cutting class and someone is cutting class with you, but behind your back they're going to night school. So in the daytime they look like they're with you, when in reality they're fronting just to appear to be down, and at the end of the year they graduate with flying colors and you're left back. Everything they criticize artists for doing they are or they want to do. That's a severe double standard.

I'm not just knocking them. I think they're needed and offer a valuable service to the Hip-Hop community, but at the same time they don't have to knock the artists that are out there. Why try to legitimize themselves by calling artists that do, or try to do, what they're doing "illegitimate"? That's fucked up and foul.

Favorite Journalists:

Errol Nazareth
James Jones
Dele Fadele
J.D. Considine
Robert Hilburn
David Hinckley
Tom Moon
Armond White
Justin Oneyeka
Stephen Worthy

In 1994 when the "Greatest Misses" project came out writers were saying I didn't sound the same. You're damn right I didn't sound the same. Instead of yelling I was more laid-back in the groove, because I wanted to do a mellower vocal. Somebody else can do a laid-back groove and be accepted, but at the same time I have to always be compared to "It Takes a Nation of Millions to Hold Us Back." That's ridiculous. That's like comparing children. Anyone that has children knows that that's not a wise thing to do.

Each one has his or her own identity and characteristics. At the same time nobody could compare to that record, so why should I try to make another one of those. People in this growing Hip-Hop press always wanted some shit to say, never had a voice before, and then legitimized themselves with a voice they created out of thin air.

That's what I wrote "I Stand Accused" about. I figured if critics can just criticize off the cuff and create their own jobs, how come the critics can't be criticized. A critic's job to me is one that should build and enhance the business that it criticizes.

> SOMEBODY ELSE CAN DO A LAID-BACK GROOVE AND BE ACCEPTED, BUT AT THE SAME TIME I HAVE TO ALWAYS BE COMPARED TO "IT TAKES A NATION OF MILLIONS TO HOLD US BACK." THAT'S RIDICULOUS.

I've heard of constructive criticism, but when it gets down to name calling and mud slinging, then you have to really question it. Say something good about somebody. I think with the amount of Rap groups out there critics should spend more of their time saying good things about the groups they like instead of spending so much time knocking the things they don't like. Someone once told me that critics, as well as radio deejays, are mostly frustrated musicians, or frustrated Rap artists who are mad that they never got off, so they found another opportunity to flourish. And most of their disgust is thrown at somebody else who's in the seat that they could never somehow get to.

After the song "I Stand Accused" and statements I made in the press about Rap critics, I was accused of trying to be beyond reproach. What I do with my albums is something different to transcend Hip-Hop. What I try to do is enhance and improve a record and make sure that my four points are lined up: the record, the video, the concept, and the performance. I think they hear Hip-Hop one way, and because they're so young and limited in their music experience they're like, "This has to be it, if it's not like this then it's not slammin." I suspect one reason they feel like that is because they never see it in action. As a matter of fact, when we released "Give It Up," it was such a hot international record because people hadn't heard from us in a while, but Hip-Hop critics in the United States still refused to give that song its props. One reviewer said, "It sounds too much like the Red Hot Chili Peppers." Since when is it fucked up to take ideas from other records and adapt them to Hip-Hop? That's what Hip-Hop is all about and has been about since its inception.

The reason I never did soft music is because it isn't conducive to performances. But if you don't see shows come to your town or you don't see groups up against each other, then that throws off your whole range of comparison. So critics and fans can only go off of what they hear or what was sent to them. They often have no real feeling for what a song is really about because they rarely get a chance to see a song in action.

HEADZ

Headz are a category of people who are into being totally immersed in the thickness of the Hip-Hop culture. Headz dictate which way the culture is running at a particular time. A lot of times the headz in Hip-Hop, those that are at the forefront of the culture, dilute the culture with a lack of proper information about Black life in general. We as Black people have had to disacknowledge a lot of things that we have done in our past. Hip-Hop's history and culture have been disacknowledged and pushed to the side, even by headz. We can't think that a lot of things that have happened in Hip-Hop have happened for the first time.

You have people out there that call themselves headz in the 1990s who can't even name the five members of the Furious Five. Whether they're headz or not is questionable.

For somebody to come off and call Hammer whack to me is a typical white-oriented statement to trigger off the ignorance of Black ill-informed "player hating." We have a crab-in-the-barrel

> FOR SOMEBODY TO COME OFF AND CALL HAMMER WHACK TO ME IS A TYPICAL WHITE-ORIENTED STATEMENT TO TRIGGER OFF THE IGNORANCE OF BLACK ILL-INFORMED "PLAYER HATING."

mentality amongst us to say, "Man, he's making it too good, fuck him." There was nothing wrong with Hammer rapping over what he was rapping over. He was rapping to the best of his abilities coming out of the West Coast. He danced. A lot of Black people on the East Coast were like, "What the fuck is that?" without even taking into consideration that dancing is part of our makeup. He didn't do anything different. He danced, he rapped over a certain aspect of music that he picked. But what I saw as being the first strain of the virus was when Black kids were saying, "Man, he's getting too big. Fuck Hammer." White kids would jump on and mimic the same sentiment. When white kids started repeating what they heard of the jealous "player hating" in the Black community, it ended up being written about in magazines and newspapers.

I remember meeting Hammer in 1987 with Daddy-O of Stetsasonic. He started his own independent thing out on the West Coast like many guys did: Too Short with his whole operation, Eazy E, and all those guys out on the West Coast. I saw him go from "Let's Get It Started," then he did the song "Turn This Mutha Out," which moved him into the next realm where he used a Parliament Funkadelic sample, and rapped and danced over it. This turned a lot of Black people on around the country. A lot of Black people gravitated to Hammer at first. The Rap community in New York looked down upon his style because it was Rap that was coming from another place with another feel to it. So the rappers in the east thought it was corny. That was still player hating because when rappers went to perform in Houston, Texas, and Hammer would be on the show performing with them, Hammer would get the largest crowd response. I've seen it happen in front of my own face.

Favorite All-Time Rap Albums:

Raising Hell by Run-DMC: The one that pushed Rap to the front.
Death Certificate by Ice Cube: Death sides last three cuts; best sequencing ever.
Looks Like a Job For by Big Daddy Kane: Show skillz that are unmatched.
License to Ill by the Beastie Boys: Introduced a collision of culture; sound attitude.
Tougher Than Leather by Run-DMC: Underrated in a classic year for Rap albums.
In Full Gear by Stetsasonic: Stet's efforts introduced jazz fusion; underrated.
Straight Outa Compton by N.W.A: How the west was won.
Paid in Full by Eric B. & Rakim: Last Rap album to have so many hit singles (five).
Makaveli by Tupac Shakur: Intense; his best work in music and word.
Escape by Whodini: The first true success Rap album; four hits.

Then Hammer did the groundbreaking album *Please Hammer Don't Hurt 'Em*. That record came out and was tremendously popular in Black communities outside of New York because the samples could be related to by older people. Hammer's Raps were simple enough, he danced, and he put on a show. So a lot of people could relate to that. The Rap purists from the East Coast, who were Black, trashed the idea. They were killing the idea. Just like they "player hated" and killed a lot of ideas that were coming from places outside of New York. Artists that had accents in their

voices were relating with their audiences a lot better than artists from the Northeast. Artists that used funk in their records were getting better results than artists that used faster aspects of soul in their records. Artists that were doing more things with their shows were getting results. Therefore it fostered this "antisentiment" toward anything that didn't come out of the Northeast. When white kids follow Black culture they don't come in with their own point of view or opinion, they follow the Black opinion. Then they come with an opinion on top of that. That's where the danger comes in. It was like, "Hey, I'm white, I'm inside the culture now because there's this Black antisentiment toward this situation. I agree with that and now I can add more fuel to the fire." A lot of the white kids would pick up information that was lying around the side and actually be legitimate in their criticism, then whites would go from just criticizing to damn near being considered authorities. When white folks consider themselves authorities on something Black we have to watch that.

Hammer didn't do anything different on *Please Hammer Don't Hurt 'Em* than anything he did before. He rapped on nontraditional Rap music: things like Rick James and the Chi-Lites, rapped over them in his own particular way, performed well over them, brought a whole different performing style that was not traditional to the Rap game, and I saw Hammer go from starting out on a Black vibe to this thing that everybody thought was nonBlack. I couldn't understand where the nonBlackness was in it. He was dancing, which we do. He was using the Chi-Lites and Rick James, which we listen to, and he was rapping over it in his own way, which we do. As a matter of fact he was using aspects of gospel that had never been used. When I saw that happen to Hammer that's when I started to see the dreaded apocalypse for certain things that eventually happened to us. I never tried to do things for white acceptance. I did things that I thought cut through as being different and against the grain of the expectations. Hip-Hop is bigger than any one person's opinion of what it should be.

REMEMBER THE DEAD AND IT MAKES ME
CURSE
WHEN THEY DON'T INCLUDE 100
MILLION
OF US BLACK FOLKS
THAT DIED IN THE BOTTOM OF BOATS
I CAN CARRY ON 'BOUT KILLIN' TILL
DUSK AND DAWN
AND WAR AIN'T THE REASON THEY
GONE

—"Hitler Day"

AFRICA

My first visit to Africa took place in 1992 when we visited Ghana. That trip brought me to the reality that I was doing and saying the right things regardless of what anybody else says. Going to Africa was the most rewarding trip of my career. Brother Akbar Muhammad, the International Representative of the Nation of Islam, set up the opportunity for us to go to Ghana to be part of the Panafest Cultural Festival, which takes place every year.

Earlier that same year we had a commitment to go to South Africa, which eventually fell through. At first the security was to be provided by the African National Congress (ANC), but at the time they were having some drama with the Zulus so arrangements were worked on with the Zulus to have a cooperative security arrange-

ment. The ANC and the Zulus were still having a small beef with each other and things weren't organized properly, so finally they said that the South African police would do the security along with us. We were like, "Fuck that." It just so happened that Flavor broke his collarbone at the same time, so we couldn't go anyway.

Going to Africa made it clear to me that we as a people, around the diaspora, have been oppressed and exploited to the benefit of European countries and their people.

We left for Ghana the second week of December in 1992. We flew on Egypt Air so of course the first place we landed was Egypt. Cairo is the oldest city I've seen. I didn't like the way it seemed to be evolving. It was old and had some deterioration that appeared to be long-standing. The city was packed, and it seemed like *everybody* smoked cigarettes. Cairo is definitely a one-of-a-kind place. We went on a tour while we were there and checked out different places and different areas of the city. We stayed in Cairo for two days, so the second day, early in the morning at one o'clock, we met at this windy road that led to the plateau of the city. I remember the tour guide saying, "To the left is the city of Cairo," we were all looking over to our left at the plateau, and I was thinking, "Yeah, okay." By that time it was about five o'clock in the morning, we had an eight-o'clock flight out of there and needed to be at the airport by 7 A.M. Then she said, "To the right are the pyramids." We all turned to our right, and it was like POW—the most gigantic structures I've ever seen. They just snuck up on us. I was fascinated. I couldn't believe it. The first thing that struck me about the pyramids was their size. When you see them in magazines and books you can't get a full grasp of how big they are. It was like, "WHOA," unbelievably gigantic.

We had Def Jam pay for a film crew because we wanted to document the trip, so we had a three-man film crew come along with us on the tour. They got footage of a couple of us riding camels, and the sun rising behind the pyramids. We took a lot of pictures in front of the pyramids, which were way off in the background, one of which ended up being on the *Muse Sick-N-Hour*

Mess Age album insert. After we left Cairo, we viewed the historic spot where the former President of Egypt, Anwar Sadat, was shot.

The airport in Cairo made me feel like I was in the 1950s. There was nothing available to eat, we had a long wait, and people

> WHEN WE LANDED, FLAVOR AND A COUPLE OF THE GUYS KISSED THE GROUND, AND I LOOKED AT THE GROUND IN A WAY LIKE, "DAMN, THE MOTHERLAND." IT WAS SUCH AN EXUBERANT FEELING.

were trying to get as much shit on the plane as possible, negotiating and arguing with the airline people and the customs officers. The plane ride from Egypt to Ghana was so bumpy it felt like a bus. We also stopped in Kano and Lagos in Nigeria, which is where we waited in the airport for our flight to Accra.

When I looked down as we were landing in Ghana it hit me, "Damn, Africa." When we landed in Egypt, technically, we were in Africa, but when we took off to go to the west coast of Africa I really felt it. I looked down from the airplane and the landscape looked like Texas.

When we got to Accra I remember seeing a whole lot of people standing on top of buildings because it was Panafest and everybody was checking out the incoming visitors. When we landed, Flavor and a couple of the guys kissed the ground, and I looked at the ground in a way like, "Damn, the Motherland." It was such an exuberant feeling. We had been everywhere else but now we were back on the Motherland. They stole us and took our ancestors away in boats, now some of their progeny were coming back home in an airplane—on our own terms. We looked at that whole trip very differently.

As soon as we got into the terminal, the national TV station interviewed us. I just kept thinking, "I can't believe we're here." It was so organized, nice, green, definitely different from where we had just left. Egypt. This was *really* Africa, and we really felt good about it.

Isaac Hayes was coming in the next day to be a part of the mu-

sic fest along with us. Me, being a big Isaac Hayes fan, had brought my Isaac Hayes CDs and tapes for the trip. Isaac Hayes was one of my heroes as a songwriter, from his works back in the Stax Records days and the songs he had done as a soloist. I was overwhelmed that this brother was there with us, or that he even knew us. We were present when Isaac Hayes was instooled as a chief of an African village, which gave Flavor the inspiration a couple of years later to also want to be instooled as a chief. So besides being known as Flavor Flav, in his village in Ghana he is known as Nana Qwabina Obobe and was given three acres of land as well. A chiefdom is not taken lightly, it's something that you have to earn by having the respect of the people.

Brother Akbar Muhammad was definitely a steady source of information throughout the whole trip. Brother Akbar is the most technical, knowledgeable person, with a level of street sense, that I've ever met. He'll give you dates, exact figures, facts, and bring it to you in a way that is exciting. He was formerly known as Brother Larry X, and was the Nation of Islam's Minister in East Elmhurst, Queens, back in the 1960s. As we were traveling he gave us every little bit of information that we needed to know about Ghana.

Riding through Accra I saw things that made me happy but at the same time there were also things that made me mad. For example, seeing a big poster of a white Jesus in the middle of one of the streets. Christianity is running rampant over there, and all I could think about was the so-called "Christians" who went to Africa over four hundred years ago, and we all know what that led to—the most dreadful ac-

> I WAS PISSED. I WAS ALSO TOLD THAT THERE WAS AN INORDINATE AMOUNT OF BLEACHING CREAM BEING SOLD IN THAT PART OF AFRICA—PEOPLE TRYING TO BLEACH THEIR BLACKNESS OFF.

count of human enslavement that the world has ever known. They even had the nerve to name one of the first slave ships *Jesus*. Now that's some shit to think about. Another crazy experience was going into the market in the middle of Accra and seeing a white Santa Claus in the window of a shop, with puffed-up cotton balls on the outside and "Jingle Bells" playing out the window. I was pissed. I was also told that there was an inordinate amount of bleaching cream being sold in that part of Africa—people trying to bleach their Blackness off.

The highlight was the warmth of the people. If you waved your hand you got a wave and a smile back no matter who it was. It was just normal custom. You could actually see the natural warmth of our people. It was something that I'll never, ever forget. The way they balanced heavy objects on their heads was unbelievable. I saw one brother walking down the street and he had balanced a cooler on his head. I saw another brother do some incredible tricks with a soccer ball when we were on the beach. When I saw these things I thought, "Damn, we can do anything."

Out there when they make a law or rule they take it serious. One time we were outdoors doing this show and a lot of people started crowding around the door, and the policeman said, "Hey, hey, make a line, make a line, and don't act wild." The people were still crowding around the door, and more people started to come. Krunch, my assistant and light man, told me he saw a policeman pull out his gun, point it in the air, and start firing, then he brought that shit down to head level. The crowd was in line quick, fast, in a hurry.

We performed for President Jerry Rawlings in the country's entertainment building, also at the University of Ghana and other places throughout the country. The last few days we played at the Culture Fest in Independence Square in front of fifty thousand people. Fifty thousand people at Independence Square, and I know that we could go to five or six cities in one country and there would be fifty thousand people a pop. In the Western world, especially the United States, to fill one of those stadiums would be a problem. Meanwhile groups like The Rolling Stones and The

FIGHT THE POWER
157

Who can travel throughout America and Europe and pack stadiums without a doubt. They have the population going for them, they have the income going for them, and they have the complexion going for them. So in Africa the tables are turned our way.

We rocked "Fight the Power" and all the records that we had. Brothers were coming up to me saying, "Y'all are slamming. I have your albums." It just reconfirmed in my mind that the reason that Black groups can't get like The Beatles or The Who or these big white groups is that we're in the wrong places. We could get as big as those groups if we were in our own hemispheres. A country like Brazil, which has the largest Black population of any country outside of Africa with seventy-five million Black people, is a prime example. Bob Marley is a giant whose music, meaning, and message were universal and appealed to Black people all over the planet, as well as white people. I'm not saying that Public Enemy is going to be the group that's going to make Rap universal, but the personal agenda that I have is to expand the horizons and boundaries of Rap music to make it possible that another group can fit into the new boundaries that we help to open up. We weren't the first Rap group to go to Africa—L.L. Cool J and Stetsasonic had both been to Africa before us—but we definitely had a giant impact over there.

We also performed at the "Castles of Elmina," or what are more appropriately referred to as the slave dungeons. The structures were some of the earliest-known European buildings in the tropics, and still remains to this day after nearly five hundred years. It was built under the Portuguese in the 1480s as a trading post, and eventually the trade in slaves became the dominant activity there. To the Portuguese who built the structures and later for the Dutch colonialists who took it over, they were castles but in my

WE WENT DOWN INTO THE DUNGEONS AND ACTUALLY SAW THE LIVING CONDITIONS THAT OUR CAPTURED ANCESTORS HAD TO COPE WITH.

book they are nothing but slave Dungeons with a capital D. That shit will never be referred to as "castles" by me. Fuck that.

We went down into the dungeons and actually saw the living conditions that our captured ancestors had to cope with, it gave us the feeling of having been there. We saw the limited space where they used to pack hundreds and hundreds of our people in a room and lead them off to what they called "The Door of No Return." Countless ships would continually dock next to the dark and damp dungeons and they would cartel enslaved Africans from the dungeons right onto the boats, which were connected by narrow tunnels to the oceans. They were never to be seen again, which is why they called it "The Door of No Return." We were told stories that had been passed down of what had happened hundreds and hundreds of years ago.

For example, we were told that they used to throw a little food down into the dungeons from a little hole. If they threw a limited amount of food down to hundreds of starving people, there was going to be some serious mayhem. When somebody throws food down and you haven't eaten in a straight week, you'll do anything to eat. Experiencing that was some real shit that was thick. It left a real bad taste in my mouth. I could smell, taste, and feel the death in there. Not just death from the mistreatment but also from the competition for food or the lack of food, especially if you were down in the hole for a month and a half. It was dark, hot, and people were dying.

DO YOU KNOW WHAT THAT TWO FEET WAS FULL OF? BONES, FLESH, AND DECAY HARDENED OVER TWO HUNDRED YEARS, TWO FEET THICK.

One of the most alarming facts we learned is that when they first went inside the dungeons about twenty years ago to renovate the building for historical purposes, the floor of the dungeons was actually two feet higher than it was when we stepped in there. Do you know what that two feet was full of? Bones,

FIGHT THE POWER

flesh, and decay hardened over two hundred years, two feet thick. By the time we walked in there they had cleared out two feet of death and disaster. Those who made it through that ordeal to make it to the boat had to be superstrong.

Olaudah Equiano, an African who was actually captured and enslaved in the 1700s and later wrote about his experiences recalls: "The stench of the hold while we were on the coast [African] was so intolerably loathsome. . . . The closeness of the place and the heat of the climate added to the number in the ship, which was so crowded that each had scarcely room to turn himself, almost suffocating us. This produced copious perspirations, so that the air soon became unfit for respiration, from a variety of loathsome smells, and brought on a sickness among the slaves, of which many died. . . ." When somebody tells you that the boat trip was relief it makes you realize that the slave dungeons and the Middle Passage are aspects of our existence that every Black man, woman, and child need to be taught with the same passion and conviction that Jewish people teach about Nazi Germany and the death camps. Then to make it to America. That's one of the reasons why we're interbred with some of the strongest qualities because our ancestors from way, way back had to be strong-ass survivors to make it through to this point.

> GETTIN' ME BRUISED ON A CRUISE
> WHAT I GOT TO LOSE, LOST ALL CONTACT
> GOT ME LAYIN' ON MY BACK
> ROLLIN' IN MY OWN LEFTOVER
> WHEN I ROLL OVER, I ROLL OVER IN SOMEBODY ELSE'S
> 90 F—KIN' DAYS ON A SLAVE SHIP
> COUNT 'EM FALLIN' OFF 2, 3, 4, HUNDRED AT A TIME
> BLOOD IN THE WOOD AND IT'S MINE
> I'M CHOKIN' ON SPIT FEELIN' PAIN
> LIKE MY BRAIN BEIN' CHAINED
> STILL I GOTTA GIVE IT WHAT I GOT
> BUT IT'S HOT IN THE DAY, COLD IN THE NIGHT
> BUT I THRIVE TO SURVIVE, I PRAY TO GOD TO STAY ALIVE. . . ."
>
> —"Can't Truss It"

I put my mind back into their reality. Isaac Hayes, who had been there before, you could see the emotion reemerge on his face. He and Dionne Warwick had previously done a short film on the experience. I could see the emotion on everybody's face. Everybody's emotions ran real deep. Thinking. It was crazy. Being there, right down in there like that was something we had never experienced before.

One thing I loved about Ghana—I've never seen so many Black people in my life. Over there you have to prove you're Black, you just can't say, "Yo, yo, give me a break brother, I'm Black." Everybody is Black. There's black on black on black, blue black, black on top of black. You can't just say, "Yo, I'm your brother," you have to prove that you're a brother. That's African law, you have to prove it.

I remember staying in Kumasi and going out in the hood to get some food, and it made me realize that Black people are the same all over the world. I had some *grupas* (fish), cabbage, and rice. I could have sworn I was in Mississippi. A lot of people in the United States think, "Africa, what are you going to eat? Elephant." They just don't know. We performed in Kumasi and met some good Muslim brothers up there. We went to the big market, it would be called a swap meet in L.A., and the market was packed. There were thousands of people in the market and you could see that everything was running as it always has.

Driving out of Kumasi, which was a four-hour trip, I saw landscapes that I had never seen before on any other continent. I was told that in Ghana they can have a harvest every two and a half months, which means you can put something in the ground and two and a half months later something is coming

> I REMEMBER STAYING IN KUMASI AND GOING OUT IN THE HOOD TO GET SOME FOOD, AND IT MADE ME REALIZE THAT BLACK PEOPLE ARE THE SAME ALL OVER THE WORLD.

up. That tells me that potentially Africa could feed the whole planet. The Western region of Africa could feed the whole continent. I think the Western region of Africa could feed the world but it's been divided by colonialism, imperialism, and neocolonialism. So the Western region of Africa is not feeding the African nations that are starving. The Western region of Africa can't supply other parts of Africa with that which it needs. Whenever you have to get approval from Europe to feed fellow human beings, what the fuck is that about?

Since Africa has been partitioned by European countries going back to the Berlin Conference of 1884–1885 and has so many rich resources for the future of many businesses and countries around the world, you'll see speed rails in Africa, you'll see Africa united, you'll see travel routes from country to country, you'll see resources going to different parts of the world and all throughout Africa. The downside is it will probably be controlled by Western Civilization: the United States, Europe, Canada, and even Asia and Middle Eastern countries with controlling interests in that mix.

Brothers and sisters in Africa have been lied to about us just as we've been lied to and misinformed about them. A lot of people think of Africa as people back in the bushes and zebras, but it's not all like that. They had heard that Black people in America didn't want to come back. That's what the people I spoke with were thinking based on what they had been told. They had stories passed down that we were captured, but that we didn't want to come back and thought less of the Motherland. They were lied to and told that when we were captured and shipped off that we really weren't captured, we just went off to another place and built a civilization somewhere else because we couldn't make it there. Those were the old stories that were

> BROTHERS AND SISTERS IN AFRICA HAVE BEEN LIED TO ABOUT US, JUST AS WE'VE BEEN LIED TO AND MISINFORMED ABOUT THEM.

passed down. In modern times they look up to Black Americans very highly because they say, "To be such a small percentage of the population, how do you do so well and dominate?" There's still a lot of misunderstanding on the way that Black Americans feel about the Motherland. So our first Panafest was like a meeting of the minds and a reemergence and reunderstanding of how things actually were on both sides.

While there we received a lot of information about former Ghanaian President Kwame Nkrumah. Nkrumah was one of the first African leaders to talk about Pan-Africanism as a viable term. At a speech on African affairs he delivered in 1960, Osagyfo Kwame Nkrumah stated: "Potentially, however, an African union could be one of the greatest forces in the world as we know it. . . . A united states of Africa is inevitable. As I have stated elsewhere, there are three alternatives open to African states: firstly to unite and save our continent; secondly, to disunite and disintegrate; or, thirdly, to sell out. In other words, either to unite, or to stand separately and disintegrate, or to sell ourselves to foreign powers." Dr. Nkrumah tried to electrify and modernize Ghana and tried to unify Africa into being the United States of Africa— one unified body with one language, one government, one military force, one monetary currency, like European countries are now instituting. Unfortunately, Kwame Nkrumah had to fight opposition from puppets within his own nation while of course fighting opposition that came from Europe and the imperialists. He was later exiled, and only recently has the legacy of Kwame Nkrumah been recognized as a true one for African people. As another Kwame once said, Kwame Toure, formerly known as Stokely Carmichael, "We must fight for the unification of Africa. That's what Pan-Africanism is all about. The unification of the mother continent at this time must take priority. The unification of the African continent is entirely different from African unity. They are two different things. They are two different terms and they are two different things. African unity means you have different states who come together and talk, talk, talk, talk. Unification of Africa means you have one state—Africa."

Africa and all the areas of the "Third World," which I call the First World, have been raped, maimed, and robbed of their power, solidarity, and structure. I recognize that Black people are a world majority and it will take a lot of work for us to unify that effort.

RACE AGAINST TIME

PEOPLE OF COLOR
GOIN' OUT LIKE NO OTHER KIND
MADD DRAMA GENETIC GETTIN' WRECK
PROTECT DA NECK CHECK THE EPIDEMIC
DRUG USE ADDICTION AND MURDER
I HEARD A PREGNANCY
INFANT MORTALITY
REST IN POVERTY
NOT PIECE
DISEASE TILL DECEASED
STERILIZED
REALIZED
THAT BEAST
SO HERE'S A WORD TO THE WISE
WE'RE RUNNIN' OUTTA
TIME—TIME

The song "Race Against Time" from the *Muse Sick-N-Hour Mess Age* album is a takeoff of the Chambers Brothers' "Time Is Going to Come." I remember that record when I was growing up because it would start off at an exciting pitch, then it would slow down, and then the pace would pick back up again. "Race Against Time" is actually a description of our race against time. Time is the only commodity that you can't purchase. Time is the only commodity that you can't go backward on. Time goes forward and you can't stop it, you can't buy it. Our race against time is questioning biological and chemical warfare against us as a people, and looks at Africa as being one of the most beautiful continents on the planet, populated by our people, being wiped out. Millions are dying per year because of this disease they call AIDS and other ailments that have yet to be given names, which have been pushed into Africa.

According to the World Health Organization, 2.5 million sub-Saharan Africans have AIDS. The United Nations organization UNAIDS reported that nearly 13 million men and women in sub-Saharan Africa have the killer disease. In the United States it is estimated that 300,000 people have AIDS. Whether there are actually as many people infected with AIDS in Africa as reported or if it's a case of Europeans and Americans going into Africa with prejudiced minds and reporting what they want to report for their own devious purposes, the truth remains that infectious diseases that have symptoms similar to AIDS like tuberculosis are plaguing, and have been plaguing, African people for years due to inadequate clinical and social conditions.

Africa has been the refrigerator for the rest of the world. People have used it for their resources and sucked it dry. I foresee Africa as being a place like Australia: modern buildings, speed rail, airport systems, everything like the United States or Australia has times two. But I also see Africa in a situation where it would be half populated by Black people and the Black people there would have less power and become workers for a larger white establishment. When Africa becomes united, which was the original goal of Kwame Nkrumah, will it become united underneath a white supremacy jurisdiction? That's the question. That's what we must fight against. There will be a lot of Black faces there, but what will the governing rule be? And how will it fit into the New World Order that America, Europe, and the multinational corporations that control the world have devised? I'm not with that New World order, but I am with Curtis Mayfield's vision of the "New World Order." Over the last fifty to seventy years things have been heading the wrong way. Roots were planted back when the Portuguese, Dutch, Belgians, Germans, French, and English went into Africa and tightened their hold and gave African countries the illusion of independence to deceive the world order at that

FIGHT THE POWER
165

AFRICA HAS BEEN THE
REFRIGERATOR FOR THE
REST OF THE WORLD. PEOPLE
HAVE USED IT FOR THEIR
RESOURCES AND SUCKED IT
DRY.

time, because they didn't want to be known as the new Nazis. So they made believe that everybody had their own shit, but in reality the countries were still dependent on them and were coerced into "swinging our way," as Ill and Al Skratch would say.

South Africa was a brilliant start because South Africa has a lot of the resources, a lot of financial power, and a lot of the assumed leadership to take it to the next level. If South Africa does well and controls itself it could help the whole continent because it could set a precedent on how everything is supposed to run, but that's ten to twenty years off. And the key struggle in South Africa has yet to be waged—the control over the economic infrastructure. As Dr. John Henrik Clarke asserted, "Apartheid is not the main issue in South Africa, bad as it is. If the whites in South Africa eliminated apartheid tomorrow, the Africans would still be in difficulty because they would have no economic power and their land would still be in the hands of the foreigners."

Today Africa is heavily dependent on other countries for technology, investment capital, and physical and human capital. Africa has the largest share of foreign ownership and control of economic activities and resources, and is one of the least industrialized of all major regions of the world. The saddest part is that the current poor state of the African economy cannot be attributed to a lack or shortage of natural resources. African resources, however, have been drained away from Africa for the express benefit and enrichment of other parts of the world. In the book *African Perspectives on Development*, edited by Himmelstrand, Kinyanjui, and Mburugu, the following assessment of the African state of economic affairs is made. "Analysis of Africa's problem shows that dependency is one of its root causes and that until this major structural feature is changed, the continent will remain a peripheral appendage in the global economy. Africa's dependency syndrome is today easily observable in the nature of production: pattern and orientation of external trade; the sources of capital and financial resources; the nature of technology; the sources of skilled manpower; and the ownership and management of economic enterprises."

Ghana's President Rawlings has to go through all sorts of pressures, and I could see the strained look on his face from the pressures he was getting from other nations to allow them to be involved or have their piece of advice in his nation's affairs. He had this look on his face like, "Y'all don't even know what it takes to just keep a nation of people to this ideal with foreign nations trying to control our destiny." He was caught between a rock and hard place for sure.

He said the only way that Ghana could continue to exist is if a pipeline were established between Black people in the diaspora, recognizing it for what it is and for what it represents—our future. In America the school systems don't teach anything about the continent of Africa. For the thirty to forty million Black folks in America, Africa is becoming a dwindling subject of interest. One of the most derogatory things I've ever seen is in New York City where there's a lot of brothers from the African continent hustling and trying to make a living selling merchandise on the streets, and Black people in New York look at them like they're some creatures from outer space. Black folks in this country are quicker to align themselves with white Americans, the children of their former slave masters, than their own African brothers who have come here to try to set up a way of life and make a living for themselves. That's terrible. I've seen it in Atlanta, in Houston; wherever there's a large population of Africans, brothers always tell me how people treat them and talk to them like they're strangers, and how lonely they feel in this country even though there's so many Black people here. They say, "You know, Chuck, they just don't understand. They think it's about grass skirts and jungles, and when I try to have a conversation with most of them they treat me like an alien."

I tell them to understand that they're dealing with a nation that has been damaged mentally by a one-sided, twisted belief system.

We returned to Ghana two years later for the Nation of Islam's annual Savior's Day convention, which was held in Ghana in 1994. I left the United States after everyone else to attend the last three days of the Savior's Day event. Everybody else was there for about ten days. We played the festival the night before the commencement speech. We performed along with Black Girl, Jermaine Jackson, and other musical groups from Ghana and the United States. The crowd was really receptive. The first time we played in Ghana in 1992 we let people come up on the stage, and a lot of people remembered us for that. This time the security kept the crowd about twenty feet away from the stage. We were trying to tell the brothers from the FOI that they didn't have to be United States minded over there because there's way more love and respect over there. It was still a very receptive crowd.

The night we did the festival I was hanging out in the audience with about fifty young Ghanaians and they were like, "Yo, what's up? It's good to see you back. We don't understand what's happening with Black people in the United States rapping about 'niggers' and 'bitches.' "What's up with that? Why are they doing that?" I was telling them that "Rap is a two-way street and other forces have swung it into another direction and it's pretty much a reflection of what they see. It's become popular, rappers have been tricked." They were like, "Damn, that's fucked up. There's millions of us over here and our thing is to always stay conscious

> **BLACK FOLKS IN THIS COUNTRY ARE QUICKER TO ALIGN THEMSELVES WITH WHITE AMERICANS, THE CHILDREN OF THEIR FORMER SLAVE MASTERS, THAN THEIR OWN AFRICAN BROTHERS WHO HAVE COME HERE TO TRY TO SET UP A WAY OF LIFE AND MAKE A LIVING FOR THEMSELVES.**

and to stay afloat and survive, and you have people over there just giving their lives away." One brother came to me and was like, "We used to look up to Black Americans as being the cornerstone for our future, but I don't know so much now because over here we fight for an education but there's too many confusing messages coming out of the States to follow. It sounds like too many people have become the white man's slaves. It's entertaining, as far as athletes, singers, and rappers, but nobody is really standing up for Black people all over the world." This kid was about sixteen. There was about fifty of them just hanging. They had on jackets, White Sox hats, the whole nine. It was like being in the hood but the consciousness was on another level. To summarize their questions for me: "Bitches? Blunts? 40s? Why?"

Record companies have little clout in any of those countries, especially in the countries where the government can change any day. They're reluctant to go in and set up an office in certain countries in Africa. Big corporations settle in stable areas. The big white record companies are set up in South Africa, where there was previously a stable white government. People invest and divest depending on the perceived government's stability. In places where there's a Black man running shit—like in Ghana with President Rawlings—they're probably afraid that somebody is going to just flip and say, "We're taking everything. Get out." In a way that's good. Over in Africa bootlegging is real big. They sell bootleg tapes throughout the continent.

In developing countries with tight economic conditions bootlegging can be advantageous because at least demand gets built that way. With bootlegging you don't receive a dime, but if your tape gets bootlegged in an area you can go out there to perform, and you stand to make something that way as opposed to nothing at all. That brings back one of the original qualities of Rap and one of the four dimensions that I feel is necessary for an artist's career: performance, records, videos, and concept presentation. Bootlegging promotes your music more than the record companies do, especially in those markets. We have to start somewhere and believe me it's not going to start off with people

THE IMPORTANT THING IS ONCE YOU UNDERSTAND AFRICA, YOU'LL FIND WAYS THAT YOU CAN MAKE YOUR TREE GROW THERE.

buying a nine-dollar CD. Even if they could buy a CD, they won't buy a CD without a CD player.

An idea I had a couple of years back when I was signed with Sony was to make a real cheap cassette player and give out a million of them in Africa. Then you could start trafficking tapes because without hardware there's no need for software. That's like having a TV set with no electrical outlets, you can't plug it in anywhere. Everything is a stepping-stone process. It's different than when you go to Brazil. When you go to Brazil they have shit down there, but Africa is still underdeveloped but it's getting there. The important thing is once you understand Africa, you'll find ways that you can make your tree grow there. That's what we did. We seized the opportunity. In the future when we get our structure tightened we want to be able to do an African tour. The best way to do that is through the government's sponsoring it: the people come in for free, the government pays the artist and reaps all kinds of rewards from the people for the cultural fest. As far as the white companies making a move in those countries, keep them the fuck out. They have everything else under them already.

The following day after the festival we were on the podium when President Rawlings and Minister Farrakhan gave their speeches. There was a football field across the street where there was a soccer game going on between the national teams of Ghana and Mali. Those two countries have a big rivalry between them so the stadium was packed. Mustafa Farrakhan, Minister Farrakhan's son, asked if we would go over to the stadium with him to make an announcement at the stadium that after the game President Rawlings and Minister Farrakhan would be speaking. We went in the stadium. It was a tight game, the score was one to one, and they take their soccer serious over there. We made the announcement at half-time and when the game was over a whole lot of people swept from the stadium and went over to Independence Square where the speeches were being held.

Both leaders gave tremendous speeches about joining the Black forces around the diaspora. The Savior's Day event attracted the largest congregation of Black people ever to go back to Africa at one time. We felt proud to be participants in that. On the stage were people like Bob Law, Na'im Akbar, Haki Madhabuti, amongst others.

The craziest thing is Independence Square is right off of the water because Accra is right on the coast. As Minister Farrakhan was speaking, clouds were hovering over us and it looked like it was going to pour down raining, which would have put a damper on the event. A drop or two fell and the clouds were gray and dark the whole time, but the rain held up. At the end Jermaine Jackson sang a unity song for peace. Jermaine told the people to come closer, so the same people that were there the night before for the festival and were kept twenty feet away were allowed to come closer, and they gave the real reaction. It was the warmest feeling to see thousands of people singing along. It was mad love. Straight up.

Going to Africa was an enlightening experience because in the people I could see the potential that Africa has, but it was also a damper because I saw what was in the process of happening. It was a bittersweet visit. Everything I saw that was supposedly an advance, I saw as being an advance for the conqueror and not for the native people of the land. The sweet part of Africa was seeing that the continent is not over and done with. The sweet part of Africa was seeing the warmth of the people and them embracing us and welcoming us home to get involved to help make a change. The sweet part of Africa was actually seeing African history in motion.

Traveling to Africa was the final frontier. That was the only place we hadn't been. We had touched every other continent. When we went back to Africa it was a great feeling.

FIGHT THE POWER
171

CHUCK D
172

The bitter part of Africa was seeing the exploitation, and all the forces that were in Africa to keep it from being what it could really be. I think it's the overall plan of the world to have Africa be the future of the

world. Africa is definitely the future for our existence as a people. Not only do we have to be in line with Africa mentally, but we have to be in line with Africa physically. Africa has to be a physical reality. People from other nationalities have a place to go and call home. The Italians go back to Italy, back to their motherland, the Japanese have Japan, the Chinese have China, the Irish people go back to Dublin and get reconnected. Right on down the line. There are some Black people who say, "I want to go to Rome. I want to go to London." Black people have to go back to Africa. If we can't physically go back, we need to develop an African state of mind. People from the Caribbean have the closest thing to an African state of mind because they had less of a cultural breakup than there was in the vast continent of the United States.

BIG PAYBACK

Stolen Africans, out of the ocean, out of the wombs of the slave ships, shackled in leg irons and enslaved. Step out of the acres of cane fields, and cotton fields. Lynched in the magnolias, swinging on the limbs of weeping willows, running food for the vultures. Tied, bound, and whipped from Brazil to Mississippi, in Jamaica, in the fields of Cuba, in the swamps of Florida, the rice fields of South Carolina, from Alabama to Suriname, up to the caves of Louisiana; raped, slave bred, castrated, burned, tarred and feathered, roasted, chopped, lobotomized, bound, and gagged. You African Ancestors.

That accurate yet painful description of the transatlantic slave trade opens up the graphic and powerful movie *Sankofa*, which depicts the slave trade in glaringly brutal detail and also captures the feelings, and helps lay the foundation for the feelings of rage that continue to be felt by many deeply pained descendants of the African continent.

Most people are familiar with the African slave trade, and believe that the history of Black people begins with the colonial period and the slave trade. The preslavery greatness of African Kingdoms on the western coast of Africa such as Ghana, Mali, and Songhay are not well known. Senegalese scholar Cheikh Anta Diop records the stability and power of the Kingdom of Ghana prior to the Europeans' presence in *Precolonial Black Africa* in the following manner: "The Empire of Ghana was defended by 200,000 warriors, forty thousand of them archers. Its power and reputation, renowned as far as Baghdad in the East, were no mere legend: it was actually a phenomenon attested to by the fact that for 1,250 years a succession of Black emperors occupied the throne of a country as vast as all of Europe, with no enemy from without nor any internal tensions able to dismember it." As the Kingdom of Ghana declined, it was replaced by the Mali Empire, which consisted of at least 500,000 miles and became known for its legendary trading and learning centers, Timbuktu and Djenne. The Songhay Empire rose to greatness in the 1300s, and continued to carry the torch of African greatness forward at least for another century. Without a knowledge of the past, not just the slave past, people around the world will continue to hold a warped and negative view of Black people in any country, as they currently do. A reading of Dr. Khalid Abdullah Tariq Al-Mansour's enlightening book, *Betrayal by Any*

> WITHOUT A KNOWLEDGE OF THE PAST, NOT JUST THE SLAVE PAST, PEOPLE AROUND THE WORLD WILL CONTINUE TO HOLD A WARPED AND NEGATIVE VIEW OF BLACK PEOPLE IN ANY COUNTRY.

Other Name, gives a thorough picture of ancient African Kingdoms of Northern, Southern, and Eastern Africa, as well as details of the African biological roots of historical figures such as Moses, Buddha, Jesus, and Muhammad. An honest review of history reveals the potential greatness of Africa and African people for self-determination and self-rule.

Contemporary African leadership has had to struggle against remnants of the doctrine of white supremacy and the colonial past. In Africa the leadership is attempting to seize control or maintain independent control of their respective countries, its people, and their resources. At the same time they face a myriad of other problems that are hitting them from all angles: poverty, rising unemployment, political instability, wars, decreasing commodity prices, and foreign indebtedness. Colonialism, imperialism, and white supremacy are the root causes of the tragedies that are taking place in Africa today, which are well-developed monsters. They are thousand-year-old programs—five hundred years in the thinking, and five hundred years in the execution.

The traumatic ordeal, which has transplanted millions of stolen Africans to various parts of the globe, has never really been addressed. A crime against humanity took place and the criminals have yet to be brought to justice. There would be a significant stride toward healing and bettering relationships between the races if the United States of America and European countries, which were involved in the plundering, despoiling, oppression, and enslavement of African people, returned some of the spoils that were accumulated during the centuries-long slave trade and made collective reparations for partial compensation for the losses incurred.

There have been precedents previously set with the reparations agreement between Germany, Israel, and the survivors of the Holocaust, and, more recently, the United States reparation payments to Japanese-Americans, and an apology from the United States of America to individuals and families who were illegally detained in concentration camps during World War II.

I've drafted the beginnings of a sample reparations agreement between the United States and African leaders based on the actual agreement signed by the governments of Germany and Israel obtained from the book *German Reparations: A History of the Negotiations* by Nana Sagi. The Jewish people were successful in their material claims against Germany for the suffering they endured and the costs incurred by the refugees who fled to avoid the persecution and murder they faced in Europe. It is worthy to note that over twenty-four powerful Jewish organizations from around the world, including the United States, France, Argentina, Britain, Canada, South Africa, Australia, and Germany among others, were involved in the agreement and were instrumental in applying universal economic and political pressure on the government of Germany to pay up. It is only with that kind of unity amongst African countries and leaders that the demand for reparations will be heard and eventually fulfilled.

Agreement Between the United States of America and the
Organization of African and African-American Unity
Whereas
unspeakable criminal acts were perpetrated against the African people during the transatlantic slave trade,
and whereas
by a declaration in the Supreme Court of the United States and the President of the United States on
December 31, 1999 the Government of the United States of America made known their determination, within
the limits of their capacity, to make good the material damage caused by these acts,
and whereas
the countries of Africa have assumed the heavy burden of the loss of so great a number of its natives and
valuable natural resources and have on this basis advanced a claim against the United States of America for global
recompense due to the destruction, colonization, and enslavement of those lands and its peoples,
now therefore,

the United States of America and the Organization of African and African-American Unity have agreed as follows:

Article I
a) The United States of America shall, in view of the considerations herein before recited, pay the OAU OAAU the sum of four trillion, four hundred billion dollars.

This is where our leaders, legal minds, and nationalist organizations like the Republic of New Africa and NCOBRA (National Coalition of Blacks for Reparations in America) can further work out the details and lay the case for reparations for Africa and the people of African descent worldwide.

Slavery is a very serious issue. Africa, reparations, Pan-Africanism, the future of Black people around the world, are all very serious subjects to me. These are some major issues that Black leadership needs to address as a unified body and voice.

If you want to announce the official date of Blacks in this country as 1609, I prefer to say slavery began in 1555 based on Congressional records. But if you go from 1609 to 1865 that's still 256 years of legalized importing of bodies, minds, souls, disorientation of philosophies, robbing and raping of culture and women. What Black people went through in that period between 1600 and 1900 we have a right to be mad at shit. Because slavery was still going on in big droves in South America, especially Brazil. Brazil didn't stop slavery until 1888. With that mad trafficking of human personnel we have a right to have an attitude. And a right to demand reparations.

BLACK LEADERSHIP

In America as well as Africa and every place on the planet where Black people exist, we must realize that we have to save ourselves and stop relying on other people to come up with great answers for us. We have to save ourselves. We have to look within ourselves. Black people in America are destroying themselves and people are looking at today's youth as being the spokespeople. Youth should never be looked upon to be the spokespeople for the entire race. The youth may be the spokespeople for the sentiment and the expressions of rage being reflected, and they may be asking a lot of questions about what's going on, but you have to have adults who have experience and control over certain aspects to be the spokespeople. White America looks at our youth, the athletes and entertainers, for answers, which is a ridiculous concept. In any other country they don't look at the athletes and entertainers to explain the state of their people. Most of our athletes and entertainers are afraid to even say shit about the government. Here in America they're asking Charles Barkley. He can't be serious about thinking he can be governor of Alabama. It's fun to say, it's fun to be joking, but do you think those crackers love him because of his mind? They love him because he can dunk backward and lead his team to victory. They ask rappers like myself the state of the Black situation. I say, "The people you need to be asking you're afraid of." Ask Ben Chavis, Minister Farrakhan, Kwame Toure, Al Sharpton, deal with them. No, they want to quickly shuffle them off as being racist, and many ignorant Blacks follow suit because we're programmed to think less of them because the program that they offer would benefit us. Of course they're going to talk about a program that benefits us. We're the ones who have been exploited the most. The so-called mainstream Black leadership has to update themselves to the realities of today and the Black situation.

Suggested Top Eleven Music Books:

THE DEATH OF RHYTHM AND BLUES by Nelson George
RAP ATTACK VOLUMES 1 & 2 by David Toop
DROPPIN SCIENCE: *Critical Essays on Rap Music and Hip Hop Culture* by William Eric Perkins
FUNK by Rickey Vincient
MICROPHONE FRIENDS: *Youth Music/Youth Culture* by Andrew Ross and Tricia Rose
THE NEW BEATS: *Exploring the Music, Culture and Attitudes of Hip Hop* by SH Fernando Jr.
BREAK IT DOWN: *The Inside Leaders of Rap* by Michael Small
THE SCIENCE OF RAP by KRS One
CULTURE BANDITS VOLUME 1 by Del Jones
IT'S NOT ABOUT A SALARY: *Rap, Race, Resistance in LA* by Brian Cross
BOMB THE SUBURBS by William Upski Wimsatt

I've heard so much criticism of Jesse Jackson by the average Black person that right now I'm appalled by that because I see when there's a crisis that pops up, he goes there and tries to do something. Jesse Jackson's schedule is berserk. People may say this and that about Reverend Jackson, and I look at them like, "Who the fuck are you? What the fuck have you done? You don't have a pot to pee in and a window to throw it out of talking about this man and how he's doing his thing." At the same time they're afraid to tell their boss, "I need a raise." They can't even tell the welfare line to raise their monthly checks, and they're talking about somebody else. "Jesse Jackson is on both sides of the fence." And what side are you on? People may have their valid points but usually people who stack up and find those valid points

10. Whose world is this? Hard to describe the bitter-sweet feeling in front of the Pyramids and the Sphinx. Cairo, Egypt, 1992.

11. In African garb witnessing Isaac Hayes becoming chief. Flav's to my left and Brother James Norman is right up front. (1992)

16. On the set of *An Alan Smithee Film—Burn, Hollywood, Burn* with one of the great old/new school rappers, Coolio. (1996)

17. Shaking hands with the great Tupac Shakur, 1993. After helping to break him into touring with Digital Underground, I appreciated his respect for me. His incredible energy and talent are missed.

> **PEOPLE MAY SAY THIS AND THAT ABOUT REVEREND JACKSON, AND I LOOK AT THEM LIKE, "WHO THE FUCK ARE YOU? WHAT THE FUCK HAVE YOU DONE?"**

aren't doing anything themselves. I'm like what the fuck have you done? That's my biggest question. Before somebody should criticize a person that's doing something, they should look into their situation and analyze what they've done. Unless somebody is doing something against the community that's just straight-out foul, then you can say something. It's like when people watch a sports event and talk about how a player isn't any good but they're sitting in a chair in their living room with a beer can talking about, "Barkley ain't shit." Barkley came up with a perfect comeback for people that were criticizing his rebounding at one point in his career. Barkley said, "Hey, that's my job. I don't tell you what to do at your job at 7-Eleven." When we talk about attacks on the community, a lot of times we attack the community ourselves because we're misled with misinformation.

People criticized former New York Mayor David Dinkins. They failed to understand that when David Dinkins was the mayor he was the mayor of *New York*. All of the communities that were tight and together put pressures on him that we can't even understand. It's true, Black people helped get Mayor Dinkins elected, but once he became the mayor you have to know that he's going to be ripped apart by communities that are tighter than ours, that have organized pressure, and they're going to get things adhered to first by being an organized voice. Even though we put Dinkins in office, we were organized in the voting process but we weren't organized in the community. Unified, we could have kept him in office, yet our voice was a distant whisper. Dinkins got pressures from all over and everybody was like, "You're the mayor." He was the mayor of New York, not the mayor of Black people. Those were the pressures that Dinkins had to face every day and Black people were the first to come out of the bag criticizing Dinkins

without understanding the whole method of being elected. That goes with a lot of our Black elected officials. The pressures are going to come quadruplefold. A lot of times you do have politicians that go out there and run for office, and then the accountability factor to the Black community is lessened because they're being stretched in other places. We need to be able to see that and be more aggressive as a people on some of the things that we need done, and not rely on one person to get things done like a miracle worker.

Not long ago when I appeared on the *Tom Snyder Show* they were saying, "Criticism has come because Black people don't have that one Black leader." I responded, "We're a nation of millions, it's not about having *one Black leader.* It's about having a cabinet of leaders who are able to drop their tags and badges when they come in the community and represent a united force of different philosophies when they're dealing with the outside. Whether it's Minister Farrakhan, Jesse Jackson, Ben Chavis, or Cornel West. It's the philosophy of the Honorable Elijah Muhammad, If you're looking for a leader, be one. As long as we're united and standing in the same pattern of what progresses us as a people, that is what's important."

One thing I try never to do is criticize Black leadership. I stopped doing that around 1990. I made a concentrated effort not to criticize Black leadership in a public forum. I've decided if I'm going to use any time speaking with the media I'm going to use it to the most positive advantage and not spend my little time talking about what Black folks are *not* doing. Even when I get questioned about the ineffectiveness of Black executives in the music industry, I stress that behind the

> YOU HAVE TO BE REALLY FOCUSED ON YOUR ATTACKS AND BE READY TO DEAL WITH WHATEVER COMES.

Black executives is the disgusting corruption and racist politics of the music business which led them to be that way.

Any man or woman should not let pressures silence them. Of course you shouldn't be off the hook and just blast off attacks. That's like having a gun and pointing and shooting it anywhere. You have to really be focused on your attacks and be ready to deal with whatever comes, and I think Black leadership should be trained and well schooled in doing that. I think the recent African-American Leadership summits are well advised because they show the people who are representing. I think it's a wonderful move. There are very few people from the Hip-Hop generation represented in those summits, however, and that's one of the areas that I'm working hard to represent. But first we have to really tie up some areas in the Hip-Hop Nation: the Zulu Nation, the Rhyme Syndicate, any organization is good. It's just that we have to drop those badges when we come down to dialogue and figure out how to help our people who are disorganized. That's what it's all about.

SHOULD HAVE CHECKED WITH ME
BEFORE YOU WROTE IT
GOT IT FROM ANOTHER SOURCE
AND QUOTE IT
                —A Letter to the *New York Post*

APOCALYPSE '91: The Enemy Strikes Black

As a dispatcher of information who has taken stances on numerous sociopolitical issues throughout my career, I've had a tumultuous relationship with the press in general and I really question the so-called "Black press" and their lack of leadership in certain crucial areas.

When Flavor Flav had an incident with his girlfriend, the Black magazine *Jet* didn't cover it until a month after his arrest. I had a big beef with that. When *Jet* put it in their magazine it became big news in the Black community and *Jet* didn't even do their own homework but relied on another paper for a quote from Flavor Flav.

Then when Kool Moe Dee had some financial difficulties *Jet* wrote an article about that when I feel they should have just left that alone. The headline was like, "Kool Moe Dee

Loses His Car to Internal Revenue." That was disgraceful. Fuck *Jet* for that shit. In my opinion if you're in Black media, your obligation should be to present your people in the most positive manner possible. I'm not saying you have to paint a pretty picture all of the time, but being that Black people are presented as garbage in Western society, I feel that Black media has a responsibility to combat that image.

I have been one of the most interviewed artists in the world over the past ten years, partially because of the controversies that Public Enemy as a group has stirred up, but also because I have become somewhat of a spokesman for the Hip-Hop community and the feelings and sentiments of rage expressed by Black youth.

I cherish the relationship that I have developed with the press overseas. They have really played an important role in our music and our message being accepted or at least understood by international audiences, partially because they take the music and what we're saying considerably more seriously than their American colleagues. Whenever we would travel overseas we would hold press conferences and the turnout would always be packed.

That was a great help for us because in some of the countries their principal language is not English, so the press in those countries became an integral part of getting our message across to people who might otherwise not know what the hell we were saying.

On our 1994 tour in Europe I was asked a question by a German reporter at a news conference held in Vienna. "Your music has a lot of messages that deal with racism and other important issues. How do you think your message is received here?"

My response to him was, "That's why I hold press conferences and you are here. You guys are the middlemen between us and the public over here, because if there is a language barrier or if there is a misunderstanding with a concept that we present, we do press conferences and interviews to make sure that we clarify to you, so you can clarify to the people what we're about."

In the United States there's a lot of things that are misunderstood, because in America the press and the public are into subtleties.

The most that we can ask when we are in any country is that they take our word for what we're about and what we're trying to do.

So our relationship with the international press has remained respectful over the years, but our relationship with the American press has been a bit more rocky because of the way they have misrepresented us.

How to Kill a Radio Consultant

> Pusher of the button
> Talkin' loud ain't sayin' nuttin'
> The mack of the format gettin' fat
> Ain't funny 'cause my neighborhood
> Is flowin' money
>
> Only black radio station in the city
> Programmed by a sucker in a suit
> Slick back hair he don't even live here
> Raps the number one pick so I draft it
> I don't care about all the other demographics
> When the quiet storm come on I fall asleep
> What dey need is Arbitron on the funky jeep
> —"How to Kill a Radio Consultant"

On the "Greatest Misses" project in 1992 I did a song entitled "How to Kill a Radio Consultant." Of all these radio stations that play "Black music," people don't realize that a very small percentage of those radio stations are Black-owned. Black people are trained to think that just because a station is playing Black music that it's Black-owned. Consequently, people turn on the radio and say, "Yo, that's the station," and get programmed and fed anything.

About seventy-eight percent of the white stations that own "Black radio stations" have the nerve to hire radio consultants. So if somebody is listening to music in Memphis, Tennessee, do you think that the music comes from what the community wants to hear

in Memphis? Often not. The music they're listening to in Memphis could be programmed from a white boy sitting in L.A.

One of the biggest Black radio station franchise owners is Summit Broadcasting. They have radio consultants who they pay a decent amount of money per year to program radio stations in different areas.

The people in the community don't choose what they want to hear, the radio consultants choose what gets played. That's not much

> PART OF A RADIO STATION'S RESPONSIBILITY IS TO SERVE THE COMMUNITY WITH INFORMATION. IF IT'S NOT DOING THAT THEN WHAT IT'S DOING IS PURELY EXPLOITATION.

different than the situation that George Orwell predicted in his book *1984* where "Big Brother" is listening or watching you.

I think broadcasters should be required to communicate to the community and know what the community needs and wants and how it operates. That's their responsibility. The job of the radio station is not to just play music, its job and responsibility are also to service the community with information via communication. If it's not doing that then what it's doing is purely exploitation. What I mean by exploitation is they're taking in the advertising dollars from the businesses, not communicating properly to anybody that's listening, and letting people go on their own interpretation of what they hear.

A lot of times if a radio station plays fifteen R&B songs in a row talking about, "Baby, you need to turn over and give me some of that ass," and you have a nine-year-old girl listening and she doesn't get anything else communicated to her that's different from that, then what you have is a community that's being run by somebody else's leash treating the community like one big dog. The majority of the R&B music is full of sex, singing about "Do Me," and the stations are playing that music throughout the day for anyone to hear, and they want to talk about Rap. They actively promote their stations around the country as playing no Rap or "Music for the whole family to listen to." I don't know any self-respecting parent that would consider that type of song music that they would want their whole family listening to, especially if they have a few young sons and daughters in the house. What is their message based on? It's not love, it's lust. I don't have a problem with what it is, just that they don't have the right to look down on Rap or anything.

As a former deejay myself, my job was to use the microphone not just to introduce records or to make people feel good and happy, but also to disseminate information and to help the struggle of Black people.

My focus in "How to Kill a Radio Consultant" was to express my feeling that the radio consultants have ruined the aura of Black radio because the Black radio stations no longer communicate like they should with the community that they are supposed to service. The answer to "How to Kill a Radio Consultant" is to put pressure on the radio station that plays the music to get them to play music that the people want to hear in that community.

In Nelson George's book *The Death of Rhythm and Blues,* which is one of my favorite books, he talks about how jocks like Jock-O Henderson, Jack "The Rapper" Gibson, Captain Boogie, Dr. Jive, Georgie Woods, Frankie Crocker, Gary Byrd played the records *and* communicated to the people. The radio station was basically all the people had as far as Black information was concerned. And Black information is what kept people going and kept people supporting the few Black businesses that were there. Black information kept you aware of the people who were not only in entertainment and sports but also important people that were in other areas: politics, law, business, education, medicine, etc. It gave you a sense of self and a sense of solidarity and the radio jocks communicated it best.

In reading the very informative and important book by James Spady, *Georgie Woods: I'm Only a Man* on the life of the Philadelphia "mass communication specialist" Georgie Woods, there is a reference to a speech made by Dr. Martin Luther King,

Jr., at an annual convention at the National Association of Television and Radio Announcers (NATRA). Dr. King stated, "I have come to appreciate the role which radio announcers play in the life of our people. For better or for worse, you are opinion makers in the community. And it is important that you remain aware of the power which is potential in your vocation. The masses of Americans who have been deprived of educational and economic opportunity are almost totally dependent on radio as their means of relating to the society at large . . . One need only recall the Watts tragedy and the quick adaptation of the 'Burn Baby Burn' slogan to illustrate the pervasive influence of the radio announcer on the community. . . . We would certainly not have come so far without your support. In a real sense, you have paved the way for social and political change by creating a powerful cultural bridge between black and white."

In the 1980s the large corporations started taking over the radio stations and as a result, the Black seemed to come out of everything. That's when it became "more music, less talk." Program directors must have started getting instructions from higher up to tell the disc jockeys to shut up. If you shut up the deejay, then you're left with an unclear picture of what the music is really about. All of a sudden, the music becomes the only communicator, and the music isn't always the best communicator.

The music was the second-best communicator to the deejays. It seems to me the corporations were at odds with the deejays and probably didn't want to pay them what they were worth. The deejays knew how much advertising was coming through and knew how much money they were making for the radio stations, and recognized that they were the ones with the golden touch that the people were going to follow. Today, the deejay has been largely cut out by corpo-

> "MORE MUSIC, LESS TALK." THAT'S SOME BULLSHIT.

rate America. Again, "More music, less talk." That's some bullshit. Why less talk? If the deejay is saying something of substance, then of course you want to hear him. What they're going to do is train a whole new set of listeners into thinking that there's not supposed to be a deejay. The deejay is about as important as a broadcaster in a basketball or football game when you're watching TV. I remember when the NFL tested broadcasting football games without a sports announcer. Those games were boring as hell and the test failed miserably.

In general, the Black press have been followers and not trendsetters in this area. There's positive in everybody. There's positive and negative energies in everything on this planet. Dr. Dre, Snoop Dogg, Tupac, whoever you want to name, they have some positive messages in some of their records but those records have to be pumped up and given media attention because they're good, as opposed to waiting for something shocking to happen and then covering those records dealing with negative subjects. MC Eiht talks about, "I'm trying to go right, but society won't let me go right, it's hard." The media just doesn't focus on those positive songs, they'd rather dwell on the negative. Nature is positive and negative. Nature will give you a sunny day with flowers, and nature will give you a monsoon and wipe away people and millions of dollars in property. That's nature. Nature will give you a nice puppy, and nature will give you a pit bull. So we just have to be able to squeeze out the positive. That goes for the Black press, that goes for Black radio, that goes for Black television, and that goes for Black music, and all of the surrounding elements of the interpretation of our lifestyle, culture, art, and religion.

CHUCK D
190

RAP GROUP HEADS FOR ARIZONA
Their Mission: Justice for Martin Luther King

TALKIN' MLK
GONNA FIND A WAY
MAKE THE STATE PAY
LOOKIN' FOR THE DAY
HARD AS IT SEEMS
THIS AIN'T NO DAMN DREAM
GOTTA KNOW WHAT I MEAN
IT'S TEAM AGAINST TEAM
—"By the Time I Get to Arizona"

My plans for 1992 were to lay back a little. I thought I was going to be able to lay back in 1991, but I ended up doing the *Apocalypse '91* album and things took off again. In the beginning of 1992 we came out with our second video. We shot it in December of 1991 and the name of the video was "By the Time I Get to Arizona." I called a press conference right after we finished our last tour date in 1991. The press conference was held in front of schoolchildren and members of the press. It was a video that protested the lack of a holiday in Arizona dedicated to Dr. Martin Luther King, Jr. There were two states, Arizona and New Hampshire, that refused to acknowledge Dr. King's holiday, and Arizona had this cocky attitude like, "We're not giving that nigger a holiday."

So a movement developed to garner support and resistance to the position that the state of Arizona had taken. Most of the resistance was coming from whites who were saying, "You need to have a King holiday or we won't have the Super Bowl in the state." Yet the state was still like, "Fuck it."

The year before there was a general population vote and the holiday had been voted down. That's what made me write "By the Time I Get to Arizona." In the song I depict Public Enemy with the S1Ws (Security of the First World) taking a plane trip to Arizona to knock some politicians off. People had the nerve to question what I was talking about in the video. I said, "Call me Steven

Spielberg. This is my damn video, and I can do what I want to do with my song in video."

At the end of the video there's a big explosion, and the press who were present were so shocked. They were like, "I don't believe that you brought schoolchildren in to see

THE GOVERNMENT KILLED DR. KING, SO HOW WOULD YOU FEEL IF WE KILLED REPRESENTATIVES OF THE GOVERNMENT IN A SYMBOLIC OR FICTIONAL WAY?

this type of video." I was trying to stress the seriousness of what they were saying about our hero, Dr. King. That's a serious matter to me. They were trying to say that our hero who died by one of their bullets wasn't shit.

A large part of the opposition we received from the video came from people on the conservative right and the Black clergy in Phoenix. They were blasting us. "Who is Public Enemy to come and take our leader and speak in a blasphemous manner like that?" They thought we were wrong to involve Dr. King's name in the use of violence. Dr. King was peaceful and loving and all of that but he needed three brothers behind him with some straps at all times. The world is not peaceful and loving like that. You can be fair and loving and all but you need leopards behind you to protect that. So people used Dr. King's philosophy against what we were trying to get across in the video. I was making a point and a gesture that Dr. King is our hero too, and all of his philosophies we love and understand, but there are different people out here who don't. Everybody is not going to believe in turning the other cheek. Some people believe in justice the old-fashioned way—the Mosaic Law way. Later on people were asking, "How do you think Dr. King would have felt?" *My response to that was how do you think Dr. King would have felt if he would have lived after he had gotten shot?*

We believe that the government had something to do with the destruction of Dr. Martin Luther King, so we flipped the script on

the government. Politicians represent the government. That was the meaning of the record. The government killed Dr. King, so how would you feel if we killed representatives of the government in a symbolic or fictional way?

I'd like to see the same kind of aggressive pressure that was used against us used against white supremacist groups that are causing havoc and death because of their terrorist activities in real life. In the book *The COINTELPRO Papers: Documents from the FBI's Secret Wars against Dissent in the United States,* edited by Churchill and VanderWall, a 1967 directive from J. Edgar Hoover announcing a new counterintelligence program is cited. The current director of the FBI needs to refocus the FBI's attention on white terrorism. The new memo based on the original 1967 version should read something like this: "The purpose of this new counterintelligence endeavor is to expose, disrupt, misdirect, discredit, or otherwise neutralize the activities of white nationalist, hate-type organizations and groupings, their leadership, spokesmen, membership, and supporters, and to counter their propensity for violence and civil disorder. . . . When an opportunity is apparent to disrupt or neutralize white nationalist, hate-type organizations through the cooperation of established local news media contacts or through such contact with sources available to the Seat of Government, in every instance careful attention must be given to the proposal to insure the targeted group is disrupted, ridiculed, or discredited through the publicity and not merely publicized." The Oklahoma City bombing was not a random act of violence. It was a link in a chain of violent activities by the far-right, neo-Nazi Aryan Nation. The neo-Nazis have attacked and killed innocent people, killed police officers, robbed banks—they do that shit for real. They represent a real problem for America because they're white and America has been focusing their energies on suppressing Black, Brown, and Red people,

> THE OKLAHOMA CITY BOMBING WAS NOT A RANDOM ACT OF VIOLENCE.

and now an enemy has come up within their own ranks. They're sleeping with the enemy for real.

When the "By the Time I Get to Arizona" video was released and hit the wire I was on a plane looking back at the States, heading for another European tour—this time with Anthrax. When I called back to the States, people were telling me the video was being discussed all over. I got a call—they wanted to interview me on *Nightline.*

While overseas doing the European tour I had to take one day out just to handle all of the media. MTV had a call-in during the daytime asking the audience should they show the video. Over seventy percent said "Yes" and about twenty percent said "No." That poll was reaching the kids and the younger audiences. The older audience had their opportunity later that night with *Nightline.*

Ice-T was in the video because I saw him while he was in Arizona, and asked him if he wanted to be in the video. He said, "Cool." As a matter of fact I wore a Body Count jacket in the video. Sister Souljah was also in the video. She introduces the song and narrates through the beginning of the video as we head into Arizona. Eric Meza, who shot the video, said to me, "Do you want to do some shit that's going to be worth something?" I said, "Bet." He said, "We might only get it shown once or twice." I said, "Bet. I want some shit that will get the point across on one showing." When we had that press conference and showed the video, it may not have been played a lot of times, but that motherfucker made it to *Nightline.*

I did the interview with *Nightline* from a hotel in Hamburg, Germany, at five o'clock in the morning because of the six-hour time difference. I was trying to prepare myself, but there is really no way to prepare for an interview at five-thirty in the morning. *Nightline* came on at 11:30 P.M. in the States. They had me on the screen where the viewers could see me, but I couldn't see anything. I was just talking into a camera. I couldn't see the other people.

All I could hear was the other panelists—J. D. Considine, who

was a music journalist for *The Baltimore Sun,* Clarence Page from the *Chicago Tribune,* and Forrest Sawyer, who was the host of *Nightline* that night—debating.

The white guy, J. D. Considine, was on my side. Clarence Page, a Black man, was saying that I was coming off wrong. So here I was listening to them and *Nightline* opened up talking about Public Enemy, then they started talking about Rap, then they dropped some information about us and our past controversies leading all the way up to the new video. So before I got a chance to say a word they had prepped the audience for about eight minutes, telling them what we were about. Then all of a sudden they said, "On your mark, get set, go," and I had to explain my piece.

I wasn't nervous but I may have looked nervous because the hearing device that I had to put in my ear, which was supposed to stay in my ear while I talked, for some reason kept slipping out. So in the beginning of the interview as I was trying to get my point across, I could be seen trying to keep the little piece in my ear. It can be distracting when you're trying to get your point across and keeping something in your ear at the same time.

I handled it though. I gave myself a grade of eighty-two to eighty-five, a solid B. I got by. I got my point across. J. D. Considine dropped some science. As for Clarence Page, the last thing somebody truly Black wants to do on TV is make themselves look bad in front of another Black person. I don't know if Clarence Page was concerned but I didn't want it to look like I was attacking him. So I was making my points and when I talked to Clarence Page I was cordial. It would have looked crazy for me to be on TV arguing with him. I couldn't see what was being shown but I wanted to make sure it looked civilized. I'm not with arguing on TV with another Black person. A lot of times when somebody is on TV who represents Rap they come across looking uncivilized, to the point where the only thing a viewer gets out of it is ignorance. Forget what's being said, they sound ignorant so people get turned off to Rap. People put up blinders or a deaf ear to what a lot of rappers say due to the *way* it's said. So I just tried to make it look civilized and respectful. *I believe my performance on*

Nightline *defused a lot of people.* When we came back to the States from Europe the controversy had settled a little bit. That video and the uproar it caused was one of the biggest of the many prophetic things that have happened in our career. What were the two biggest Rap issues of the year 1992? Ice-T with "Cop Killer," which was some deep heavy shit, and Sister Souljah with the President Clinton remark. The first controversy at the beginning of that year was "By the Time I Get to Arizona."

Our whole philosophy is that controversy is good if you can handle it. You have to handle controversy. You can't have controversy take over because controversy can kill your shit. In that case we defused it, knocked it down, and got our point across.

MTV decided not to play the video anymore. Even though they got approval from the audience on it, they just didn't play it. But the message was made and the message was that Dr. King was our hero. Just because his philosophy was different, not everybody that loves Dr. King had the same philosophy, and it was basically a respect thing. This is our hero, our leader, and you can't come off having a state that's going to say he won't be respected.

During that time we were getting supportive letters from people around the country, almost everybody Black. However, a lot of white fans were writing us letters as well, agreeing that we had to fight for what we felt was right.

Although the controversy wasn't immediately resolved, the long-term impact was positive and today they do have a Martin Luther King holiday in Arizona.

When I write explicit lyrics and develop politically charged concepts for songs, the idea that I have in the forefront of my mind is to speak unwaveringly and unequivocally for the concerns of Black people and to present issues from a Black viewpoint and interpretation.

The "By the Time I Get to Arizona" controversy was not the first situation, nor the last, where the message I was attempting to get across became the focal point of heavy criticism and a barrage of attacks. However, I have maintained the position that it is imperative for someone in the entertainment industry, particularly in the

CHUCK D
196

Rap game, to dispatch information that is unfiltered and untouched about subjects that are blasphemous to the Black existence.

CHUCK D DEFENDS BLACK HEROES/SHEROES THROUGH VIDEO AND SONG

One of Public Enemy's most popular songs, which was featured in Spike Lee's film *Do the Right Thing*, was entitled "Fight the Power," and its hard-driving message became an anthem for frustrated youth around the world. The last verse of the song states:

> ELVIS WAS A HERO TO MOST
> BUT HE NEVER MEANT SHIT TO ME
> HE WAS A STRAIGHT OUT RACIST
> THAT SUCKER WAS SIMPLE AND PLAIN
> MOTHERFUCK HIM AND JOHN WAYNE

I saw the necessity to address the legacy of Black music and attempt to bring it up to be recognized. The attack was not really directed toward Elvis Presley because Elvis was a talented performer, there's no question about that. The attack was directed toward the *institution* of Elvis, where white people think and present Elvis to the world as being the "be-all and end-all" when there were Black originators before Elvis who have never gotten their respect and props. I was dealing with racist America portraying that Elvis *invented* that level of quality soul, bluesy, rock 'n' roll singing when there were brothers before him. I don't think that it's right for talented and influential performers such as Chuck Berry and Little Richard to

> THE ATTACK WAS NOT REALLY DIRECTED TOWARD ELVIS PRESLEY BECAUSE ELVIS WAS A TALENTED PERFORMER, THERE'S NO QUESTION ABOUT THAT.

be written out of the history books, hearts, and minds of the American public when it was these same performers and many others who were the strong influences on

THE "DISCOVERY" OF THE AMERICAS WASN'T REALLY A DISCOVERY, IT WAS THE BEGINNING OF GENOCIDE.

Elvis Presley, himself, and other rock supergroups like The Beatles and The Rolling Stones.

That would be like thirty years from now reading about the history of Rap music with all of the books and documentaries of that period focusing on the impact that Vanilla Ice had on Hip-Hop. There's no doubt that Vanilla Ice has had an impact—a white boy who could Rap and dance like that—but it would have to be placed in the broader context of time and place for his impact to be really appreciated and not be a misrepresentation of reality.

Later in 1994 on the *Muse Sick-N-Hour Mess Age* album I also addressed two more issues that struck me as being important to interpret from a Black perspective. One song addresses the inappropriateness I feel about a holiday being named after Christopher Columbus. In 1992 there was the worldwide quincentennial celebration of Columbus's voyage in 1492 in which he "sailed the ocean blue." But what does that day represent to Black, Brown, and especially to the indigenous people of this part of the planet. The song I wrote to address that issue is entitled "Hitler Day" and the song's introduction begins:

500 YEARS AGO ONE MAN CLAIMED
TO HAVE DISCOVERED A NEW WORLD
FIVE CENTURIES LATER WE THE PEOPLE
ARE FORCED TO CELEBRATE A BLACK HOLOCAUST

HOW CAN YOU CALL A TAKEOVER
A DISCOVERY?

"Hitler Day" is a knock on Columbus Day. Columbus Day is one of the most asinine holidays that they could ever have on the face of the earth for people of color. The "discovery" of the Americas wasn't really a discovery, it was the beginning of genocide and the beginning of a takeover. When Columbus stepped foot on what is now known as the Bahamas, because he never did reach the mainland, he started a chain reaction that led to the enslavement and death, by murder and disease, of millions of Native and African people who were brought to slave for the Spaniards' colonial conquests and desires.

It's crazy when you see Columbus Day celebrating five hundred years of people being maimed, robbed, brutalized, and killed. There are opposing sides about the validity of Columbus Day. A lot of people will say that I and those who oppose such a day are crying over spilled milk, but everything seems like crying over spilled milk if you don't take it seriously.

Imagine what would happen if someone said, "Let's have a celebration for Adolf Hitler and what he did for Germany." People from all over the world would be on your ass like white on rice because Hitler represents the death, torture, and destruction of millions of human beings, particularly Jews. There would not be one Jewish person anywhere on this planet who would not rally and unify on that point. That would be a ridiculous concept. For me, that's what Christopher Columbus represents to Black, Brown, and Red Nations in North America and throughout the world because he opened the gates for five hundred years of mayhem, as I say in the song.

HANGIN' HEADS AND SNAPPIN' NECKS
SPLITTIN' UP KIN
MAKIN' FAMILIES WRECKED
TURNED THIS PLANET INTO A SEWER
PROVIN' TO ALL JUST A LI'L GRAB WILL DO YA
OR DO US

Let someone go out there and say, "I think all white people should die of AIDS." They will call you crazy. So I'm naming some things that are slaps in the face to the Black existence.

Other issues that I dealt with in the "Hitler Day" song are the lack of recognition of important Black persons and historical events, such as the Black Holocaust of unparalleled proportions, otherwise known as "The Middle Passage," for which estimates indicate as many as one hundred million enslaved Africans died in one way or another during the transatlantic slave trade. When I pull out the dictionary and look up the word "holocaust" it doesn't tell me that the word is to be used exclusively for any one group of people. The dictionary says that a holocaust is widespread and complete destruction. Well, I'd like to see someone argue that Black people's sojourn here in America for the past five hundred years does not qualify under that definition.

At the same time I raise questions about other recognized national holidays like the Fourth of July, also known as Independence Day. Whose independence? In 1776 Black people were far from being independent. I like the way the freedom fighter and abolitionist Frederick Douglass analyzed the Fourth of July in his oration at Rochester on July 5, 1852. He said, "I am not included within the pale of this glorious anniversary! Your high independence only reveals the immeasurable distance between us. The rich inheritance of justice, liberty, prosperity, and independence, bequeathed by your fathers, is shared by you, not by me. The sunlight that brought life and healing to you, has brought stripes and death to me. This Fourth of July is *yours*, not *mine. You* may rejoice. *I* must mourn."

That's a clear example of my point that what may be true in the eyes of one person or one group of people is not necessarily the way another person or group of people may feel about the same subject. It's not a matter of being ungrateful, it's a matter of facts

and dealing with the two realities that exist in this country and which have existed in this country since we've been here.

What should Black people think about American heroes like George Washington, the first President of the United States, Thomas Jefferson, and a long list of other American "heroes" who don't mean shit to me? All we are told about George Washington coming up in the educational system is that he chopped down a cherry tree and never told a lie. What relevance does that have to me as a Black man or to the Black men, women, and children who have been taught this about George Washington and are still being taught that about this "American hero"? What is of concern to me is how did George Washington feel about, and treat, the over three hundred slaves he eventually owned, or the twenty slaves that his father, Augustine Washington, owned. As a matter of fact, I don't really care how he felt about them, it pisses me off just to know that he owned slaves in the first place! What kind of treatment did my great-, great-, great-, great-, great-, great-grand-parents who lived during his time period receive? That's how I'm looking at that situation and that individual.

The second song on the *Muse Sick-N-Hour Mess Age* album is entitled "Ain't Nuttin' ButterSong" and addresses the American national anthem, "The Star-Spangled Banner."

I ALWAYS THOUGHT DAT POWER
WAS TO THE PEOPLE, WE THE PEOPLE
O SAY CAN I SEE WE AIN'T THE PEOPLE
WHEN I PLEDGE ALLEGIANCE
I SHOULDA GOT A STICKA
1ST GRADE/2ND GRADE
I SHOULDA JUST KICKED A
VERSE THAT WORKED
IN THE MIDDLE OF CLASS
INSTEAD OF SINGIN' 'BOUT BOMBS
LIKE A DUMB ASS
LAND OF THE FREE
HOME OF THE BRAVE

AND HELL WITH US NIGGAS WE SLAVES
THAT SHOULDA BEEN THE LAST LINE
OF A SONG THAT'S WRONG FROM THE GET
SO WHEN EVERYBODY STAND
I SIT
—"Ain't Nuttin' ButterSong"

That's how I feel. That's something that's very important to me and I'm sure that I'm not the only one feeling that way. Mahmoud Abdul-Rauf, previously known as Chris Jackson—the former leading scorer and playmaker for the NBA's Denver Nuggets—felt so strong about his opposition to America's national anthem that he was willing to sacrifice his salary of $2.6 million a year. He gave up $31,707 for the one game that he missed because he chose to sit while the national anthem was being played before one of his games. He was subsequently suspended by the NBA for that protest. He said that he felt the American flag was a symbol that represents "oppression and tyranny." He was willing to sacrifice more than most people for his strong belief in that principle.

Imagine if more Black professional athletes in unity protested against social injustice and white supremacy. Imagine if Dream Team 1, which won the gold medal in the 1992 Olympics in Barcelona, Spain, Dream Team II, which won the gold medal at the 1994 World Championship of Basketball held in Toronto, or Dream Team III, which won the gold medal in the 1996 Olympic games in Atlanta, Georgia, decided to make a quiet, yet powerful symbolic statement about the conditions and destiny of Black people in the modern world? What could David Stern and the NBA realistically do? Look at the Black superstars in the lineups for those "American" all-star teams: Michael Jordan, Magic Johnson, Scottie Pippen, Karl Malone, Charles Barkley, David Robinson, Clyde Drexler, Patrick Ewing, Alonzo Mourning, Reggie Miller, Shawn Kemp, Shaquille O'Neal, Hakeem Olajuwon, Grant Hill, Penny Hardaway, Glenn Robinson. What could they do except respect the cause, and begin to take the matter seriously?

FIGHT THE POWER
201

The precedent has already been set by two of my heroes, Tommie Smith and John Carlos. There should be a commemorative stamp of them standing with their Black fists raised in the air during the medal ceremony at the 1968 Olympics. Part of a statement issued by Tommie Smith about his participation in the Olympic boycott read: "I also recognize the political and social implication of some Black people participating for a country in which the vast majority of Black people suffer from unthinkable discrimination and racism. It is my obligation as a Black man to do whatever is necessary, by any means necessary, to aid my people in obtaining the freedom that we all seek. If I can open a single door that might lead in the direction of freedom for my people, then I feel that I must open that door. I am not only willing to give up an opportunity to participate in the Olympics, but I am also willing to give up my life if there is even a chance that it will serve to dramatize, much less solve, the problems faced by my people." Due to the stand taken by Tommie Smith, John Carlos, Lew Alcindor (Kareem Abdul-Jabbar), Muhammad Ali, and other athletes and supporters of the Olympic Committee for Human Rights, they were also able to get the support of thirty-two African nations to boycott the 1968 Olympics.

"The Star-Spangled Banner" is nothing but a song to me. If you want to talk about stickering Rap records for being violent, that's one of the most violent records ever made, and all athletes and a lot of Black people are required to sing that song or salute the American flag before they start their sporting events. There haven't been any dramatic changes in Black people's re-

> IT IS MY OBLIGATION AS A BLACK MAN TO DO WHATEVER IS NECESSARY, BY ANY MEANS NECESSARY, TO AID MY PEOPLE IN OBTAINING THE FREEDOM THAT WE ALL SEEK.

alities here in America since Tommie Smith and John Carlos in unity defiantly protested with the wearing of the black gloves and holding the power fist up in the air during the singing of the national anthem at the 1968 Olympics in Mexico City.

When I talk about the flag in the song, I say that the red in the flag is for the blood that we've shed. I look at the flag differently. We should look at the American flag like a Jewish person looks at the swastika. Interpretations go two ways, there are two sides to every story. The stars in the flag represent the stars that we saw when we were getting our asses beat. The blue in the flag is for the sad songs that we sang throughout our history, singing the blues and singing church songs, thinking that we're going to go to heaven to live in paradise while the white man has heaven right here on earth and we're living in hell. The stripes in the American flag are for the whip marks on our backs. The white in the flag is for the obvious—there's no Black in the flag. So "Ain't Nuttin' ButterSong" deals with how we look at things differently.

Don't look at it like I'm crying or screaming all the time. It's rightfully so that we demand the right to speak out on what we don't have today and that we demand changes because we've been used, abused, and exploited. The next step is to reach our youth, teach them the truth, and instill in them some pride—Black pride—so they won't submit to the bullshit of the American shitstem.

All-Time Favorite Movies:

1. *Dead Presidents:* I watch this Hughes' bros flick religiously.
2. *A Soldier's Story:* Adolph Caesar and a cast of brilliance.
3. *A Rage in Harlem:* Bill Duke made us go back and feel the fifties.
4. *Hollywood Shuffle:* Underrated Townsend always sharp.
5. *Mo Better Blues:* I feel this film personally.
6. *The Five Heartbeats:* A must for every Black entertainer.
7. *School Daze:* Spike uncovered the Black college phenomenon.
8. *Nothing But a Man:* Ivan Dixon ahead of his time.
9. *Boyz N the Hood:* John Singleton put a lump in my chest.
10. *Harlem Nights:* Eddie Murphy underrated flick. Pryor, Foxx, Robin Harris, what?

In the United States the move to label Black voices in the 1980s and 1990s as anti-Semitic, whether it was Jesse Jackson for his "Hymietown" remark, Minister Farrakhan in his defense of Jesse Jackson, and the Professor Griff incident with Public Enemy, has occurred through isolated incidents that have been taken and projected into a war zone. It's like, "You said this, this means war."

Most Black people have never looked at Jewish people as being any different from other white people. We basically look at people that play a part in our oppression as being non-Black. We don't look at their religious affiliation and say the person oppressing us is Jewish, Christian, or Catholic, that really doesn't matter. As a race we're not generally anti-

BLACK AND JEWISH RELATIONSHIPS

Semitic, but we are definitely antioppression and anti the white man with his foot on our necks.

Black people can practice Judaism, Islam, or Christianity, but we're still going to be looked at and judged on our visual characteristics. "That person is Black. Fuck what he believes." That's why it's so deep with us. In this country, a lot of Jewish people chose to hide the fact that they were Jewish in order to progress and have full access to the "American Dream," a choice the overwhelming majority of Black people will never have. With someone that's Jewish it's hard to distinguish them from any other white person, other than by their name, which could easily be changed, and many have changed and have assimilated and melted into the pot. It's very hard for Black people to melt into the pot. When we melt into the pot we usually become the charred crust at the bottom.

In recent years there have been comments made about there being an anti-Semitic attitude amongst rappers. One thing that can be said about rappers is we say what we feel, and one feeling that most of us have had in common is the feeling of being exploited and jerked in this business by unscrupulous "businessmen." Black artists in the entertainment business have a legitimate beef, and rappers are just the ones who are most vocal about what's taking place. There's a real legitimate beef. It really has nothing to do with what a person believes, it has to do with the criminal aspect of handling business.

Conservative white Anglo-Saxon Protestant businessmen sewed up a large portion of the larger more mainstream businesses and intentionally stayed away from the entertainment world, and a disproportionate number of people from creative Jewish backgrounds saw the void and filled it up. The beef is really with the business tactics and practices of those in the entertainment industry in general. Fair business practices aren't, "I know the game and you don't so I'm going to throw you a nickel and I'm going to keep ninety-five cents while you think I got ten cents." That's the whole game of the music business. That's been the game of what is supposed to be a "buddy-buddy" business system. It's been a trick. That's been the upsetting quality of the relationship.

The game of America has been learned well by people that have been able to stay together while being attacked, but Black people are still trying to rebound from the long period of self-hate that we've been through. Even though we now know the game, we don't know if we're players on the same team or not. Then there's the mistrust between the people that know the game and call themselves our teammates. We're like, "Okay, we'll be teammates," but at the same time we're not getting the ball. Rappers have a legitimate beef. It can't be branded as being anti-Semitic. We have to lay it down in human terms. One category of people has suffered in this business and don't have shit today, and the other category of people has shit.

Of course a rapper is going to have a Dr. Khallid Muhammad on their record, and Dr. Khallid is going to drop some factual information with some justifiable anger behind it. America as a whole fears the anger of the Black man but it's anger that has to come out. You can't suppress the anger after all of these years. It's like when you stab a finger, the initial stabbing action may take a second but the pain is going to be around for a while. The screaming and hollering have to be heard, and they're coming through Rap. That's like a guy getting hit by a truck and expecting him not to yell. Black men have anger coming back from slavery when they dunk a basketball on somebody. That's why you can't find too many interracial boxing matches anymore. You can't find any kind of interracial physical competition anymore. There's too much anger and rage involved. Now the anger and rage have gravitated to a vocal and intellectual level and that's the biggest fear, because once young brothers get intellectual who knows what they're going to come up with next. "How do we suppress this?"

People say if you come out and say something against Jewish people that's the end of your life in the business. That's demeaning and derogatory because Blacks have been thrown all over the

business, we've been the number-one casualty of the business, but at the same time we can't talk about what the fuck has been done. Individualizing the culprit is the best approach, but if you weigh the facts at the end of the day and count the people, if you want to count backgrounds, we are terribly overrepresented on the side of the casualties, chaos, and disorder done to us by a so-called caring group of people. I don't buy the concept of the "caring group of people." I believe that there have been individuals who a lot of times in their ignorance have felt they can do and say whatever they wanted, and put whatever image of Black people they wanted to out to the world, receive the benefits and the profits that poured in from it, and go on like nothing ever happened. I'm challenging that shit.

People have used the shield of religion to do devious shit. It's not who or what you say you are, it's how you act. If a person is foul, it's not that the person is Jewish or Black and acting foul— the person is just fucking foul. One person can say she's Muslim, another can say she's Christian, another can say she's Jewish— now prove it. If your religious book says you have to do certain things, then do what your book says. If you're saying one thing but not following what your book says then you're not that. You have to prove it with your deeds. The following statement by Michael Lerner in the book *Jews & Blacks* with Cornel West captures my feelings on the issue as it relates to Jews, Christians, Muslims, or any other set of organized beliefs that a person claims to follow. "All these flowery words seem empty if Jews [Christians, Muslims] ignore that we live in a society where African-Americans are being systematically demeaned, where racism continues to flourish, and where economic oppression yields degradation and daily suffering. It becomes immediately obvious that this reality poses an immediate demand on the Jewish [Christian, Muslim] people: to challenge those who believe that the suffering cannot or should not be alleviated, to join in the struggles to change all those societal institutions that perpetuate poverty and racism, and to connect with the oppressed in a way that recognizes their fundamental humanity and fundamental similarity with us, our sisterhood and brotherhood with them. To do this in a way that is not condescending, that does not assume that we are "morally higher" or "better," but rather out of a deep recognition of God's presence in each human being, is our challenge." Talk is cheap, actions are what count.

There's been lots of devastating acts that have been committed against Blacks by people that have hid behind the shield of a religion as protection for their individual dastardly deeds. We have to identify the culprit. We can't be silent. A person may say, "I'm Mr. Tannebaum." We don't attack him for being Jewish, we attack him for being foul. Then we tell the rest of the Jewish people that he's making a bad example for them.

If we would be more precise and focused in our attacks then people would have to look at the facts of the matter. Identify the culprit and take all of the glow off of people, strip them naked, identify their crime, and the average person will be able to see where the situation is foul. Black people in New York had one of their roughest periods when Ed Koch was the mayor of the city. From my vantage point, he didn't give a fuck about the Black situation in New York at all. He was foul. He was one of Public Enemy's harshest critics, saying that we should have been jailed for some comments we made as artists that were catching heat.

> YOU HAVE A LOT OF PEOPLE THAT HIDE BEHIND THE SHIELD OF RELIGION BECAUSE IT PROTECTS, ESPECIALLY IN THIS COUNTRY.

I haven't seen a large outcry from the Jewish population against what some Jewish individuals are doing, and them repudiating their actions. You talk about the Anti-Defamation League and the Jewish Defense League and some radical factions, they protect their people. Some say that they're out to protect all races, but they protect their own first.

Anybody that's Jewish who reads this, your beliefs are your beliefs, your philosophies are your philoso-

phies, if you read the Torah that's your business. This beef has nothing to do with the God-fearing person who wants to practice his or her religion. That's why I don't believe in me picking up a religious belief and just wearing it for protection and not being into it. You have a lot of people that hide behind the shield of religion because it protects, especially in this country, without true belief. I say this confidently, Black people have more serious issues and concerns than to think about the religious and philosophical beliefs of a person. We're struggling for our survival as a people and striving to get people's feet off of our fuckin' necks, not to get people to drop their philosophical and religious beliefs.

Over the years people have questioned me about my loyalty to Minister Farrakhan. I follow Minister Farrakhan for a lot of different reasons. My whole point, and I'm not speaking for Minister Farrakhan, is that I'm pretty sure he doesn't want to spend most of his time talking about Black-Jewish relationships. He wants to talk about the building of *our people* and that's what he's always been about, and that's what I'm about. All of this other shit has come about with the disorientation of the media and the news taking his statements after he was protecting Jesse Jackson after Jewish organizations were attacking Jesse because of his New York "Hymietown" remarks. Minister Farrakhan went in there as a force of protection to say, "You protect your people, we're going to protect our people." It was as simple as that.

Then all of a sudden media organizations like the *New York Post* made a big thing out of Minister Farrakhan's speech. To me it seemed a big fabricated issue whether Minister Farrakhan and the Nation of Islam were anti-Semitic, and it stuck because the United States is a country that does not have the highest level of independent thinkers. The United States is a country that operates on sound bites and what views are spewed down to it in its simplest, oatmeallike form. Therefore, it was very easy to build hype up on the matter and not only get Minister Farrakhan neutralized, but chase Jesse Jackson out of the Presidential picture.

The bottom line is that Black people do not have any type of anti-Semitic sentiment on their brains. We are thinking about coming up and whatever foot we perceive to be on our shoulder, that's the foot that we're going to try to knock off even if it's a Black foot.

Many people know that Public Enemy has also suffered in the past from the label "anti-Semitic" from some comments made by Professor Griff in 1989, and subsequently from the release of the song "Welcome to the Terrordome" in 1990, which recounted my feelings and experiences of that turbulent period. I may not have agreed with everything Griff said, I don't agree with everything anybody says, but I defended his right to speak as an artist. And the one thing I was not going to let happen was for people outside of our inner camp to attempt to divide and conquer us as has been the case too often in our history. I read the accounts of what happened between W.E.B. Du Bois and Marcus Garvey, I'm familiar with the wedge that was created between Malcolm X and the Nation of Islam, and most recently I saw what happened with Reverend Jesse Jackson and Minister Farrakhan as they came together in a bond of brotherhood in the 1980s. I wasn't going to let that happen with us. Public Enemy has a rule amongst ourselves: "None of these people were our friends before we got into this, so it really doesn't matter if any of them are our friends when we leave." It doesn't matter to me. What does matter is that I stand up as a man and pick and choose who I will associate with on my own.

When you read magazines, newspapers, and books, they make it look like I fired Griff. Fuck them, they don't know the real story. The real story is in this book. The shit was mad drama.

DRAMA

In 1989 after the release of *It Takes a Nation of Millions to Hold Us Back* the constant traveling started to take its toll on all of us. By 1989 everybody had started families, continued families, and added on to families, so we were all dealing with family life. It

FIGHT THE POWER
211

IN 1989 AFTER THE RELEASE OF IT TAKES A NATION OF MILLIONS TO HOLD US BACK THE CONSTANT TRAVELING STARTED TO TAKE ITS TOLL ON ALL OF US.

takes a lot of mental preparation to be on the road. When I'm on tour I limit my phone calls and concentrate on being a public servant. I take care of all of my family responsibilities because that's part of my duty, but educating through music is what I was meant to do.

When I decided to start Public Enemy, I wanted to bring the Unity Force look with us. Since Hank and I both already knew Griff from the Spectrum City days, and he founded Unity Force we kept dealing with him, rather than deal with each member of Unity Force, which was about twenty people. We wanted to deal with one person and that one person could talk to the twenty. Griff was the contact point for us. I renamed Unity Force the Security of the First World (S1Ws) inside the group and Griff's first duties with us was as road manager for Public Enemy. Onstage Griff was an S1W but he was set apart from everybody else because he was a mobile S1W.

Originally it was Flavor and me with the microphones, then Griff started picking up the mic, which wasn't a bad idea because I definitely needed more help, so that became part of the act. With Public Enemy just because you were onstage didn't mean that you didn't have another job to fulfill. Everybody had to double up on their duties because we weren't bringing any extra people out on the road with us. Especially on the first tour when we were netting six hundred dollars a week.

The road-manager situation got real tough for Griff because Flavor's actions were chaotic. I could see the friction between the two because Griff and Flavor are like night and day. Flavor comes from the street, and at that time he was grappling with his street self and his disciplined self. Flavor runs twenty-four hours a day. Trying to get him places on time was close to impossible. Griff was disciplined. Griff did an excellent job the first couple of years controlling his temper. Sometimes I would be unsympathetic because I would say, "That's his job. If I have to go look for Flavor what's his job?"

I remember one night when we had a show to do in Trenton, New Jersey, and Flavor was nowhere to be found and Griff had to try and find him. Flavor popped up like everything was cool about four hours after we were scheduled to leave for the gig, carrying this big-ass radio. Griff looked at him and said, "I don't believe this. He comes in here walking like everything is all right." Griff picked up the radio and kicked Flavor in the chest. Flavor disappeared for the rest of the night.

We went to Trenton and performed anyway. At the time we hadn't done any videos yet so people didn't know how we looked. I asked James, one of the S1Ws, to put on Flavor's Troop jacket, twist his hat to the side, and play Flavor Flav for the night. I told James not to move around like Flavor, just slump over in the corner and act like he was sick. I went out there and told the crowd, "My man Flavor Flav has strep throat and a bad fever, but he's out here giving one hundred percent. Usually people would be laid up in bed, but he's out here like a trooper. The show must go on. Put your hand up, Flavor." James put his hand up. Then I said, "You stay right over there and don't say anything. I'm going to dedicate this show to you." There was one guy out of the whole audience who was going off. He was screaming, "That's not Flavor Flav. That's not him." I asked Griff to go and speak with the guy and try to calm him down but that just made the guy even crazier. Eventually Griff got the guy to calm down and the show was going smooth, and as I was getting down to "Rebel without a Pause" James started moving around a little bit. When I turned around as I was moving from side to side on the stage I hit James directly in the mouth with the microphone. All you could hear on the microphone was "Uuuggghh." After the show James took his shit off in the dressing room and was like, "I'm not ever playing this Flavor shit again."

Flavor had stayed back, because he didn't like the way he was

being treated. Flavor missed a couple of shows, and not long after that Griff was like, "I can't do this looking out for Flavor anymore." Flavor has burned out many different people since then but Griff was the first one. I removed Griff from his road-managing duties and he brought John "Pop" Oliver on the road to handle Flavor. Mike Williams and James Norman took over the road-managing responsibilities. I had Griff start helping me to coordinate the tours.

I noticed that there was tension growing between Griff and the other S1Ws.

A lot of the guys didn't like the way they were being shuffled in 1987. Two brothers would come out on the road, then two brothers would go back, and they would rotate. Griff was in charge of that. Some of the S1Ws resented that he was in a power position and thought he was mismanaging and misusing that power.

After being on the road so much we became like a family. Like with any family, petty beefs would pop up between members but I used to turn my head to those situations and be like, "We're all men. They'll work through it." Especially when it came down to the S1Ws because, since they were brought in as a preexisting unit, I didn't want to dictate and manipulate what was going on inside an operation that was none of my business. What I thought was none of my business got to be looked upon as not being interpersonal enough. People would say, "You need to be more open with people." The shit was new to me. I was never somebody's boss before.

Besides not wanting to seem like I was a dictator, I also didn't want to get too close to anybody because when they got sent off the road they might come back to me and say, "Can you keep me on the road?" It happened once with this guy named Jacob. He had a hard time on the road in 1987 because he smoked cigarettes and he ate meat, which the rest of the S1Ws wasn't with. He was sent home after this gig in Memphis. Jacob kept requesting meetings with me, trying to see if he could stay out on the road. All I could say was, "I wish I could help you but that's none of my business." I kept a distance from all of that as long as I had enough brothers onstage and people were doing their jobs. I'm a firm believer in a structure within a structure.

As the leader of the group, since I brought everybody together, I should have been there to check things before they got out of hand. What I learned that year is as the leader and the person responsible for bringing the whole situation to where it was conceptually, legally, and financially, I should have been there to check everything because

> AS THE LEADER OF THE GROUP, SINCE I BROUGHT EVERYBODY TOGETHER, I SHOULD HAVE BEEN THERE TO CHECK THINGS BEFORE THEY GOT OUT OF HAND.

everything was on my name. But my attitude of "It will take care of itself" didn't help things at all. Either I had to be in there "big I, little you" or I had to step aside and let it work itself out. My biggest mistake in the drama that was yet to unfold was not taking the proper leadership position.

I remember one incident that really challenged me to say, "Damn, am I heading this group right or am I doing the wrong thing?" We had a rule, *nobody* in the dressing room. Magic Johnson and Don King were in the audience one night and they wanted to come in the dressing room after the show. I definitely wanted to meet Magic Johnson and Don King but everybody else was like, "No, nobody in the dressing room." Here I am in charge of the situation and Don King and Magic Johnson could have meant something for the further advancement of our situation, and once again I didn't say anything. I was in that wishy-washy position of, "I'm just here as a member." When I came out of the dressing room they were gone.

The initial plan of Public Enemy was to come out as a group, then build each of the members individually over time. When I came up with my recording contract, I saw it as my duty to figure out how many other people I could spread it over. I don't know too many people that have spread one contract over a gang of

careers. Hank got a career out of it, Bill got a career out of it, Flavor, Griff, then the touring situation, all out of one contract. It was me in the beginning, then Flavor, especially with the second album, then Terminator X, especially with the onslaught of "Rebel without a Pause," then it was Griff's turn. On the second album, Griff was placed in a more prominent position. For one, he asked me to put him there and, secondly, it made sense. So he was set apart from the rest of the S1Ws.

I was always making up names and titles, so I gave everybody a title to make the artwork look better and to create more of a mystical aura and approach. I was into Black Nationalism thoroughly so I called Griff the "Minister of Information," which is a takeoff of Eldridge Cleaver and the Black Panther Party. A few of the guys from the S1Ws were rooted in the Nation of Islam, and we would get into our debates here and there, but one thing we all agreed on—it was all for one and one for all. When we presented ourselves in public it would be in the way that was best to propel the group, it wouldn't be one person's ideology.

By 1989 we were the most interviewed music artists around. People wanted to know what we were about. I couldn't handle all of the interviews myself, and since Griff wasn't doing the road managing anymore I would have Griff, our "Minister of Information," handle some of the interviews.

I was handling seventy-five to eighty percent of the interviews, soaking in a little bit of what the guys in the S1Ws would say and adding it to what I believed. I believe pretty basic things. Like with religions, I don't believe God handed out religions like a deck of cards. When you break down Islam to its most fundamental level it means submission to the Will of God, and the Will of God is to respect your fellow man and woman, respect His creations, and respect the planet. Anything after that becomes semantics.

As a group my goal is to gel all the philosophies into one where there's a commonality that gets expressed and not a host of contradictions. What Flavor believes and what Griff believes may be two different things, but they were both a part of Public Enemy. What Drew believes and what James Allen believes may be two different things. It's my job to bring it to a center point and say what's true for all of us. "We're Black, we fight for our people, and we respect our fellow human beings." Once you start getting into tit-for-tat rhetoric, then you fall into a sea full of contradiction. We would make controversial statements for the sake of getting highlighted, then we would pull back.

After handling so many interviews our first two years, studying the media for a long time, and also being in communications, I came up with a formula for handling the press. I would take three blows, get hit by one, step back, look, hit another one, step back, disappear, come back and hit again. As opposed to going out and spewing a lot of opinions and leaving myself open to where somebody could drop a bombshell on me. My whole thing is to never let myself be thrown into a box. With all the media interviews we did during that period, it would have been a lot of pressure on anybody.

At the same time back around the way, Hank and Bill had been working to secure our own record label. Since we had been instrumental in helping to build Def Jam, we had our sights and plans on building our own label. During the upcoming months, especially after delivering "Fight the Power," which was later to become one of the most successful singles in Motown history and whose distribution was handled by MCA, we were working on a label deal with MCA. It all started with Motown through Spike Lee's movie *Do the Right Thing*.

DO THE RIGHT THING

Spike Lee first contacted Bill Stephney to set up a meeting because he was putting together his next movie. Spike Lee had previously done *She's Gotta Have It,* which jumped him off into the marketplace as being a filmmaker. More recently he had done *School Daze.* Along with Spike Lee's cutting-edge movies was his appreciation of music. His previous movie *School Daze* had a top Go-Go record jump off by the group EU. As a matter of fact, when

we were on tour the following year we performed with EU. They appeared on the Run's House tour opening up some dates. So we performed with them and it showed the power of the Black sound track. The Black movie was making a return.

Originally, during the second Black movie phase of the 1970s, the "Blaxploitation flicks," with the advent of *Shaft* and Isaac Hayes, showed that not only was the movie a trigger point for Black music but the music was also a trigger point for the movie. This technique was used by Spike Lee quite effectively in *School Daze* with EU's cut "Doin' Tha Butt." Spike was getting ready to mastermind his next project, which he said was a film he was shooting in Brooklyn dealing with the racial tension that was going down there and in New York in general. One of the causes for the tension in the city at that time was the Eleanor Bumpers situation where police used excessive force in restraining an elderly Black woman in the Bronx and wound up killing her. Another was the Michael Griffith situation in Howard Beach where a young man got killed when his car broke down. When he went to get aid to fix his car he was chased down by a mob of white youths and, while trying to get away, was hit by a passing car. There was a lot of hostility in the air in Brooklyn at that time, both on the Black and the white side. All of this on came on top of the Bernhard Goetz shooting a couple of years before, where this white man, Bernhard Goetz, claimed he was being harassed for money on the subway. He was armed and ended up shooting four or five Black youths in the *back*. Two of them suffered severe injuries, and that became front-page news. Racial tensions were at a peak, so Spike decided to jump on top of those issues with his own point of view as a filmmaker.

The meeting with Spike was held at a restaurant around the corner from Bleecker Street. I remember I ordered some bean soup because it was an Indian restaurant. I was happy to meet Spike. Spike said, "I'm putting together a film and I need a theme song." I looked at him and said, "What do you have in mind?" Then he explained the story line of the film. He said, "I need a theme song, an anthem, something to define the rage that's going on right about now. The name of the movie is *Do the Right Thing.*" I told him I had some things I was working on, then I said, "What I'll do is go overseas and do this European tour with Run-DMC and when I come back you'll have your song." It was as simple as that. Hank and I looked at Bill, then we looked at Spike, then we started talking about other things we had in common like the Mets and the Knicks because we all were big sports fans. Before we left Spike looked at me again and said, "I just need a theme song, an anthem."

What I didn't know until I saw the movie was that he was going to have the song run throughout the movie. It wasn't just a theme song, it was a backbone for the whole movie. It was like the song was one movie and the movie was one song. We really appreciate what Spike did for us with the strength of that song. After we ate we shook hands.

At the tail end of 1988 we toured Europe with Run-DMC for the latter part of October through the latter part of November. For that four weeks we had an incredible time touring. I remember writing the majority of "Fight the Power" on a couple of plane trips. When I'm on a plane or on a bus writing with my headphones up loud, I'm in my own world and people can hear me talking out loud. I started dwelling on the fact that Black people have heroes too, and our heroes aren't projected as much as the heroes that we are forced to bow to, especially in the American system.

The original "Fight the Power" was a record that was done by the Isley Brothers back in 1970–71, and it was a record I heard as a child. The record was startlingly powerful to me because it was the first record I ever heard that had a curse word. That stuck in my mind.

The song was a tribute to the fight against oppression. I start out "1989 the number." When you're writing a song for a movie

you have to think ahead and the difficult thing about that movie was I had to think nine to ten months ahead. Normally when you make a record you have to think ahead anyway, but with a movie you have to think way ahead, especially for a movie that you haven't seen. It was a record where we tried to hinge upon the feelings of defiance, pride, attitude, nationalism, a little bit of rhetoric, and deal with who we had as our heroes, who we are as a people, and give our heroes a top-notch place in history. The words are self-explanatory: "Fight the Power." Since I came up with the title, which was an easy one because it was there, writing it was not a difficult task.

I remember Jheryl Busby, who was then President of Motown, came to New York and we were talking about the "Fight the Power" song. He was very interested in the minds that we had and the way we operated. MCA was one of the majors that decided to get up on the Rap scene because they knew they could make some money. So they moved in and offered us a label deal. All of this was on the table around April of 1989 when we got back from Japan.

We went to Japan in March of 1989. We were having clusters of meetings about the tensions that were building within the group. Everyone was dealing with family pressures, undetermined futures, and wanting to grow within their capabilities. I had a meeting of confidence with Griff where I told him, "Don't worry about anything, you're a very important part of this group." That meeting of encouragement with him was looked upon as a dis to everybody else.

The whole situation was rough for me because I knew how to Rap and make a group happen but I wasn't trying to get into philosophical bullshit. On my end, I could have stepped up my involvement because we had had a meeting the year before in Richmond where everybody got a chance to express their feelings on how they were being treated. I tried to keep everything cool but the general feeling was one of, "Fuck that, Chuck, this is some shit that's really deeper than what you can see and you need to just sit over there and listen." I still didn't want to get in the middle of that shit. Then somebody told me, "If you're going to be the leader of the group, be the leader. You can't be half here, half not here." My leadership qualities were being challenged. I didn't have any tension with anyone, to me we were like a family. My problems came from having to step in between the other individuals within the group.

The Japanese tour was exciting, playing in places like Kawasaki. We played in five cities over there. I brought my daughter and wife over on that tour. We all brought people over for that tour and we had a great time. That was the time when the Japanese Prime Minister Yasuhiro Nakasone made some racist comments about Blacks in America, and there were also Japanese companies that had manufactured and sold products depicting demeaning, stereotypical images of Little Black Sambo dolls, toys and beach wear, so we did massive interviews and checked a lot of people. Sony had just taken over CBS, so going to Japan being affiliated with Sony, and also going over there and dropping mad information made people say, "Damn, this is some revolutionary shit. They're not taking kindly to any of that Sambo shit." The Japanese have been brainwashed just like people all over the world with propaganda from America about Blacks in America. We went over there and showed them we were serious. When we performed, the Japanese kids were loving it because they were heavily into Rap and were also rebelling against the older generations. We developed some good friends over there, Kan Takagi, and the Japanese crew Major Force Possé. We found a whole new B-Boy world the first time we went.

As a writer I can have stacks of deep material but the key is how to use them in a song—bit by bit, piece by piece, is my method. I do not give people everything I know and I don't want to make people think that I know everything. I give enough information where I don't get placed in a box.

Until we had more jams, five-minute speeches were part of our show. We knew how to keep an audience on our side but at the same time say enough to make them feel guilty, then at the end make them feel like they're with us even though they fucked up.

That was a technique that worked very well. Sometimes Flavor would talk before the records or Griff would give a speech that would set it up for me.

One time we did this gig at USC and the audience was full of USC and UCLA students. In the middle of the show, Griff started getting into some real heavy issues. As Griff was giving his speech a white student stood up and challenged him. They got into a debate in the middle of the show. Another kid jumped on-stage and had a seizure.

Our whole philosophy is at the end of the night we want the people on our side because we're dropping the truth and we're teaching them something that's contrary to what they know. We're a music group but we are bending the rules and the philosophies of what music groups do to the extreme level.

"Fight the Power" was finished and was placed in the movie *Do the Right Thing.* I saw a screening of the movie and I thought, "Damn, they're playing that song a lot." When we made our final mix I was satisfied with it. We finished it up at Greene Street and it was really, really strong and it became the anthem Spike was looking for.

In May we did a spot date in Washington, DC, and I remember Griff telling me on the bus about a personal problem he was having in his family that was building up. That was on top of all the other drama that existed.

We arrived in DC and were staying in the Comfort Inn in Chinatown. I had a radio station interview to do, along with five or six other interviews. When the writer from *The Washington Times* arrived, Griff called up to my room and said, "*The Washington Times* is here, are you going to do the interview?" Darryl Brooks, who was a tour promoter at the time, wanted to sit down and talk to me about hooking up another tour. I told Griff that I had to meet with Darryl across the street. I was going to tell Darryl about the "Fight the Power" song that was featured in Spike's movie and was going to blow up in the summer. He was getting ready to promote L.L. Cool J's Walking Like a Panther tour so I wanted to see if he could put us on some of those dates. Griff already had something to do but I was like, "You have to knock it out for me." As I went across the street for my meeting with Darryl, Griff handled the interview for me.

The reporter from *The Washington Times,* David Mills, wanted to interview me on what we were doing and also about some comments Griff had made two weeks prior on BET about the connection between Jews and jewelry. Some real deep, deep slave shit.

Our whole philosophy is not to go deep, deep, deep when people don't understand the simple. Keep it simple. Let them get mad in bits and pieces but then drop it to make them look stupid. Our plan was to make people put their own foot in their mouth if they challenged us. Not to go so deep where someone could attempt to dismiss us as being crazy. We could be right in what we were saying but we could be right in the wrong environment. That was our method of handling situations. If I had handled the David Mills interview when he wanted to ask me about Griff's statements, I would have sidestepped the issue in many different ways, then I would have dressed the whole situation up. I was knocking out so many interviews per month, more than anybody in music. I had developed a technique because I was doing it every day, every week, and no shit came up in our face, so obviously I was doing it right.

> OUR WHOLE PHILOSOPHY IS NOT TO GO DEEP, DEEP, DEEP WHEN PEOPLE DON'T UNDERSTAND THE SIMPLE. KEEP IT SIMPLE.

Griff was gifted at doing interviews too. As a matter of fact he took it to a further extreme, but just when he got close to the edge he would cut back to sting the opposition. That way they really couldn't accuse us of racism. He had the technique down after two years of handling interviews. That was my right-hand man. If I had two interviews scheduled, I would have Griff handle one and we'd knock them out.

FIGHT THE POWER
223

I don't know exactly what happened during the interview with Mills, but Griff got ticked off. Griff knew the lines of pushing it to the extreme and then pulling back, but Griff didn't really like that reporter from day one. Griff wasn't even on speaking terms with David Mills, but I asked him to handle the interview for me.

Griff told me later on when I finished meeting with Darryl Brooks, "I handled it, Chuck, but it's going to be some shit. I'm going to have some problems with this guy." I was mad tired, looked at him, patted him on the shoulder, and said, "Don't worry about it. Get some sleep," and I went up to bed.

> GRIFF REPEATED SOME COMMENTS HE HAD MADE ABOUT THE CONNECTION BETWEEN JEWS AND THE JEWELRY INDUSTRY, THE JEWISH CONNECTION TO THE SLAVE TRADE, AND THE JEWISH ROLE IN THE APARTHEID REGIME IN SOUTH AFRICA.

In the interview, Griff repeated some comments he had made about the connection between Jews and the jewelry industry, the Jewish connection to the slave trade, and the Jewish role in the apartheid regime in South Africa. He was like, "Is it a coincidence that the Jews run the jewelry business and it's named jewelry? No coincidence. Is it a coincidence to you that probably the gold from this ring was brought up out of South Africa, and that the Jews have a tight grip on our brothers in South Africa?" Some of the comments made during the interview obviously bothered David Mills. It could also be added that David's girlfriend at the time was white and Jewish and was at the interview, and she may have been offended by what Griff said, which I suspect sent David into another zone. David Mills contacted our headquarters and wanted to set up a follow-up meeting. He said he was going to hold off on writing his piece until he could speak with the entire group.

They set a meeting with David Mills, and James, Roger, James

Norman, and Mike asked me to come down to our headquarters for the meeting. I had an attitude of, "Fuck him. I'm not talking to him if he thinks he's going to sell us out like that." They asked me to come up there and I said I wouldn't. Mistake number 2. If it's your problem, handle your mistakes, nip the shit in the bud, and eliminate it. The situation turned from a spark, to a little campfire, to a brushfire.

Instead of going to the meeting with Mills, I went to California for some other meetings. I called Griff and asked him what was going on back in New York. He was like, "Everything is cool." I said, "Well, if anything comes up you'll handle it, right?" He said, "Yeah." Still I left it alone. I later found out from the S1Ws what happened at the meeting in New York.

They told me that when David Mills came in they sat down and talked with him for about two and a half hours, showing him books and facts to substantiate some of the comments made by Griff. Mills had further questions about the points Griff had made. During the meeting the S1Ws provided the names and dates of Jewish people who owned slaves and described the wider role that Jews played in the African slave trade. They referred to the DeBeers Consolidated Mines based in South Africa and controlled by Harry Oppenheimer who reportedly controls nearly eighty-five percent of the world's total of diamonds and rare gems. The initial problem with Griff's statements was that he didn't explain any of what he said. He didn't give any references. The S1Ws gave Mills references to books, like the *Secret Relationship Between Blacks and Jews,* which were authored by Jewish people which substantiated the claims Griff had made. David seemed to be taking the information one way, and kept saying, "Show and prove to me what's going on."

Then Griff came in the room. The S1Ws said that Griff kept asking the reporter if he could listen to the original taped interview. He was like, "Can I listen to the tape? I want to listen to the fucking tape."

That approach evidently got them nowhere, and David eventually left the meeting mad and faxed the transcript of the interview

to newspapers around the country. A few days later a friend read an article in the Rock Beat column of *The Village Voice* written by R. J. Smith, which reprinted excerpts of David Mills's interview with Griff. He faxed a copy of the article to me in California. I looked at the article and said, "That shit will disappear." I crumpled it up and went on with what I was doing. I played that shit off like, "We're Public Enemy. They can't expect any spook shit coming from us."

Later David Mills regretted writing the story and apologized to Griff. He was quoted as saying, "Not because I agreed with what Griff said but because he told me, 'Go read your history books,' and I wrote a story before I had done that." David Mills later requested to write a follow-up story for *Spin* magazine, which was interested in a follow-up to the story, but when Mills told them he wanted to shift the story's focus to the Jewish role in the slave trade, the magazine passed.

At first I didn't worry about the *Voice* article because the interview we had done the year before with the Studd Brothers in Switzerland was blistering. Then there was the interview with *The Face* on the bus where Griff chewed this motherfucker up. It would only take one thing to get Griff set off in the wrong way and he was dropping it on somebody. I would tell Griff not to take any of it personally because these people were looking to set a trap for him to fall into.

Then things started getting hectic. I didn't do anything or say anything. I ignored it. Mistake number 3, ignoring it. This was some shit that was attached to me but I was looking for somebody else to fix a mistake that I should have been fixing. Week by week the controversy was mounting. People were going off of *The Village Voice* story more than the original *Washing-*

> IT WOULD ONLY TAKE ONE THING TO GET GRIFF SET OFF IN THE WRONG WAY AND HE WAS DROPPING ON SOMEBODY.

ton Times article. *The Village Voice* had just named Public Enemy "Group of the Year," and the story was getting bigger and bigger. It mushroomed. It became an issue. I was pissed trying to figure out why this was even an issue.

Then in August a Jewish radical with the Jewish Defense Organization named Mordechai Levy was arrested for shooting at people. Then we started receiving notes and letters from the JDL.

After the drama started hitting the fan, we all got together and tried to figure out how we were going to deal with it. That's when Hank and Bill were like, "Fuck it, the group is over with. Y'all are through, finished. Y'all have to handle that shit." It was over cause we didn't handle our business. We were letting a loose cannon go off and I wasn't displaying proper leadership skills. Something like that should have been nipped right in the bud.

Now remember, me, being bullheaded, said, "Fuck him," and didn't go to the meeting with Mills, which could have settled the issue. Griff had five or six different pressures on him. Once the situation got to the point between him and the rest of the brothers in the S1Ws where they weren't talking or kickin' it for various personal reasons—I'll call them PE reasons—it seemed like Griff developed a "well, fuck it then" attitude. That was the major thing that bothered us. It wasn't what he said. Everyone has a right to say what they feel and many of the things that he said were based on facts. It was the "well, fuck it then" attitude that didn't sit well. You can have an "I'm not getting along with everybody" attitude but try to work it out. Everyone would have had to humble themselves and shrink their egos.

Normally when pressure came on us we'd come together regardless of what was going on. The S1Ws usually became tighter than tight but this time it was just crazy.

By the time June came, the drama was affecting the pending deal with MCA and Bill, Hank, and myself. Bill and Hank were still moving forward with the label situation and Bill was like, "This is your situation and we're trying to close this deal down, you need to handle it." I was a part of the partnership with Bill and Hank with MCA, and Al Teller, who was the president of MCA at

the time, was Jewish and had lost his parents in the Holocaust. The MCA deal didn't mean as much to me so I offered to drop out of the picture so Bill and Hank could have their deal, which they did get: SOUL Records. I figured if I was going to cause that many problems at the table I didn't need to be there. Instead of having a multimillion-dollar-label deal, I chose to stick with the group. I didn't make a mistake on that.

I was trying to ignore the shit before but couldn't ignore it any longer because the pressure was starting to come down on other people. In mid-June I got a call from Spike asking what was going on. Spike said he'd propped us up like mad and was now getting mad drama with the film people.

Walter Yetnikoff, a big wheel up at Sony, wasn't putting heavy pressure on us.

They couldn't fuck with us directly so what they did was go after everybody around us to see who they could fuck with. They were fucking with Russell at Def Jam, messing with the MCA negotiations, and fucking with Spike Lee. The biggest problem was with the film companies and Spike.

Russell Simmons was also getting mad pressure put on him from different angles. He was already bald so I guess he started growing an Afro with all the pressure. Bill Adler, who was the publicist at Def Jam and who is also Jewish, was saying, "Chuck, when you handled your interviews you made people that were oblivious and foreign to what you guys were about sympathetic to your cause, you swept them into your fold. You have to do something."

All the problems began with small, interpersonal relationships that got turned inside out to the outer world and festered into a mushroom cloud by the end of June. I thought the biggest controversy we were going to have was me talking about Elvis Presley and John Wayne in "Fight the Power," instead we had this shit.

I didn't have any clear-cut answers. All I knew was we had traveled the world together, had our own family structure, and when we took care of things the world would know. At the same time some people were doubting me.

By that time we had already done "Bring the Noise" and "Don't Believe the Hype." My initial goal in working with the S1Ws, especially those heavily oriented in the Nation, was to use my lyrics to help clean up the bullshit hype that had come out about Minister Farrakhan that started after the *New York Post* article. I felt through popular music and entertainment I could help bring his name into a positive light and have white kids singing a song

WE ACTUALLY HAD WHITE LISTENERS WANTING TO GET INTO THE MIND-SET OF MINISTER FARRAKHAN AND LOOK AT HIS WORDS FOR THEMSELVES AND DISCOVER THAT HE WASN'T WHAT THEY HEARD HE WAS.

with Farrakhan's name in it, and we could change the whole complexion of how he was being looked at. Minister Farrakhan was gaining so much momentum in 1984 that when the *Post* came out with that bullshit story about "Farrakhan Says Hitler Was a Great Man"—when, as it suggested buried in the text of the article, he actually described how Hitler's greatness was used for wicked purposes—their wicked reporting turned the whole Nation movement back. When "Bring the Noise" came out and said, "Farrakhan's a prophet I think you ought to listen to," and "Don't Believe the Hype" said, "A follower of Farrakhan, don't tell me that you understand, until you hear the man," we actually had white listeners wanting to get into the mind-set of Minister Farrakhan and look at his words for themselves and discover that he wasn't what they heard he was. We had turned that whole sphere around and were going to lead into the "Fight the Power" theme with rebuilding the Nation with a perception of "Damn, they have a lot of young followers." Of course, there would be the old-time battlers but by 1989 we had helped turn that around with our own form of media—Rap music. That one interview with

FIGHT THE POWER
229

Griff and Mills wiped all that shit away and threw us back to 1985.

Griff had introduced me to tapes of Farrakhan back in 1980 and I almost had Bill Adler listening and convinced about Farrakhan. But when this new shit came about, we were in the same position as Minister Farrakhan—between a rock and a hard place.

One day I was having a telephone conversation with Russell Simmons who was frantic from all the pressure. He was like, "So you're still protecting your man? This shit is about to go down, everything is going to crumble around you." Russell had pressure, Spike had pressure, CBS was starting to get pressure, the MCA situation was gone for me because Hank and Bill had pressure, but I didn't have any pressure. But your boys can give you pressure! For example, you might not be feeling any pressure but if somebody gives your wife and your child pressure, are you going to have pressure? That's exactly what happened.

With all of the pressure coming down on the people around me I decided I had to do something. I got together with Bill Adler and said, "Let's write a press release. I'm going to have to put Griff to the side for a minute." The S1Ws wanted me to consult with them first but I didn't. Mistake number 4. I did the press conference with Bill Adler but I worded it a certain way. At first I said Griff would be suspended. Then Bill said, "You won't get the pressure off of everybody else if you just say he's suspended. They'll think you're bluffing. You'll have to say he's no longer with the group." Everybody took that as me saying he was fired. I had no intention of firing him but at the same time if he wasn't going to get in front of the press and say what he had to say to fix the situation himself, then I had to do something. My problem was I was doing it two months too late. Doing that press conference was the craziest, dumbest thing I could have ever done. I should have spoken spontaneously instead of reading some shit written up as a joint project between Bill Adler, Bill Stephney, and myself, and approved by all these other people in order to get the pressure relieved. Mistake number 5. I was operating off of emotion.

The night of that press conference I went right over to Griff's house, sat in a car in front of the house, and told him, "Look man, you're going to have to just lay low for a while. I moved the pressure off of you but you just have to lay low. This shit is deep, it's serious. What are you, a martyr? You can hear about a person being brave and beating their chest and saying, "I'll fight the world," but that's not realistic. Somebody can just come up and blow you away with a gun." I said, "If you want to die, you want to die and be right but you don't want to die and be stupid based on a statement." I promised Griff that he would still get paid when we performed because I knew he had a family to take care of. "I'll take care of your situation, but at the same time you're not the hero today. You cannot be a hero at everybody else's expense. It's all going to die down, and in some creative way I'll bring you back into the fold." He said, "Cool."

A few weeks after the press conference we had a gig in Philadelphia. We played in the Spectrum on L.L.'s tour, which was one of the original things I talked to Darryl Brooks about in Washington. "Fight the Power" had come out in June, we did the video and it was smoking hot. Critics who saw that Philly show said we got blown away by N.W.A. What they don't understand is that we got onstage and had limited time. We were forced to do a quick set and get the hell out of there. N.W.A didn't blow us away, we hurried up and got up out of there because we had drama. N.W.A didn't have any drama.

When Griff was so-called "kicked out of the group" to knock some of the pressures away, we knew people would be trying to check to see if we were bluffing or not. These other people were not my boss or my mother or father, and they certainly were not my God so I didn't feel I had to tell them anything. In Philadelphia, because it's so close to New York, we told Griff not to come near the stage. He was still traveling with us as we were doing some fill-in dates, and on some shows he actually came onstage with us.

After the Philly gig we went back to the hotel and there was a

discrepancy on the financial situation. I had promised Griff that he
would get his normal share, but that
was me saying it. When we got to
the group meeting it was voted by a
majority of the group that he would
get paid but he wouldn't get his regular fee. I explained that the final decision didn't come from me, it came
from the group meeting. He was

> WE ALWAYS MADE SURE THAT WE MAINTAINED OUR EXISTENCE AS A GROUP AND TRIED TO DO THINGS AS DEMOCRATICALLY AS POSSIBLE.

like, "You promised me . . ." and that was more drama. That was
drama between him and me.

I didn't know how to handle it. Should I have told everybody,
"Fuck it, I'm giving him the full fee?" In this business you can do
things as an individual, as a king, or as a group—you can't
choose all three. You have to do shit one way. We always made
sure that we maintained our existence as a group and tried to do
things as democratically as possible.

During that time I was making erratic moves to keep outsiders
guessing. I shut down the group, then I started the group again
without Griff. I only did that to be confusing. My whole thing is if
you're vulnerable, be confusing. I didn't have to answer to anybody so I could be as confusing as I wanted to be to save grace.
My whole thing was to duck and weave, bounce around. Ali shuffle 'em, to keep them off balance.

We were scheduled to be in Chicago for a show in July, so we
went through the proper channels to have an audience with Minister Farrakhan in Chicago and sought his advice and counsel
on how to handle the matter. Since we knew a lot of Jewish organizations would probably be looking at that Chicago show, we
told Griff not to make himself visibly present. One reporter spot-
ted him in the crowd and reported, "Professor Griff was in the audience." The next day we sat down with Minister Farrakhan. The
minister said, "You guys made a mistake." He basically said that
the comments were unwise and that we would go through a
turbulent period. "You don't know when it's going to be the

> All-Time Underrated Rappers:
>
> Too Short: Been doin' it, doin' it, doin' it . . .
> Queen Latifah: Comes harder and ruffa than most guys and multi-talented.
> Guru: Smooth as hell; a cool brother also.
> Chubb Rock: Intense; a wordsmith.
> DJ Kool: Been around a long time; a true fan of this music.
> Schoolly D: Versatile and aware.
> BIZ Makrkie: This guy will always be in Hip-Hop doing something.
> MC Ren: Scottie Pippen to Ice Cube's Jordan Sharp.
> Heavy D: Versatile; will find a way to make a hit record.

right time for you to get back on your feet, so continue to lay low."

The entire group went through a thirty-day silence of not talking to the press, and on August 1, which is coincidentally both of our birthdays, I disseminated a press release saying Griff was back in the group.

I told Griff when I brought him back in, "Don't talk to the press, just be here, get down on shows, and you'll get your full pay again. Let's move forward. We'll look back at this time as something to laugh at." There was still inner tension and animosity inside the camp and now there was a little animosity toward me.

I told people from the press that CBS had stopped our next album just to hype up the situation, and I said the next album was called "Fear of a Black Planet." I hadn't stepped in the studio for one day and had not written a song, but everybody was like, "Yo, they stopped the album." I just wanted to create more hype. When in doubt confuse them.

The same day Griff was officially brought back in we were in

Kansas City. Lyor Cohen, the manager of Rush Productions who is an Israeli, came over to me in the lobby of the Kansas City Hyatt and said he had seen Griff talking to a reporter. I looked over his shoulder and saw Griff was sitting there talking to a group of brothers with a white reporter sitting nearby. Shortly thereafter the *Kansas City Star* had a press release they were faxing around saying, "Professor Griff is back with Public Enemy." Yeah, so what? The release went on to say that when asked about his previous comments, Griff reaffirmed that everything he had said previously was true and he was not backing off. The shit all started up again. The reporter was on MTV that same night, "Yes, Professor Griff is back in Public Enemy, and he says everything he said previously is true and stands behind his statements."

By then it was major-league drama between the group and myself because the group looked at me as being a sucker. They were like, "You're giving him four or five lives. It's more than just him, all of us have to roll with this and why is he trying to be a hero at everybody else's expense?" After that I told Griff not to say anything to the press until November, which was three months.

A lot of people say we kicked him out but it was more like he was bailing out. Not only was he bailing out, but bailing out and leaving grenades in the plane and taking the pins with him. At that time it was real rough doing the shows. I wasn't getting on the bus because the bus was crazy. That bus was hot. It was a silent bus. Everybody had on headphones. The whole bus was quiet.

We continued doing gigs. Griff was on suspension from talking to the press and he was following that rule—so I thought.

In October I did the Miami Music Awards, and Luke Skywalker and MC Hammer were there. Luke and Hammer were telling me about

> NOT ONLY WAS HE BAILING OUT, BUT BAILING OUT AND LEAVING GRENADES IN THE PLANE AND TAKING THE PINS WITH HIM.

some business opportunities they were developing. I was telling them I wanted to do some independent things but I was contractually locked in, so I suggested maybe Flavor could do something. Then I realized Flavor was also locked in with a vocal contract. Then I suggested that Griff could do an album. By then he had a name, good or bad, and could move some records. It was a good idea for Luke at the time and numbers were exchanged. With all the notoriety Griff had received, I was saying, "You can do your own album and still be within the group." Following that he got together with Luke and started recording cuts for his own album.

From October 1989 through February 1990 we were in the studio. In October I cut "Welcome to the Terrordome." We had the track, which was a raw James Brownish type of track that Keith had. I took two or three samples, which will go unnamed so they don't try and sue, and figured out how to cut through the noise. There was so much drama for me in September and October that one Friday night I jumped in my Bronco and took a drive to Allentown, Pennsylvania, where I knew some people. I listened to Chuck Chillout's show, played the track, and just started writing. I stayed out there and drove back the next morning and finished writing. I came back and we cut it in Greene Street Studios. I just let all the shit that had built up inside of me come out. "I got so much trouble on my mind, refuse to lose. Here's your ticket, here the drummer get wicked." That was some true shit. I just dropped everything I was feeling—Welcome to the Motherfucken Terrordome. You want to talk about drama? Welcome to the Terrordome was written during that period and I wanted to release it right then and there.

When we released it in November/December there was drama attached to it. The JDL, Jewish people, white people, everybody went through those lyrics with a fine-tooth comb. Inside the song I explain what happened: "Crucifixion ain't no fiction, so-called chosen frozen, apologies made to whoever pleases, still they got me like Jesus." Aw shit, drama again.

This time it had nothing to do with Griff, but when they came asking me about the lyrics I was dropping it, ducking, weaving,

FIGHT THE POWER
235

dropping it. The minister told me, "Be crafty about the way you deliver your words." It's just like boxing. You have to box with the media. You have to get your point across to explain what you're about. I was explaining the whole situation that went down. I wasn't saying I was Jesus. I was saying Jesus was a Black man who caught hell from a whole bunch of people that were misinformed. The song came out and made it to the news. The press made a big issue out of that.

We all played together at The World in New York on New Year's Eve. The place was packed. The first record we played when we came out was "Welcome to the Terrordome." The place went berserk. 1990—Welcome to the Terrordome. What does it mean? The 1990s are coming and if we as a people do the right thing we'll be all right. If we do the wrong thing, the Black situation is out of here by the end of the decade. The terrordome is the 1990s. People thought the terrordome was my brain. That was a metaphor that it could be compared to later on, but the terrordome is really the 1990s. I got the title from an article I saw in *Melody Maker* magazine called, "Welcome to the Terrordrome." I changed it to Terrordome—the house of the 1990s.

Around that time for various reasons, including legal reasons, I came up with the name the "Bomb Squad" because we were known for dropping bombs. The Bomb Squad was Hank, Eric, Keith, and me. We had tight dealings with MCA and were talking about taking three guys that were left over from another project and coming up with an album for them. The three happened to be Ricky Bell, Michael Bivens, and Ronnie Devoe, later to become Bell Biv DeVoe. Ralph Tresvant had been slated to do a solo album for years. Bobby Brown had left New Edition and blew up in 1988 and Johnny Gill had just been recruited to come in, but Johnny Gill had come off a solo career and could always go back to that. At MCA Hiriam Hicks, who was their

> THE TERRORDOME
> IS THE 1990S.
> PEOPLE THOUGHT
> THE TERRORDOME
> WAS MY BRAIN.

manager, and Lowell Silas, who was running the show, were like, "Yo, these kids were left out in the cold, can y'all come up with something for them." It was a task that Hank, Keith, Eric, and I took on to try to put some kind of Hip-Hop-flavored R&B shit down for them. Subsequently, what happened in the four weeks of December was the Bomb Squad knocked out a large piece of the production and arrangement on Bell Biv DeVoe's three-million selling album *Poison*.

In January we knocked out *Fear of a Black Planet* in four weeks, and we knocked out Ice Cube's album "AmeriKKKa's Most Wanted" in four to five weeks in February.

I first met Ice Cube from doing shows together during L.L.'s tour. We would be the group that would fill in some dates on L.L.'s tour to bring more people in. N.W.A would be that other group because "Straight Outta Compton" was ripping that year. Ice Cube, Easy E, Dre, Yella, and MC Ren were a five-man arrangement. When I saw their show I said, "That shit is amazing." I couldn't even explain it. They came onstage from different areas like a rotisserie.

I remember during the fall of 1989 I was doing a TV show hosted by Jesse Jackson with Quincy Jones, Ice-T, and me, and Ice Cube was there in the audience. After the show Cube was telling me he was having some problems with the N.W.A camp. He was like, "I got this platinum record hanging up on my wall and my moms is saying, 'You hanging that up on the wall, but Dre and them have houses.'" Cube said the drama started when he went to Easy E and told him he was going to get his own lawyer and accountant. He said, "You can't have your own lawyer and accountant, this is what happens here." I would give him little pieces of advice but I didn't want to get in the middle of that. I was still dealing with drama within my own camp. Cube called and said he wanted to stay with N.W.A and wanted to do a solo album too. So he went to the head distributor, which was Priority, and they granted him a solo deal. He asked Easy would he and Dre do the album and Easy told him he had to wait. Then Cube said, "I don't have to wait, if y'all can't do it, I'll get somebody else."

FIGHT THE POWER
237

Easy was like, "Who are you going to get?" Cube said, "I'm go-ing to have to get the Bomb Squad to do it. Hank and Chuck and them." He said Easy rolled his eyes like, "If you do that your shit might go gold." Cube was calling me up and I was like, "I'm not getting in the middle of that." I gave him some numbers of other producers to call. Cube would call me up and say, "Yeah, they're all right, but what are y'all doing?" I was like, "I have mad drama in my camp, right now we can't do it."

Ice Cube was coming back and forth to the East Coast looking at different producers, which is how he got down on the "Burn Hollywood Burn" song. We had just finished the BBD project and were in the middle of *Fear of a Black Planet*. Hank, Eric, Keith, and I were in the room and Cube told us what Easy had said to him about us. That's when Hank said, "Fuck it then, we'll do it. We'll do it, rock it, then throw it back and it will be the bomb." After completing *Fear of a Black Planet* we went right into *AmeriKKKa's Most Wanted*, which was a combination of myself, Eric Sadler, Keith Shocklee, Hank Shocklee, Ice Cube, Sir Jinx, and Paul Shabazz. On the fifth week I left for another tour over-seas. We went through a fourteen-week period, and did Bell Biv DeVoe, which turned out to be a number-one album. *Fear of a Black Planet*, which turned out to be a number-one album, and *AmeriKKKa's Most Wanted*, which also turned out to be a num-ber-one album. Three number-one albums completed in the span of fourteen weeks. That shit never got written about.

We lifted Griff's suspension in November and I was thinking everything was cool. Then a three-page article came out in *Spin* at the end of February called "The Repentant Professor."

We sat down amongst ourselves and decided we were not go-ing to go to the press and explain anything, it was nobody else's business. I sat down with Griff in England and I asked, "What's up with this article?" Griff said he had done the interview in Oc-tober. By that time he knew he had to leave because we had put him on press suspension and he wasn't supposed to talk to any press from September to November. That's why people think he

THAT WAS THE LAST SHOW BACK THEN WITH PUBLIC ENEMY AND PROFESSOR GRIFF—THE END OF AN ERA.

got fired a second time. That wasn't the case.

We were in Wimbley Arena during the DMC Music Awards presentation and Griff said, "Chuck, I'm just going to step down. I don't want to cause you any more problems." I didn't know what to say because I had given the situation nine lives. Personally, I didn't like the fact that my public image took a beat down trying to protect something where I could have said "Fuck it" from the jump. I wasn't spewing details out in the public, I was trying to protect situations from getting worse.

Griff stepped down. He received a small financial settlement and was off and flying with his own thing. We did a couple of other dates, then we said we would go back to London to play our last show. We played in London at the Brixton Academy. We lit that motherfucker up. If you were looking at that show you would have thought there was nothing wrong. All of us were in the right form that night: the S1Ws, Griff, Flavor, Terminator X, and myself. We tore that show up. That was the last show back then with Public Enemy and Professor Griff—the end of an era.

CAN'T UNDERSTAND WHY A MAN
GOTTA USE A TRIGGA
ON HIS OWN, SUPPOSE TO ACT
GROWN
CRACKA IN DA BACK
WATCH A BROTHER PULL A TRIGGA ON
ANOTHER BROTHER
—"So Whatcha Gonna Do Now?"

GANGS

I first heard about the Crips and Bloods and the problem with gangs in Los Angeles back in 1985. I remember when Dre, from Long Island, and his group Original Concept came out with a record called "Knowledge Me." In the record there's a line that says, "Yo, cuz." When Dre came back to the radio station (WBAU) after doing a show in L.A. he told me how much the people in Los Angeles loved that record. He said it was like some kind of gang anthem. They would go off whenever they heard the word "Cuz," which on the West Coast has a totally different meaning than on the East Coast. We came to find out later that calling someone "Cuz," was the equivalent to calling them a Crip.

Back in those days I thought that L.A. was just about the *Soul Train*

dancers, palm trees, and blue skies. I looked at *Starsky and Hutch* and they would say "filmed on location in Los Angeles," and I would see Huggy Bear and thought that's how brothers in L.A. were living. I never knew that L.A. had much drama. Then in 1986 during Run-DMC's Raising Hell tour in Long Beach, California, some gang members started gang-banging at the show and that was the first time the gangs in Southern California became national news.

We first went to L.A. in 1987. We were playing on the Def Jam tour in the Los Angeles Sports Arena with L.L. Cool J, Whodini, Doug E Fresh, Stetsasonic, and Eric B. and Rakim. It was one of the first gigs we participated in that used metal detectors. It was also the first time I met Ice-T and Afrika Islam. Ice was driving the same Porsche that he was driving on the cover of his *Rhyme Pays* album. I spoke with Ice for a while, then he said, "Yo, we're about to get up out of here 'cause some shit is going to break off in a minute. We're out of here. I'll catch y'all."

We went back into the Sports Arena and I noticed while performing that the Sports Arena was only half full, when there was definitely a full crowd on the outside. Later on I heard that there were some incidents that took place on the outside, and I realized, "Yo, this is for real."

One thing about Public Enemy, when we went to L.A. we brought along a message. When we went into L.A. we played at World on Wheels, which is a skating rink in a heavy Crip hood. One time we played at Skateland, which was deep in the middle of a Blood hood. If we played World on Wheels we had to play Skateland because no Bloods were going to come over to World on Wheels, and vice versa. One time when we played World on Wheels, DJ Pooh and Bobcat were rolling with us in the limo. I remember Pooh saying, "I have a neutral thing going on out here because they know I do music, but I'm not going in there. I'm out of here." We would go in the skating rinks and as part of the show I'd say, "This is our color, black. We love y'all." Back then they mostly identified themselves as Bloods, Crips, or Cuz. So the way we came off was shocking, informational and educational at the same time. And they loved it. We could feel the warmth from the community that wasn't down with the bullshit.

All of a sudden Public Enemy had cut through the L.A. barrier. It helped that we had some roughshod records: "My Uzi Weighs a Ton," "Riot Starter," and "My 98," which talked about cars. We were able to relate to Los Angeles more than the average group out of New York because we were from Long Island. On Long Island we drove cars and L.A. had car clubs. We would roll in big groups, we were the first group that actually had six members. We looked like a gang, and we appealed to that mind-set but we tried to take that mind-set to another level.

When I would go to the radio station out there, which at that time was one of the most influential radio stations ever in Rap, KDAY, with DJ Greg Mack and J. J. Johnson, it always came down to, "Yo, Chuck, say something." Especially when "Rebel without a Pause" got hot all the way up to "Fight the Power." Right after "Fight the Power" KDAY shut down. I always gave them an outside, older point of view like, "Hey, we come from New York, y'all don't know how privileged you are just to have seventy-five-degree weather in January. Where I come from we don't have gangs because it's too cold." I would always give a worst-case scenario of the East Coast. "It's cold, people can't find shit to eat, they're not thinking about ganging up because they have real life to worry about." KDAY was a station that was community oriented and through the process of Rap let people know that there were positive options.

We would hear of problems that groups would have going into Southern California. One time in 1986 we heard that Grandmaster D from Whodini was hanging out in a Crip area with a red sweatsuit on and somebody stepped up to him who didn't know who he was. The guy threw up some gang signs that he didn't pick up. Somebody stepped in and said, "That's Grandmaster D." The guy said, "I don't give a fuck who he is, he'd better change something with all that red he's wearing." Of course these stories got back around so everybody knew that when going into L.A. you'd better wear black. We were wearing black

anyway, but straight up, you better believe that when I went to L.A. I was wearing more black than ever.

On the *Muse Sick-N-Hour Mess Age* album I was inspired by the concern for, and benefit of, my brothers out there killing themselves in gang violence to write the song "So Whatcha Gonna Do Now?," which I consider a love song of sorts. The Bloods and Crips out of Los Angeles and the whole Southern California region have roots going back to the Black Panthers; in Chicago, the Black P Stone Nation, the Black Gangster Disciples, and the Vice Lords have roots going back to Noble Drew Ali and the Moorish Science Temples and parts of Islamic teachings. Those are some complex situations because they are two, three, sometimes four genera-

> THEY'RE NOT LISTENING TO THEIR PARENTS, THEY'RE NOT LISTENING TO THEIR TEACHERS, THEY'RE NOT LISTENING TO PREACHERS, AND THEY CERTAINLY ARE NOT TRYING TO HEAR WHAT ANYONE FROM THE "CRIMINAL JUSTICE" SYSTEM HAS TO SAY.

tions old and have now escalated to the point where they're about vendettas and forgiveness, and finding that balance.

I speak at thirty-five colleges a year and I speak at many high schools, both Black and white. In speaking to young people in cities around the country, hard-core gang bangers in many instances communicate best with others who are older than them who have gang-banged. They're not listening to their parents, they're not listening to their teachers, they're not listening to preachers, and they certainly are not trying to hear what anyone from the "criminal justice" system has to say. One comment that really stands out from a revealing book about gang life and how some of the brothers have changed their lives for the positive—*Uprising: Crips and Bloods Tell the Story of America's Youth in Crossfire*—was made by a brother who is now R.I.P., but who left some words for brothers in gangs to think deeply about. General Robert Lee, who had gang-banged since the late 1960s, was shot by a Crip, and lived in a wheelchair for over twenty years, shared his thoughts and offered a solution to the senseless gang violence: "The police beat us and kill us all the time, but we can still tolerate to see them every day without shooting at them. Yet once we see that blue rag or that red rag, we think that we have to kill somebody? You're looking at people whose families raped our ancestors, killed them, and hung them up by the testicles, tarred and feathered them. . . . Now if we can forgive and walk around people like that every day, then we ought to be able to forgive each other easily. I don't know one brother that has skinned another brother alive, put salt on him, boiled him in oil, and killed him. I don't know any brother that has done another brother like that. White people have done us like that a lot, and we forgive them. So if we can forgive things like that, then we sure can forgive a brother for shooting another brother who really didn't even mean it. . . . We've got to forgive each other, we've got to let everything go." I agree.

The gang problem is not just in L.A., Chicago, or New York. The gang *problem* is in the middle of those major cities that you rarely ever hear of: Little Rock, Arkansas; Houston, Texas; Jackson, Mississippi; Birmingham, Alabama; Memphis, Tennessee; Louisville, Kentucky; Indianapolis, Indiana; and many others. They're heavily influenced by the news media coming from the bigger cities. The copycat gangsterism occurs in places like Kansas City, which is the wildest situation that you ever want to confront because in Kansas City you have people that have become Crips and Bloods from just choosing sides after seeing the movie *Colors*.

In the beginning of our career we used to go down to Nashville, Tennessee, and it used to be strictly Nashville. And we would go to Austin, Texas, and it would be strictly Austin, and other parts of the country had their own style and identity, but now since Black life has been so popularized and mass produced through the mainstream media, especially television and videos,

a lot of kids want to act in a similar manner, look the same, and talk the same way. If they hear somebody from Philadelphia say they're going to "gaffle somebody up," or they hear somebody from New York say, "you know what I'm saying," a hundred times in their vocabulary, they will imitate that and that's when a new style starts to pop up everywhere. So where something was considered "country," laid-back, and reserved to itself, soon it becomes a national issue.

Youth crime, guns, and gang violence are now national issues. The more they get covered and interpreted on the news and in the media and also glorified in films, videos, and records, the bigger they become. You have people over in Germany throwing up gang signs because they're impressed by the culture of it. If you speak with someone who is eight, nine, or ten years old who is highly impressionable—and peer pressure is stronger than it's ever been at that age—you have a lot of deprogramming to do.

I started to see remnants of gangs taking off in other cities after the movie *Colors*. After *Colors* and a lot of West Coast Rap started coming out, young people from other areas started looking into the world of Rap for more information. And youngsters, no matter who they are, are impressionable. If someone is projected through television or videos they're looked upon in a greater light, even if they're talking about the reality in their own neighborhood.

I don't think it stems from migration either, because one person leaving L.A. is not going to make big, big changes in a city. Somebody that's strong and powerful enough can convince and show people a particular type of game, but each city has its own thing going on. I can't see a person coming into another city and just taking over. That's some far-fetched shit. By 1990, 1991, I started seeing people in different areas, whether they were from L.A. or not, taking on Crip and Blood titles because it was a so-called exciting, young, impressionable thing to do with no accountability. It was the dark side of a culture. People in other cities were taking on gang names that they didn't even know the original meanings of because the lifestyle was being projected through the movies, videos, and music.

The problem is when you see fourteen- and fifteen-year-olds with no historical reference whatsoever who get into it for the trendiness of it. I decided to confront the issue of the "coolness" of gangs because I thought it was getting silly. The silliest aspect to me was in the music that they consider "gangster Rap" and its glorification in videos and in the news as being a phenomenon for white folks' entertainment, while real brothers were killing each other all over the map.

Gangsta Rap

Stylin' now its gold plated medallions
I didn't know under fros
We got so many black Italians
—"Generation Wrekkked"

Black people have been murdered ever since we stepped off the boat in America. The murder or destruction of a Black mind, body, and soul goes right along with the American program. The murder of Black people has been packaged, marketed, sold, and accepted to be an effective strategy in the implementation of our genocide while large corporations and the government benefit off of our demise.

The terms of Rap music aren't clearly defined. Gangsta Rap is one phase and segment of Rap, which has many segments. People ask, "What is Rap?" Rap is a vocal over music. It's a vocal style. Asking if Rap will disappear or play out is like asking, "Will singing records ever stop?" It's a vocal application that started back in the days as overdub by Jamaican toasters who would grab the microphone and rhythmically speak in their patois lingo over reggae dub beats. Guys like Kool Herc would be up in the Bronx with his Caribbean Brooklyn style of DJ'ing, and he had guys with him who were straight American and these

FIGHT THE POWER
247

CHUCK D
248

> GANGSTA RAP IS A LEGITIMATE POSITION BECAUSE IT TALKS ABOUT CERTAIN ASPECTS OF LIFE.

guys would MC over the instrumental breaks of different types of records. Therefore, the technique was similar but the records were different, which developed into the early stages of Rap. The music is already defined. You can Rap over rock like Run-DMC or a Rage Against the Machine has proven, you can Rap over jazz like Gang Starr or A Tribe Called Quest has proven, you can Rap over funk like Snoop Dogg, Ice Cube, Too Short, and other West Coast artists have done, you can Rap over soul, blues, blends, or hybrids of any of the two, like the Fugees are currently proving to the world.

Rap music is a formula. Hip-Hop is a subculture of Black culture. It's another term for Black creativity. We've been a creative people for thousands and thousands of years but the creativity of the last twenty-five years could be called Hip-Hop. We'll always be a creative people and new creation will generate another term. Rap music is here to stay because it's vocal over music, and as the music changes the vocals can remain the same because it's one of the few live vocal styles ever used for recording music. It's actually a vocal style that runs parallel to singing. That's its advantage.

Gangsta Rap and political Rap are terms and categories that are not bad. It's like a baseball team with different players. Someone will play first base, someone will play second base, and someone will play shortstop. These are just positions. Gangsta Rap is a legitimate position because it talks about certain aspects of life.

The term "Gangsta Rap" was first coined by N.W.A who had a song called "Gangsta, Gangsta," which dealt with the reflections of gang life in L.A. The first hard-core gangland-style rhymes I know of actually come from Philly with Schoolly D and his "PSK What Does It Mean?" and of course the "OG" of Gangsta Rap, Iceberg (Ice-T). Some artists call it "reality Rap." Gangsta rhymes do have a legitimate reflection. They talk about certain realities of street life. One of the best writers of our time, Ice Cube, was very clear in explaining aspects of that life early on.

I tell hard-core and Gangsta Rappers that they can say what they want to say in song, but can they also walk the walk, go into the jail systems, and talk to some youngsters, or go into different communities and offer ideas and solutions to help fix certain situations. Don't cop out and say, "I just say it the way it is. I'm out to make the money." You're making the money on someone else's back. Most recording artists that have records aren't gangsters. Most Black "gangsters" that consider themselves gangsters aren't really gangsters.

Should Gangsta Rap be scrutinized by society, scapegoated, picked on, and censored? I don't believe a story shouldn't be told. I believe every story should be told. As a matter of fact, I see Gangsta Rap as potentially being a plea for help, expressing a viewpoint that doesn't get represented by the mainstream. Certain aspects of it should be commended for being informative and, until the problems in the poorer communities get fixed, certain elements of what's termed "Gangsta Rap" will not disappear.

If artists like Spice 1, MC Eiht, or Tupac are highlighted in times of trouble, then artists like A Tribe Called Quest, De La Soul, or Common Sense should also be projected. There is an imbalance in the projection. A lot of times when the mainstream media projects the problem areas, they make the problem areas appear to be bigger than life. They'll project problem areas on the cover of *Newsweek, USA Today,* on the news, and the exposure makes the artists and the art form take a rebellious stance. Then more people gravitate to it because it's perceived as being rebellious, even if at the same time it's self-destructive. Since we don't have control of our own Rap stations or the interpretations that come out of major magazines, the problem areas get magnified more than anything else. Then people say, "I see this is a problem, I heard about it, my moms heard about it, let me check it out for myself." I believe the mainstream exposure of the problem areas and the rebelliousness involved have led to greater interest and sales for that

genre. Gangsta Rap has been propelled into a fashion statement.

There were no major movements to censor and shut the music down when it was perceived as being confined to the Black community, but when it started to reach white kids in the suburbs it became a politically viable issue to address. That's when the alarm was rung.

There's never been a time where we've had as many Black voices yell and speak out like we're hearing now, and be so popular. Angry Black voices. That's Rap music. Previously there was the voice of discontent and rage being expressed through rock music, but many of those voices were from young whites protesting against the condition of society at that time. Rap is angry Black voices yelling and speaking out and being heard, and sometimes followed by Black and white kids around the world. Censorship and the attacks on Rap are an attempt to nip that in the bud. In this country, the Black man has never been allowed to be vocal about any situation. What you have now is like three hundred Malcolm X's, although twisted in a sea of chaos and disorder, but they're all yelling and screaming and not only being heard but they're being followed.

The problem is without control over our own environment and our reality there develops a blur between fantasy and reality. It's a serious situation when art not only imitates life, but life imitates art. When that takes place, you have art that dictates as well as reflects.

If we want to keep it real, it's hard as hell for a Black person to be a *real* gangster. We can play with the image of being a gang-

> PREVIOUSLY THERE WAS THE VOICE OF DISCONTENT AND RAGE BEING EXPRESSED THROUGH ROCK MUSIC, BUT MANY OF THOSE VOICES WERE FROM YOUNG WHITES PROTESTING AGAINST THE CONDITION OF SOCIETY AT THAT TIME.

ster or a player but we're not players and we're not gangsters. It's like when kids play "house" or "cops and robbers." Black adults are playing games. A gangster is somebody that can commit a crime, influence the law, and get away with it. That is what's called corruption: defined as "a mechanism used to nullify and to immunize groups from law enforcement, and to gain an edge in the competition for markets and contacts." Black people are definitely not a group immunized from law enforcement. They have not ever had that power in this country. The top Black "gangsters" in the forties, fifties, and sixties, like "Bumpy" Johnson in Harlem, all the way up through the seventies, and eighties, like New York's Leroy "Nicky" Barnes and Frank Matthews, all got hemmed up by the system. There may have been some individual, temporary victories, but they were short-term like a motherfucker. No one Black has ever won in that game in America. With the vigor that the U.S. prosecutors have been going after the Mafia throughout the U.S.—as witnessed in the murder and racketeering trials of John Gotti, the boss of the reputed Gambino crime family, one of the most powerful Mafia organizations in the United States—you know Black organized crime will be next. President Bill Clinton said it with his recent statements: "The message today to the Bloods, the Crips, to every criminal gang preying on the innocent is clear: We mean to put you out of business, to break the backs of your organization, to stop you from terrorizing our neighborhoods and our children, to put you away for a very long time. We have just begun the job and we do not intend to stop until we have finished." The new initiative, which they've named the "Anti-Gang and Youth Crime Control Act of 1996," makes it easier for the youth who commit violent acts to be charged and sentenced as adults and toughens the penalties for the possession and use of firearms.

One of the things that I find really offensive that's taking place right about now is the trend for people in the Rap world to criticize Reverend Calvin Butts and C. Delores Tucker for their positions on demeaning and derogatory lyrics. I feel these people have points. I was on the *Today* show with C. Delores Tucker and

we agreed on seventy percent of the issues because we're both concerned individuals trying to fix a problem.

C. Delores Tucker attacks the companies. Calvin Butts attacks the companies. They're not just attacking the artists and young Black people. The ones who are ducking and dodging their attacks are Time Warner, BMG, Polygram, Thorn EMI, Sony Music, Tower Records. Tucker and Butts are being protective of the community that they work in every day. They realize the companies are going to make two hundred to three hundred million dollars off of young people just saying anything and benefit off of our community across the board. They're stepping up right in the middle of the mix. They're demanding that the companies deal straight up with them because they care about the community. The last thing I expect to see is somebody within a company objecting to Tucker and Butts, talking some shit about, "They're fucking with me. I got to get paid." That's usually the ignorance that signifies a house nigger of the highest degree.

One day I was talking to an executive at Interscope Records who at the time was being attacked and shell-shocked by C. Delores Tucker. He was telling me he had hired a special investigative agent to spy on C. Delores Tucker so he could win a case against her and get her off of his back. I told him face-to-face, "I don't know about all that spying shit. You're white, she's Black. She has more in common with me than you. She could be my aunt. The way you get her off of your back is by being nice to her and saying something like, 'Excuse me, Ms. Tucker, what can I do to take care of your problem? I understand we're in a serious situation. What can we do to help take care of it?' " Instead he's trying to be confrontational.

I don't care who it is, if it comes down to an older Black person, there's not a white business person on the planet who can speak to me about attacking an older Black person who's trying to look out for the community in his or her own way.

What record companies do is take artists that don't know shit and make them fanatical about different movements. For example, bootlegging. They get artists mad at the bootleggers when artists should be mad at the fucking record companies that take eighty percent or more of their revenues. Those are the motherfuckers who should have the tables turned on them. The artist is the one sweatin, "bustin" his or her ass, and kissin ass to sign a contract, and the labels are able to divert the anger to a bootlegger. Black artists should take up bootlegging. I see a lot of young artists talk about bootlegging and not talk about anything in the business. They talk about bootlegging like it's a big, big issue because the majors are talking about losing money. That was the conversation in 1990, 1991, 1992. "Aw man, the bootleggers are cutting into our shit." No man, the record labels are cutting into your shit. That's the problem. I also wonder if the record companies are involved somehow with bootleggers since you need a good master to mass produce CDs and cassettes.

Today the artists are saying, "Yo man, Calvin Butts and C. Delores Tucker are trying to stop us from doing what we're doing." These are usually white people dictating to uninformed Black artists who are twenty or twenty-one years old and are just fanatical about a situation because the company says, "Hey look, they're coming after your money." No, no, no, the first ones that need to open up their wallets a little bit more are the companies.

I tell artists all the time, you're attacking the people who are in the community every day. Regardless of what you say about "Yo man, I don't see them." There's fifty states out there, there's fifty-five major cities. They're out there somewhere doing something.

The more rappers do the negative aspect of Rap music, what will happen is the school systems won't let Rap in the schools, the towns won't let rappers come to any event, and there'll be a problem between the Rap community and the people who actually govern the area. That's where we're trying to make a difference.

Once upon a time people thought the message of Public Enemy was racist. Now after seeing the real facts of what we're about and seeing the alternatives that are out there, people are looking at us like, "Public Enemy can't be that bad because what they're trying to do is teach their people pride and teach their people about their own facts, so that's not as bad as saying, 'Go get an

FIGHT THE POWER

AK and spray up the whole spot.' " We look like the good guys in today's scene, whereas in the beginning we were so radical that we looked like the bad guys but really we were good for our people. In fact, we are good for everybody because white kids needed to know more about Black people, because they weren't learning about Black people from their parents and they weren't learning from the school systems. We show the youth that we are real, and if you do what the television shows you will suffer the pain for real. If you see an artist do a drive-by in a video they get a chance to do another video but if that happens in real life the person dies.

Right now Rap is being used in a way that's negative to the existence of Black people. Jails are being built and they're being filled with nothing but more and more Black people. Black youth under the age of twenty-one are dying at a rapid rate from shooting each other. I mean at the ages of nine, ten, eleven, just shooting each other trying to emulate what they see on TV and some videos. A brother named Twilight, another voice in the book *Uprising: Crips and Bloods Tell the Story of America's Youth in Crossfire,* explained it this way; "Sit back and look at this world we live in. Look at society. I grew up watching *The Rifleman.* If the Rifleman had a problem he grabbed his rifle, right? If I had a problem I grabbed my gun. Not only that, look at all of the movies, if you go into any house where you have a large group of young men, guaranteed you will find these movies: *The Terminator, King of New York, Scarface,* most definitely *The Godfather* and *Mobsters.* . . . The media plays a major role in all of the killings. . . . If America has a problem, what do they do? They blow up the country that they have a problem with and everything is cool." This whole gangster kick, you have to ask, where does it benefit us? The sad truth is—it doesn't.

POSITIVE RAP

LISTEN FOR LESSONS I'M SAYING INSIDE MUSIC
THAT THE CRITICS ARE BLASTING ME FOR
THEY'LL NEVER CARE FOR THE BROTHERS AND SISTERS
NOW ACROSS THE COUNTRY HAS US UP FOR THE WAR.
—"Bring the Noise"

When I grew up there were people that used to have a lot of fly gear but I was one who didn't give a fuck about wearing fly gear. That's a way that people get caught up in dumb shit. Someone says, "Yo, take a hit, smoke this joint." Are you going to bow to peer pressure? There's peer pressure in the music business. You have people that say, "Damn, I'd better do that in order for me to sell records." Those are the same assholes who, when they were in high school and somebody said, "Yo man, hit some of this coke," would do it figuring, "If I hit this coke they'll love me." Those are the same people that would go to the bridge and jump because the first three people jumped off the bridge. People do stupid shit just to get props from their friends. If you're going to do something for props, try to get props from someone that has something that can help you get where you want to go. Those props are the only ones that count. Peer pressure is tough, but don't worry about someone laughing at you if you're in the eighth grade and they are all sitting in the same classroom right next to you. They are no better than you. So what if other people have fly clothes on, their parents buy them that, that still doesn't make them better than you. Just be yourself and be original. Material items do not make a person better. That's ridiculous.

> WE HAVE TO BE INVENTIVE IN OUR OWN MINDS BUT WE ALSO HAVE TO BE REALISTIC.

We have to be inventive in our own minds but we also have to be realistic. I'm inventive but I'm also realistic. I don't totally submit myself to do what someone else thinks I

RAP IS THE CNN
FOR YOUNG PEOPLE
ALL OVER THE
WORLD.

should do. I'm not here for that. I don't care about that, never did. I stand by what I believe. Public Enemy has a rule amongst ourselves. We say, "None of these people were our friends before we got into this, so it really doesn't matter if any of them are our friends when we leave." It doesn't matter. If you build a friendship along the way and it's solid based on mutual respect, that's proper. Like me and Ice-T. I didn't know Ice before our careers led us to meet each other, but we're straight. We respect each other's principles and beliefs. We've become friends through this. Anybody that just knows *of* you and tries to make a judgment and a determination without *knowing you,* gets no respect.

When Public Enemy first came out we used to say, "Public Enemy, we're agents for the preservation of the Black mind. We're media hijackers." We worked to hijack the media and put it in our own form. That's originally how we came out. Initially Rap was America's informal CNN because when Rap records came out somebody from far away could listen to a Rap record because it uses so many descriptive words and get a visual picture from what was being said. So a person that was coming up in Oakland would listen to a record from New York and get a visualization of what New York was about. When rappers came out from Oakland and Los Angeles and they were very visual with their words, people all over could get informed about Black life in those areas without checking the news. Everytime we checked for ourselves on the news they were locking us up anyway, so the interpretation coming from Rap was a lot clearer. That's why I call Rap the Black CNN.

Rap is now a worldwide phenomenon. Rap is the CNN for young people all over the world because now you can hear from rappers in Croatia and find out what they talk about and how they're feeling. Rappers from Italy, rappers from Africa. Rap has become an unofficial network of the young mentality. It just has to be directed a lot better than it has.

While in Italy in 1994 I met a mother and son from South

Africa who were fans of ours and shared some of their thoughts about Rap music and our group. The son is striving to be a Rap artist and his mother has supported him with one condition—don't sell out his people. She turned to me and expressed her feeling about Public Enemy. "Public Enemy has mobilized the minds of the youth to turn against the evil things that destroy their lives. . . . Public Enemy has brought hope to those young people who have given up hope in their lives to forget their misery. Public Enemy has helped those people reexamine their lives and their roles in society. In South Africa I was so moved and touched to see little kids in the slums, with ragged clothes, running around the streets imitating Public Enemy. Then I saw on some of the shacks PE written in big letters. We have a hard struggle and people are always out to destroy us by selling us out and destroying our kids' lives, and Public Enemy is in the forefront of fighting this evil that is destroying our children. To me you can't wish for any other message that can save a nation and the world." I hope and pray that we will continue to be able to have that kind of positive impact on lives through Rap music.

Our initial direction as Public Enemy was to market nationalism. I knew that people in music liked trends. Our concept was to wear African leather medallions or something other than gold because people were getting their heads taken off for gold back then. Your brain is more important than what you wear around your neck. The information you can store and how you can build a business or organization is more important than anything you can buy. When you buy something, you're buying it from someone that's selling it. The importance of a BMW seller is more important than a BMW owner. Big deal, you have a car, they make cars for you to buy. Big deal, you have a gold chain around your neck, someone is making those chains for you to buy. Become the producer and manufacturer, not just the consumer. We were saying that a gold brain is more important than a gold chain. A BMW brain is more important than a BMW.

We knew that if our people were going to be trendy we could at least make it trendy to have them learn about themselves and

their history. In the current Hip-Hop climate to say you are "pro-Black and positive" may not be the trend, but the information and feeling we passed on through our music are still with those who listened to it because people will go back to using it later on in their lives. They may get blunted and drink 40s for the time being but you can't be intelligent and throw it all to the side. It's in you, it's in your soul. You may ignore it for a little while but as you have more difficulty in life you'll get back to it. It's just a matter of time. It may not come from me, it could be KRS One, Eric B. and Rakim, Goodie Mob, something that you read, your parents, all of those influences can inspire you to manifest and use the information for yourself throughout the course of your life. It might not be today or tomorrow, it might be fifteen years from now. The key thing is what we said they will never be able to get rid of. Everybody has their experiences transferred in them, especially the experience of intelligence, and that's what we tried to sell—intelligence.

In my records I try to counterattack situations with my videos and songs. It might seem out of step and out of style, but the bottom line is I wouldn't sell out my people to glorify their death, to make money off of them not knowing that we're caught up in a genocidal war. There's a saying, "He who controls the culture, controls the people." Right now our culture is not being controlled by us and certain aspects of our culture are being magnified in a nonproductive way.

People call Hip-Hop a culture. Hip-Hop is a subculture. Black people's *culture* is culture. Our whole existence is culture. Kwame Toure once said to me, "Hip-Hop borrows from Black people's culture. You're able to do Hip-Hop because there were people that contributed to Black culture, which allowed you to do Hip-Hop. So since you're doing Hip-Hop, you should only do Hip-Hop for one reason: to excel in it and put back in your culture to progress your people. If you don't do that, it's self-defeating, it's nonprogressive."

One of the biggest tricks that's happening right now is our culture is being used to destroy us as a people because the negative aspects of it are being honed upon and magnified to the point where people think it's all entertainment. The killing of Black people is entertainment? It's a programmed mind game that Black people are losing.

I was always realistic in realizing that music as a communication tool is nothing new. We may be one of the groups that chooses to use Rap as a vehicle to hijack the media and give an interpretation of ourselves. At the same time there is more power on the other end pushing garbage back the other way. Rap music is like a pipeline. With a pipeline you can have the flow going either way. Anything can be pushed through that pipeline and that's what has happened in recent years. It's like we helped push the door down and now everything is coming through. We can't help it that we played a part in pushing the door down and we came through with a fully cooked meal, and most everybody else is coming through with McDonald's and other shit. The negative is reinforced in the Black community from the outside and from the inside. From the inside we were taught to hate ourselves so the negative is definitely always more attractive. We're trained and programmed to be attracted to hate ourselves.

In order to combat the negative image currently being attached to Hip-Hop and to propel the art form forward, I am starting an organization called REACH. REACH stands for Rappers Educating All Curriculum Through Hip-Hop. It's an organization that will intersperse Rap artists who are highly influential among younger people to speak in the school systems and to community-based organizations and programs. There will be a training course for the artists on how to conduct themselves in public speaking situations. If a program like this is not initiated, the negative stigma attached to Rap will be such a burden that rappers will not be able to go anywhere and the public scrutiny of Rap and rappers will be at an all-time high

FIGHT THE POWER

based on the projection of the negative. REACH is a protection as well as a building device to bring young people up.

Right now the educational system in the United States has come to a point where they've given up on ways of trying to cut through to today's "Generation X" mind-set. You have educators that are scared of the students, scared of Black children, and are just throwing their hands up. The curriculum is outdated. It's a 1954 school curriculum. That's not to say that the basics are unnecessary, of course they're necessary, but they have to be brought across in a clear way. Heads are more distracted. We're in an age of technology. A child in the 1950s, 1960s, and 1970s would have to negotiate with their parents to actually pick up other information and entertainment, like buying records. When I bought a record at twelve or thirteen I had to negotiate with my moms to hear it. Technology has allowed a child to have a Walkman, get a tape from anywhere, lock themselves in a room, and just inform themselves on a lot of different things. Now we're talking about the Internet Age, we're talking about television with one hundred channels. A child's mind can be distracted in many different ways.

REACH is a program that recognizes the people that the youth are looking at, who they idolize, and actually brings the artists into the communities in a lecture program or assembly program that goes around to different spots in the United States.

We'll approach the record companies who are benefiting off of the community and give them a chance to contribute to a program that will serve as a positive community service, which will also

> RIGHT NOW THE EDUCATIONAL SYSTEM IN THE UNITED STATES HAS COME TO A POINT WHERE THEY'VE GIVEN UP ON WAYS OF TRYING TO CUT THROUGH TODAY'S "GENERATION X" MIND-SET.

benefit them in the long run. It's almost an artist development situation that helps the record companies. The record companies in Rap music are running out of avenues. They're running out of options because of the stigma against Rap music. REACH is similar to PLAY (Participate in the Lives of America's Youth) by Nike, and the "Stay in School" program initiated by the NBA. In the late 1970s, the NBA was going through a tough time when the players, although they were multifaceted and talented, were considered as being a whole bunch of "Afro-wearing, drug-taking, gold-wearing junkies." Then all of a sudden a structure came about that helped to change that image and say, "these people are really fantastic, play a wonderful game, and are a benefit to society." REACH is hoping to be a factor in changing the direction that Rap is going in and changing the image that has been attached to it.

The cigarette industry sells billions and billions of cigarettes around the world, which have been proven to kill people. They give you a sign on the side of the cigarette box that tells you that cigarettes are hazardous to your health. At the same time if you talk about how damaging the cigarette industry has been they end up telling you how many foundations they have, the donations that they've made to different causes, and they'll end up spending so much time talking about all of the great things that they do for society, you'll forget that the bottom line is they kill people. But people don't talk about the cigarette industry as much as they talk about Rap. The talk about Rap is derogatory, "it kills people." That's not true. It's an art form that needs its positive aspects brought out. What better way than using the method of communication for education.

I'm involved with MusicCares and NARAS (National Academy of Recording Arts and Sciences), and Michael Green, who is the head of that organization, has been very open-minded about our concerns on the caretaking of Rap music and taking it to the next level. Hopefully, we can be connected to a lot of the benefit areas that NARAS does for the rock community and do some of those

things for the Hip-Hop community through REACH. Look out for REACH in the school and community center nearest you to be in full effect soon and when you hear about it reach back out and support it.

EPILOGUE

In the midst of the Nation of Islam Headquarters Palace were
the formation and foundation of a movement responding to a
crisis. The murder of Christopher Wallace, aka the Notorious
B.I.G., aka Biggie Smalls, had just taken place two weeks prior
in Los Angeles. Coupled with the Las Vegas shooting death of Tupac Shakur eight months earlier, an alarm had been set off within
the Hip-Hop Nation. Emergency. How do we save our shit?

This meeting was called together to air concerns and clear
beefs that some rappers were having within our own community.
The gathering was stellar: Snoop Doggy Dogg, Russell Simmons,
Willie D from the Geto Boys, Doug Fresh, Common Sense, Bone
from Bonz Thugs N Harmony, Keith Clinkscales from Vibe just to
name a few. Issues were addressed and mixed with analysis,
foresight, and emotion. Minister Farrakhan and the Nation of Islam served as perfect arbitrators and drew respect from the heads
of Hip-Hop. Yes, the need to organize was immediate for the survival of the industry being attacked from outside and within. I was
thrilled to be a part of, as well as a witness to, the event. What
was said inside shall remain confidential but afterward a
spokesperson spoke our piece to the press quite sharply with attitude, intelligence, and wit.

The press gathering at Restaurant Salaam was smaller than it should've been. To many it brought home the truth about Hip-Hop's interpretation by the media and validated much of what is stated in this book. Positive Black images and events are not projected as much as niggativity in this society. Willie D, who spoke for the rappers from the mid-South, told the press to roll up their sleeves and work to write about this positive event. With this organized atmosphere I was beginning to believe that this was the start of a true union. This was great and temporarily a load off my Black shoulders.

Since January 1995, embarking on a new business partnership with Walter Leaphart (a hardworking, mover-and-shaker visionary brother from Chi-town based in L.A.), I temporarily deemphasized my full-time artist profile to create structure for Hip-Hop and rebuild a frame to the Rap game. Admittedly, I remain envious of the organization and marketing of the NBA and major-league sports, so my anger and bitterness are not based on the so-called decline of my artistry (which was intentional) but at the lack of passion, protection, and Black upper involvement in the Rap game.

The industry talk of Black and white not being an issue but green being the force between is bullshit when you witness the color ratio of control. As long as this one-sided projection continues to exploit niggativity, I will continue to term the master corporations the "White Boys."

Recently the 1996 source Magalive listed the thirty power brokers of Rap Hip-Hop, and although forty-five percent were Black movers and shakers, the momentum of the nonBlack industry people (fifty-five percent in services, ownership, and commodities) showed white mainstream control of the art form. The ratio wouldn't be as alarming if not for the artistry being ninety-five percent Black. Tipping of the scales is necessary especially when the combined assets of Sugarhill Gang, Grandmaster Flash, Whodini, and Run-DMC probably don't compare to Steven Rifkin of Loud Records. Without profit sharing and with the current state of contracts, that is a problem for me. In 1995, my then-accountant told me that my concentration should be as an artist and that it would be difficult for the public to accept me as anything else. Bullshit. I considered this bowing down to an insane level of nigger shit, whereas the white boys make, take, and become anything they want. I saw this as a prime opportunity to become a spokesperson and advocate fighter for this art form to keep the culture bandits in check. I embarked on the scene to become Hip-Hop's David Stern. A five-year plan began in 1995 till the year 2000. Began in effect. My recording commitment expanded past Def Jam in 1995 with my underground label Slam Jamz at Sony and a solo deal with Mercury Recordings. Between Public Enemy albums, growing philosophical problems with Russell Simmons and Lyor Cohen forced the issue that I should have the right to record as a soloist anywhere. Talks with such luminaries as Babyface and La Reid of LA Face Records, John McClain, Jimmy Iovine of Interscope, Steve Ralbovsky of Arista, and Jeff Ayeroff and Jordan Harris of the Sony Workgroup were respectful and candid, indeed. However, I settled into a deal with Danny Goldberg who'd just headed up Mercury Records. Although I respect Danny for his commitment to the freedom of music, I was apprehensive about working within the Polygram system. Again, conversations were quite frank about my feelings for Def Jam. Danny Goldberg had a quality I hadn't seen in many head execs other than Don Jenner at Columbia and that was a major reason for going back to Polygram. Although Def Jam eventually reared their monster head and created chaos, it was a rewarding artistic experience. *Autobiography of Mistachuck* was released in October 1996 featuring thirteen cuts. Mainly groove oriented, it was a planned effort to record over different music. Cuts like the single "NO," "Mistachuck," "Underdog," and "Niggativity . . . Do I Dare Disturb the Universe" were reminiscent of some early PE. But "Generation Wrekkked," "Talk Show Created a Fool," and "Free Big Willie" offered different approaches under my voice. Also the combination of producers and songwriters like reuniting with Eric (Vietnam) Sadler and Professor Griff and working with the legendary Isaac Hayes made the project special. Reviews nationally and internationally were very favorable, but

FIGHT THE POWER
265

the politics of Black music radio and airplay by now had its lofty price.

I began to embark on solidifying REACH and furthered my quest for penetrating news on my Black-ass terms with Fox cable. Chuck D on the Real commentary seeks to fill some serious voids. My seventh year lecturing continued at various universities and organizations abroad. Spurred by my involvement in Rock the Vote, and winning the Patrick Lippert Award, I participated in MTV's Choose or Lose campaign, making an appearance at both party conventions. The Republican convention was quite memorable to most because of my interrogation of long-time reputed cracker Senator Strom Thurmond. I've gone retail with Rappstyle which hopefully can represent a line of affordable gear in department stores. I created the Public Enemy archive series, which will release catalogue projects until the year 2002. Rapstation Hip-Hop Nation is my venture of a super-multimedia network on the Web providing music, concert, video, radio information, and interaction worldwide to a starving Rap audience. The programming of Hip-Hop interactive material and enhanced CDs and DVD-CD ROM possibilities hopefully can slash the payola politics of the art and allow its own voice to dictate.

Maybe I'm a nutcase, but this Rap game has a contact-sport beauty to it. It was important to show the travels, trails, trials, and tribulations involved in my last ten years. Hopefully, a worldly character can eradicate some of the hype and stereotype. There should be no excuse to write this book off as kids' stuff. The Black community needs to understand this. The fact that spawns from this so-called ghetto creation is that Hip-Hop runs deeper than the overall mainstream-media's controversial view. In the twenty-plus years of Hip-Hop, my props go out to all my peers who haven't gotten their due for the genius that they've put down, in the past, present, and future. They also go out to my people who've struggled for freedom and equality here on the planet earth. This book is laced with facts, figures, and lists that make this a guideline for study. Keep this as your guide when the rap on Rap gets outrageous. Until next time, don't believe the hype.

RECOMMENDED READING

How Europe Underdeveloped Africa	Walter Rodney
Makes Me Wanna Holler	Nathan McCall
From Superman to Man	J.A. Rogers
Stolen Legacy	George GM Jones
Before the Mayflower— History of Black America	Lerone Denner
The Destruction of Black Civilization	Chancellor Williams
The Miseducation of the Negro	Carter G. Woodson
Seize the Time	Bobby Seale
The Unseen Hand	
Behold a Pale Horse	
Illuminati	Na'im Akbar
The Columbus Conspiracy	Michael Bradley
Changes and Images of Psychological Slavery	Na'im Akbar
Sex and Race, Vols. 1, 2, 3	
The Development of Pyschology of the Black Child	Amos Wilson
Africa	Dr. Yusef Ben Jachonnan
Countering the Conspiracy to Destroy Black Boys	Jawanza Kunjufu
Motivating & Preparing Black Youth for Work	Jawanza Kunjufu
The Missing Link	
One Hundred Amazing Facts About the Negro with Complete Proof	J.A. Rogers
The Autobiography of Malcolm X	Alex Haley
Soul on Ice	Eldridge Cleaver
The Special Spokesmen	Jabril Mohammed
The Isis Papers	Dr. Frances Cress Welsing
Up From Slavery	Booker T. Washington
Street Soldier	Joseph Marshall, Jr.

FIGHT THE POWER

CHUCK D
268

The Business of Music — Sheryl Krasilovsky

Black Face — Nelson George

Putting It All Together — Terrance Jackson

A View From Above — Wilt Chamberlain

Ebony Pictorial History of Blacks, Vol. 1

Cointelpro — Cathy Perkus

Race Matters — Dr. Cornel West

The Wretched of the Earth — Frantz Fanon

Women, Race & Class — Angela Y. Davis

Legal Lynching — Rev. Jesse Jackson

The Science of Rap — KRS-One

Blacks in American Films & Television — Donald Booe

James Brown — Bruce Tucker

The Winner Within — Pat Riley

My Life — Earvin "Magic" Johnson

By George — George Foreman

Live From Death Row — Mumia Abu-Jamal

Get in the Van — Henry Rollins

Blackball Stars — John B. Holway

Only the Ball Was White — Robert Peterson

On a Mission — The Last Poets

Message to the Blackman in America — The Honorable Elijah Muhammad

The Fall of America — The Honorable Elijah Muhammad

Black Panther Newspapers — The Black Panther Party

Final Call Newspaper — Minister Louis Farrakhan

The Spook Who Sat By the Door — Sam Greenlee

Cress Theory of Color Confrontation — Dr. Frances Cress Welsing

The Genius of Huey P. Newton — Introduced by Eldridge Cleaver

Black Power — Stokely Carmichael (Kwame Toure)

This Side of Glory: The Autobiography of David Hilliard and the Story of the Black Panther Party — David Hillard, Lewis Cole

African World Revolution — John Hendrik Clarke

Nelson Mandela: The Struggle Is My Life — Nelson Mandela

Neo-Colonialism — Kwame Nkrumah

Gifted Hands   Ben Carson & Cecil Murphy

The Black Family in Slavery & Freedom   Herbert G. Gutman

What They Never Told You in
    History Class   Indus Khamit Kush

John Hendrik Clarke

Malcolm X

Minister Louis Farrakhan

History of the Nation of Islam   Akbar Muhammad

PUBLIC ENEMY TIME LINE
DISCOGRAPHY

Sept. 1986 Public Enemy Signs with Def Jam

Feb. 1987 Public Enemy #1
Time Bomb

March 1987 Yo Bum Rush the Show

May 1987 You're Gonna Get Yours, My Uzi Weighs a Ton, Rebel Without a Pause

Nov. 1987 Bring the Noise (Less than Zero Soundtrack)

1988 Black Steel in the Hour of Chaos
B Side Wins Again

May 1988 Don't Believe the Hype, Prophets of Rage

1988 Night of the Living Base Heads (video)
Caught Can I Get a Witness

July 1988 It Takes a Nation of Millions to Hold Us Back

June 1989 Fight the Power/Fight the Power (home video)

Dec. 1989 Welcome to the Terrordome (video)

March 1990 911 is a Joke (video)
Revolutionary Generation

June 1990 Brothers Gonna Work it Out (video)
Antinigger Machine (video)
Power to the People

April 1990 Fear of a Black Planet

Jan. 1991 Buckwhylin (video)
Wanna Be Dancin
Terminator X

April 1991 Terminator X Valley of Jeep Beets

July 1991 Bring the Noize/Anthrax (video)

Sept. 1991 Can't Truss It/Move (video)

Dec. 1991 Shut Em Down (video)
By the Time I Get to Arizona (video)

Aug. 1992 Hazy Shade of Criminal (video)
Tie Goes to the Runner

Sept. 1992 Greatest Misses

Nov. 1992 Enemy Strikes Black (home video)
Louder Than a Bomb (video)

May 1994 Terminator X Super Bad
Whodini—It All Comes Down to Money

June 1994 Give It Up (video)
Bedlam 13:13

Aug 1994 Muse Sick N Hour Mess Age

Oct. 1994 What Kind of Power We Got (video)
I Stand Accused (video)

Jan. 1995 So Watcha Gone Do Now (video)

Aug. 1996 No (Chuck D single and video)

Oct. 1996 Autobiography of Mistachuck

March 1997 Generation Wrekkked (Chuck D single/video)

PUBLIC ENEMY
32 TOURS

April 1987 *License to Ill Tour*
Beastie Boys, Murphy's Law
June–Sept. 1987 *Def Jam Tour*
L.L. Cool J, Whodini, Doug E
Fresh, Eric B. & Rakim, Stetsasonic, Jazzy Jeff & Fresh
Prince, Kool Moe Dee
Nov.–Dec. 1987 *Def Jam Europe*
L.L. Cool J, Eric B. & Rakim
March 1988 *UK Tour–Ireland*
May–Aug. 1988 *Runs House U.S.
Tour* Run DMC, Jazzy Jeff & Fresh
Prince, EPMD, JJ Fad
Oct–Nov. 1988 *Run DMC–Public
Enemy World Tour*
Nov.–Dec. 1988 *Bring the Noise
U.S. Tour* EPMD, Stetsasonic, Ice-
T, N.W.A, Sir Mix-a-Lot, MC
Hammer, 2 Live Crew, Too Short
Feb.–Mar. 1989 *Japan Tour*
Major Force Posse
April–May 1989 *UK Tour*
July–Aug. 1989 *Walking with a
Panther Tour* L.L. Cool J, Big
Daddy Kane, Slick Rick, Special
Ed
Dec. 1989 *U.S. Rap Tour*
Hammer, Heavy D, Kool Moe
Dee
Mar.–Apr. 1990 *European Fear
Tour* Third Bass
June–Aug. 1990 *Public Enemy–
Heavy D U.S. Tour* Heavy D, Digital Underground, Kid N Play,
Queen Latifah, Kwame, Young &
Restless
December 1990 *PE–Australia Tour*
Upper Hutt Posse, Sounds of Unlimited Posse
July–Aug 1991 *Turn On, Tune In,
Turn Out Tour* Sisters of Mercy,
Warrior Soul, Gang of Four,

Young Black Teenagers (Alternative Tour)
Sept–Oct 1991 *Bring the Noize
Tour II* Anthrax, Primus, YBT
Nov–Dec 1991 *Greatest Rap Tour
Ever* Geto Boys, Jazzy Jeff &
Fresh Prince, Oaktown 357, Kid
N Play, Latifah, Naughty by Nature, MC Lyte, Tribe Called
Quest, Leaders of the New
School, Son of Berserk
September 1991 *Brazil*
January 1992 *Bring the Noise–
Europe*
August 1992 *Australia, New
Zealand* Ice-T, Sound Unlimited,
Upper Hutt Posse
Sept–Oct 1992 *Zoo TV Tour*
U2, BAD II, Sugar Cubes
August 1992 *Europe Tour*
Beastie Boys
June 1992 *Scandinavia–Europe*
January 1993 *Japan, Hong Kong*
Major Force Posse
December 1992 *College Tour*
Ice-T, House of Pain
December 1992 *Africa Panifest:
Egypt, Ghana* Isaac Hayes
September 1994 *PE–Ice Cube Europe* Gravedigaz
October 1994 *Ghana Africa: Saviors Day* Jermaine Jackson, Black
Girl
November 1994 *Europe–Italy
(Budapest, Croatia)* Ice-T, Five-0
December 1994 *U.S. Mess Age
Tour*
May 1995 *Japan Tour*
July 1995 *UK–Italy Tour*

ACKNOWLEDGMENTS

Mad shout-outs . . . to the book crew: Yusuf Allah Jah, Sister Shakeyah, thanks to your commitment, expertise, and persistence; Eileen Cope, Lowenstein Morel, Jacob Hoye, Dell Publishing, Dennis Rodman, believe it or not, for making this possible, Walter Leaphart, Jr. the coordinator of it all—let's get ready to rumble— Chamaine Thomas, Keith Godfrey, Silbert Mani, Andre Key, hold on, it's gonna happen; thanks, Nathan McCall, Dr. Cornel West, Spiiiiiike, I can't thank y'all enough, Rebecca at 40 Acres, Gary G Wiz, Kyle, Jason, y'all make it so easy on me, thanks.

Hodge, Public Enemy, Flav, TX, Mike, James, Bugg, Rog, Pop, Drew—let's go around the world, bro, Malik (Tony King) Farrakhan, thanks for the older bro talks, Hank-Keith, Forever Cool, Bill Stephney, Eric Sadler, we always pick up where we left off, Harry we must step the fuck up, mad luv, Ernie Pannicioli, always bro whatever, Henry Adebonojo, Raymond Boyd, Professor Griff, we know it's on, Kevin Fonville, the baddest street artist around, thanks, Errol Nazereth, my Canadian-Indian brother info connection, Leyla Turkkan, Ursula Smith, it's gonna be deep, The Drawing Board, how about that next PE, huh? Marjorie Clark, a helluva documentary fucked up by Def Jam, Daryl Brooks, my earth brother, Ice Muthafuckin' T and the Syndicate, Body Count, Evil, Hen, Afrika Islam, Crew, Anthrax, U2, Beastie Boys, Cube, I'm proud, bro, Chip, KB, B Wyze, Sister Souljah, Andre Brown, T-Money, can you believe? Nation of Islam, Supreme Capt. Sharief, Mustapha, Minister Conrad, Sis Michelle, and indeed Honorable Minister Louis Farrakhan. Sincere thank-you for blessings and support, Brother Akbar, who poured priceless African Knowledge into my dome, DaddyO, Stet, KRS One, the Teacher, look for his second book soon. Whodini, Doug E Fresh, thanks for teachin' me, Run-DMC, JMJ, thanks y'all for being students, mentors, and friends, EPMD, L.O.N.S., The Old School, Lady B, Fred Buggs, Colby, Mr. Magic, I AAAM, Tupac, Dyana Williams, thanks so

much, Rock the Vote crew, Donna Frisby, Awesome 2, Wildman Steve, Jeff Foss, Arthur 4X, Wendy Day, Red Alert, Rev. Jesse Jackson, Haqq Islam, Hiram Hicks, Isaac Hayes, Eric Greenspan, Les Abell, Princes Hemphill, Yvonne Davis, Tam Tisdell, Nalo Fennel, Heidi Smith, Kim Green, DJ Ran, Golden Boy, Ed Lover, Dave Sirulnick, thanks for the ops, Don Ienner, Armond White, Jim Brown, Havelock Nelson, Gianna Garel, Emmitt, Val1, Bro Leonard Farrakhan, the Wayans Fam, McChill, Nelson George—I relate to all your works, thanks . . . Bro Kwame Ture, Angela Davis, Reggie Theus, Charles Oakley, Pooh Richardson, Mark Jackson, Michael Eric Dyson, Shelbi Wilson, Evander Holyfield and Mike Tyson, two warriors and professionals, Rev. Ben Chavis Muhammad, Neil Lawi, Howard Wuelfing, Phil Nelson, Ralph Wiley; why Chuck D tends to always read what you write, L.L. Cool J, pound for pound the best ever, Kool Moe Dee, the smartest ever no doubt, Delino DeSheilds, Mrs. Drayton, Mrs. Boxley, Gramma, utmost dedication and love to my mother, Judy, father, Lorenzo, sister, Lisa, and brother, Erik, extended family and ancestors, in-laws, my first wife, Deborah, Mr. Mom is handlin' things, Strong Island, Andreas 13, Black media, Kendu and the Hyenas in the desert, Son Slawta Melquan, all my affiliations, hang on, gain knowledge of the game, G.O.S. Lugo-Press, the late Pinkhouse.

No doubt my reflection in spirit and soul, love, life and wife Felicia, my support and strength to go against the odds of ignorance.

"I get up after having my ass kicked, therefore I get up to kick some ass."